In Pain Almost In Vain

In Pain Almost In Vain

HANEEF YUSOFF

PARTRIDGE

ISBN: Softcover   978-1-4828-6523-3
             eBook   978-1-4828-6524-0

To order additional copies of this book, contact
Toll Free 800 101 2657 (Singapore)
Toll Free 1 800 81 7340 (Malaysia)
orders.singapore@partridgepublishing.com

www.partridgepublishing.com/singapore

Contents

Preface ix

Introduction xiii

Before Syringomyelia 1

After Syringomyelia 9

The Early Symptoms 15

Seeking Options and Alternative Treatment 27

1st Hospitalization 37

After 1st Hospitalization 41

2nd Hospitalization 85

Hospital Rehabilitation Ward 93

3rd Hospitalization 111

The Recovery Stages 137

The Visitors that Enlightened Me 159

Visitors to my House 187

Rehabilitation Stage 203

The Rehabilitation Hospital 207

Dedicated to my beloved wife Lya
and
my four wonderful children
Nana, Iqah, Umar and Uthman

Preface

I was diagnosed with Chiari Malformation Type One with Syringomyelia in October 2011. It is a rare disorder of the nervous system.

Now, after almost three years into rehabilitation since my last surgery, I think I should share the lessons I learned with everyone, all over. I have more time to reflect now. My disorder may be unique to me, but the predicament is universal, common to anyone, regardless of race religion culture or the country we live in.

When I looked back and recalled all the emotions and trials I went through with my wife in facing this ailment, I feel qualified to give you a first-hand true account of a man inflicted with Syringomyelia. After all, this ailment is the only event that has seized all my energy, focus and time the last four years. It is the closest thing to me as I am still in pain, now!

I wish there is a cure or relieve because I do not want anyone of you to suffer this ailment. Indeed, there are drugs to help me and various techniques to lessen the pain as taught by the many psychologist and therapist. I was even assigned a pain management team which taught me the many ways to relieve me of the pain. I tried a few. It doesn't work. Probably I didn't try hard enough. I must admit music therapy works, but only when the pain is not severe. When it is severe, no music can soothe our mind so as not to acknowledge and feel the pain. Aside from the pain, there are also muscle weakness, imbalance, strain and cramps of my whole body that I must deal with!

So, what is it that I want to share? My journey, from the moment I felt the first initial symptoms until now, at the rehabilitation stage. It is about the abrupt stop to my career and life. It is about my continuous pain and the moments I felt, at times like I am down and out, giving up and in vain. It is about the internal struggle and confusion between choosing the traditional and modern medicine to heal myself. It is also about all the rejection I faced on my preference to the non-physical approach of medication from family, relatives and friends. I think it is all about their perception of these methods, but I know, despite their rejection, they all want to see me healed and cured. I know they are sincere.

This is what In Pain Almost In Vain is all about! It is about understanding the chemistry of being sick and the urgency to be cured and got out of the pain. After all, what else do I want other than the cure? Others can say whatever they want, but who is feeling the pain?

I am also here to tell the world that no matter whom we are, religious or not, there is a certain level of remorse, anger, depression, hate and refusal in us when faced with any calamity, including this ailment of mine. This is only human. We are all human. Nobody likes pain, difficulty and hardship. For me, I just continue to find the cure because it is a sign of hope. Only hope can ease remorse, anger, depression, hate and refusal.

I admit, despite all the efforts, at times, I am still in denial mode. Why me? What is this? How am I going to live? How I wish I had the inner strength of Helen Keller, Stephen Hawking and Nick Vujicic. These are truly inspirational people. I do have their images flashed in my mind when I feel down, sad and depressed. Yes, I do believe disability is not inability. Nick Vujicic is truly the one "no arms no legs no worries" guy!

One thing I held on to dearly is hope. I believe hope will keep us alive. This is also about having love. Love will keep us all alive. God love us all. Our parents love us. Our partner loves us. There is a lot of love around us. It is all about having love. When there is God and love, there is happiness even in pain.

This book is about faith, hope and people. It revolves around my internal strength and where I wanted to be from the situation I was in. I thought I was strong, but the pain and difficulty I faced showed me how vulnerable I am and in fact all of us are. At times, I was in pain and almost in vain. I am at the verge of giving up because I can see everything is crumbling down, my physical condition and all. I tried to put up a fight, despite not being able to see the light at the end of the tunnel.

This book is also about the people around me who were affected, directly and indirectly. It ventures into the different people, healers, practitioners I met and types of medication I tried. In my search and struggle to find the cure, I saw and felt the sincere help and struggle of so many kind souls. I dealt a bit into how I faced my situation by actually applying some if not all of the quotes, motivation and positive thinking theory I had gathered through my adult living life. It wasn't easy. In theory all seems to work, but in real-life situation, it is not as easy as it seems.

In Pain Almost In Vain shed real life emotional stress in me and other patients that are applicable in our daily life problems and also, the soft side of life where people are actually kind and helpful towards us. It is not all gloom and doom. Indeed, there is still a lot to cheer about. Out there, life is still filled with good, sincere people ready to be with us. I was wrong all this while. I thought everyone is individualistic and void of care and concern about me. God, I was dead wrong! I learned my lesson and I wanted all of us to rethink about our approach, observation and conclusion about people.

I have been contemplating to document my predicament for quite some time, but my health was not permitting. As a patient, I do not have the luxury of sitting comfortably in front of my laptop, in my cosy room writing down my memoirs. How could anyone sit in front of a laptop feeling, on a continuous basis, prickling, stinging, burning bodily pain, itchiness, muscle cramps and numbness on most of the body? To add to the problem, the intensity of the pain can wax and wane. I want you to imagine someone standing behind you and gripping you from behind. Can you imagine the gripping pain and the pressure over your chest? That's how I feel, almost all the time.

In my earlier appointments with the doctors, this was how I described it, "I feel like I am wearing armour". You kind of feel the weight of that heavy armour all the time, on top of the pain. At times, I grasp for my breath. It is so painful. My lower limbs are partially numb and the muscles are cramp. My upper abdomen is in pain all the time. Apart from these pains, I have to spend time doing my physiotherapy exercises and taking the rest I need after these exercises. So, the journey of writing the book is a strenuous and "painful" one. At times, I didn't write anything for days just because of the pain and I have to deal with it.

However, as I wrote down the memoirs, I began to accept all my weaknesses, acknowledged my wrong attitude towards people and learned that everyone is different and that is perfectly alright! I realized everyone I met were there to "teach" me the lessons of life. There is a lot that I gained from this pain!

One important lesson I learned is "There is no guarantee that all the prevention will save us". I am an avid tennis player, cyclist and a non-smoker. I was selective in my food intake too. With all this "preventive measure", I thought I have it all set. God was I wrong. I got what I got. I have a commendable weight, height and BP. I still read in the range of 121/80 now. My respiratory system works fine. My digestive system too, I guess. I think the skeletal and muscular system is intact. What else? Based on figures, I was fine. Yes, as I said, "There is no guarantee that all the prevention will save us".

All my intent to write my memoir and share it with the world would be in vain if I do not have a diary. Who keeps all the events in a diary? It's my wife! If there is anyone I would want to dedicate this work to, it would be my wife! She deserves it. She is one hundred percent behind me through all this. She sacrificed a lot! I was in pain, getting around all over to find the cure. I was engrossed in my ailment and could only focus on easing the pain. I don't think anyone would expect me to keep a diary. I was lucky that she has a small notebook with dates and people I met. I never knew she kept it. So, it forms the basis of my writings. I simply wrote In Pain Almost In Vain based on the sequence of events that she noted down.

Introduction

You may be looking for a way to cope with an unpleasant event in your life. It can be a sickness, losing someone you love, facing a chronic disease or just adapting to a new difficult challenge. I think you have come to the right place. In Pain Almost In Vain is my real-life story. Yes, I am now in an unpleasant event of my life, inflicted with a nervous disorder, losing a big part of my physical capability, unable to go out and work and unsure of what's in it for me, in the future.

In Pain Almost In Vain is about a patient reaction to the news of the ailment and the subsequent event he went through in the search for the cure. The book highlights a few notions that are common to all of us as humans.

First, we are not in control of what is forthcoming because we really can't predict the future! In my case, suddenly out of nowhere I got a nervous disorder, attacking that one system I never thought of, the nervous system. I have been taking care of my respiratory, digestive and muscular systems all this while, but all of a sudden, I am inflicted with a nervous system disorder!

Secondly, all the prevention we may have put in place could not protect us all because where and when a certain ailment is going to hit us is beyond our control. I am not a smoker; I played tennis, swims, cycles and lived a happy and positive lifestyle. Aren't all those the correct prevention? Yet, what happened?

Thirdly, as much as we want, we can't run away from fate! In the beginning, there was denial, remorse and anger, but slowly I have come to terms with my predicament, my fate. Do you think I can run away from this predicament? I am left without a choice but to face it, head on!

In Pain Almost In Vain reveals the expected reaction, the hope and desire of a man in pain! It is indeed a human issue and when it comes to human, there is definitely a certain level of emotional and mental stress involved. Like you, I have emotions and my emotional needs. I have needs and wants. I have desires and dreams. My mind is still intact up there. It is filled with hope, dreams and desires. It never stops thinking.

As you read along, you will see how I tried to solve the three issues – control, prevention and fate. I have found out that denial, remorse and anger can be minimized and slowly eliminated when we faced fate with a clear certainty that we should never try to change things that are beyond our control, despite all the prevention we had put in place! If it is a disease, what we can do is "find the cure" not "curing" ourselves! We will be disappointed when we try to cure ourselves. Just let curing be done by the power above! See, all of us are humans and we are never in control of our fate! So, we must accept this truth in order for us to move forward with what we still have. Initially we will all go through the denial stage, but it must never let it ruin us. In Pain Almost In Vain showed how by just accepting the circumstances, we will start looking for the cure and it continues and never stops!

In fact, if we keep on searching for the cure, we will realize that, that is what everyone wants to see us do too. I have learned that not a single person I met advised me to stop searching for the cure! So, we must continue doing what we can and should do. When I keep on searching, there wasn't any short of help that I got. It is not all gloom. There is always hope and we must have the faith in hope.

If you ask me if this a motivational book, I would say yes and no. In a way it is, but the difference here is I am the patient. I am the subject matter. Unlike other motivational book authors, I am not writing about someone else's problems and giving advice on issues I did not experience! You hear it first hand from the "motivated" person! I motivated myself!

In Pain Almost In Vain can be considered as a simple life manual. The key points in this manual are simple suggestion for anyone to go find the cure and stop curing yourselves. Why? It is not in your control. Focus on what is within your control! Also, we should all approach problems in a child-like attitude with simplicity, humour and "play". You will realize that the medical fraternity pays great emphasis on simple ways to healing. Do you know that music, memories and love are also medicines?

So, if you are looking for a solution to solve whatever problems in your life, just stick to the action that you are in control and which you can take. Keyword is control, prevention and fate. Approach all problems in a child-like attitude, try everything possible, listen to suggestions and do it. Forget about results! You are not the one determining it. If you do this, you will eliminate all potential stress and disappointments. You will see out there, people will be with you. It is not that I am perfect and already successful by applying this formula, I am in that process. Important thing is that we know we are on the right track! I have learned that being with other patients is also an education. It may not solve our problems, but we have others that are experiencing what we have. In short, we are not alone.

Before Syringomyelia

I am an engineer by profession. Basically, we design and implement engineering projects. Our job involves a lot of drawings, specifications, calculations, procedures, manuals, tables and numbers. We work together with other engineering disciplines to ensure projects or systems are supplied, installed, tested and commissioned. In any industry there will be engineers if there are machines, system or structures to be built. Engineers are not good at writing long essays or novel, but only write report, technical reports. We work with codes, standards and specifications. In short, engineers are guided, regimented, systematic creatures. Engineers check compliance and deviations and will "screw" whoever deviates. They will insist that action be taken to meet the required specification.

We can be big-headed when we are the client or an obedient servant when we are the supplier or contractor. Yes we do change colours, but still are guided, regimented, systematic creatures. Boring job, isn't it? Sometimes it is boring. It depends on the types of projects and the people in it though. As we are "straight" people, we do have conflicts with commercial people, marketing and legal people who don't work according to specifications. Yes, we do have conflicts. It is fun too. In the end, we usually win because we are the ones who hold the acceptance, approval and handover certificate. Without some of these documents, no payment can be made. It is the milestones of a project. Interesting?

The good part is if we are contractors, we can get revision orders for technical changes made to the specifications. This is a bit tricky, but since I have worked on both sides, I can easily smell if the revision order is a genuine one or a fake one. It is good if you are in a project from conceptual engineering. That way, you are well-versed with the requirement including the scope of work. So, in any conflict regarding revision orders, you can challenge it. To challenge, we need to look at the contract again. So, this is where I need my legal and commercial buddies. They can review the contracts for us. After all, we hate to read thick legal and contract documents. Just pass us the technical portion please. Thank you!

Like any profession, we need to be fit, agile and always ahead on knowledge. Things change too fast. One system we install can have hardware and software revision within months. It is quite demanding to cope with the changes. We have many stakeholders to satisfy. That's where we need to communicate well with a lot of people. We do need help. We must learn. It can be strenuous, but if we have guidance from our superiors, we can shine. We need to reduce stress. Stress kills. Stress accounts for almost all heart cases. After all these years, I am grateful that I survived all the stress related to engineering. My BP is in the 120/80 range, almost like a thirty-year old! Thanks to the tennis, cycling and the "boy inside" playfulness.

I can be proud of myself. In my engineering life, I started with teaching. I was an Instructor teaching basic instrumentation and control. What is that? As the name implies, we are instrument engineers, engineering people dealing with instruments in a process, manufacturing or industrial plants that measured parameters like temperature, pressure, flow and level in those plants. This instrument then supplies signals to a central processing area where computation of the signal is done to manage and control those parameters. We are engineering people who deal with sensing elements like transmitters, limit switches, detectors and all kinds of sensing elements and final control elements like valves, power cylinders and on-off switches. We work closely with process engineers, electrical and mechanical engineers. In short, we measure a parameter, compare it with a set point and produce a signal to control the parameter.

We design, supply, install, test and commission instruments in an engineering system, machines or plants. In an Industrial plant, the number of instruments can range from a dozen to a few thousands! It is an interesting field. It is a field where electrical, electronic, process, mechanical and computer engineering converge! Basically, we need to have a strong basic of all these fields. On top of that, we also deal with pneumatic and hydraulic types of sensors and final control elements! Confused? Well, I am too! No, I am joking.

In any plant, be it power generating plants, a palm oil processing plant, a cement plant or an oil platform, our instruments are in the field outside and the control system is usually in an air-conditioned environment. In a modern control system, all engineering programs are done in a processor and controls are done by PC-based or computer-based Man-Machine-Interface. We are the ones "seeing" all that is happening in the plant from our graphic screens in the control room! We control the plant! Interesting right? We can "interrupt" a process by clicking some "software" setting in an engineering program or the operator screen! We can do it without people knowing it! Interesting? Anyway, do not do this at your plant or installation! Please don't tell others that I teach you this!

Basically, I have worked in all major industries like power, oil and gas, palm oil, cement and many manufacturing industries. Through the years, I have evolved from an instructor, application engineer, sales engineer, instrument design engineer, project engineer and project manager in both the main field – instrument and electrical. Does it look like my resume? Well, I was merely trying to explain what I did before all these pain, numbness and cramps get a hold of me.

I have done many projects, but one of the most memorable one was for the first oil and gas installation and pipeline project overseas, for a poor country. It was challenging from the design stage, detailed engineering stage done in a cold city up to the construction and installation stage in a forty two degrees Centigrade location in a desert! We got to see mules, camels and mud houses. We can be in a sprawling desert city one day and at a remote desert location the next day. We got to drive in our MPVs through the desert and fly by small planes to cover the few locations along that one thousand five hundred kilometres pipeline! It was hot, lonely and demanding. It was stressful, but the money was good. It sort of compensates the effort! The best part is we got to see the first oil! It was a proud moment for that country and we got to be part of their history!

My last assignment was for a hook-up and commissioning contractor as project manager for an off-shore platform. It was there that I begin to feel minor symptoms of this disorder. It is probably my last assignment. Now, in my current condition, I can't do much. After all, engineering is one field you can't work alone. Once in a while I just do some freelance work of my choice. Hopefully, I can recover to a comfortable state where I can do some office, engineering managerial work on a contract basis. I have done that before. Just pray for me!

By the way, I am not just an engineer. I am a proud father to four beautiful children. I am also a husband to the "most beautiful women in the world". We are happily married for more than twenty years! She is my love, a friend, my best friend, my partner, still my girlfriend, my motivator, my adviser, my mate, my teacher, the mother to my four kids and most importantly my trusted soulmate. She has given me twenty golden years, a "heaven on earth"! We still listen to our love song of twenty five years ago. We still listen to it together, today! We went through a lot together. This together is a million times more precious than being an engineer!

I can make all the money I can, do all the big projects I can and go to all the places I want, but as a man, I must be back home to a place where I am wanted, needed and loved. I want to feel welcomed! We all need to have that "feel" and meaning of life.

I may be idle the last four years, but I should never forget all the good years when I was active and healthy. I should not complain because the time I am healthy is much longer than this four years of difficulty. I used to spend quality weekends with my family visiting places, travelling, vacationing and if we do not have anywhere to go, we go window shopping!

I swim, play tennis and cycle. I am an active person and physically quite fit. I love sports, both doing it and watching it! I think I lived a hectic, but reasonably balanced life. I got all the love and support from my love, my wife. I may not be a wealthy man, but I have a "wealthy" life. I don't have much to complain about. It has been a long happy, challenging and fulfilling experience. I thanked God for all the precious people in my life and all the blessings along the way. I remember one beautiful advice from a dear friend years ago.

"There is time to play and time to pray"

I think aside from the worldly life, the family, work and sports, I am lucky to be "brought back" to the fold of religion. I wasn't much of a performing person, religious-wise in my younger days. Of course, I am raised in a simple, humble and religious family, but I am not that obedient in a way. I am, like anyone else, prone to the influence of the "greater evil" always persuading us to deviate and live an empty, wayward life. We are all constantly "challenged" to be with good or evil. It all depends on the "internal".

So, when I said that I was lucky to be "brought back', what I meant was someone showed me the way to charge the "internal". It is about the "internal" driving the "external". I remembered a beautiful analogy he gave. "If your car battery is weak, your window will be difficult to wind up, the lamp will be dim and it would be difficult to start your engine. Now, if you charged your battery everything will work fine! It is the same with you!" What a simple, but profound analogy! Do you know what? This guy is not some religious scholar from a big institution or from a religious missionary, but an electrical engineer, a graduate from a US university! In short, he showed me the key to religion – charging the internal!

All the religious rituals performed that we see are actually driven by the "internal" which in turn was driven by "the greater light" above! Confused? It's acceptable. I am just trying to explain that invisible force and dimension that drives our internals. So, when our internals are charged or lighted, the externals become voluntary. We do it out of our heart, out of commitment and freely. Performing a religious command can be summarized as follows – you do it voluntarily or you are forced to do it. If your internals are lighted by the above, all your actions will be to serve the above. You don't need money or rewards to push you. It is all sincere!

In my case, all the health, work, family and love were suddenly interrupted. It is like running against a wall. One moment everything was fine and the next moment, Syringomyelia! I was shocked and shaken. No doubt about it! It was tough. Looking back, I think it would have been worse if my "internal" is a shambles. At least now, I have a stronger "shoulder" to cry on. I have that "power" to lean and rely on. This is precious. I couldn't ask for more!

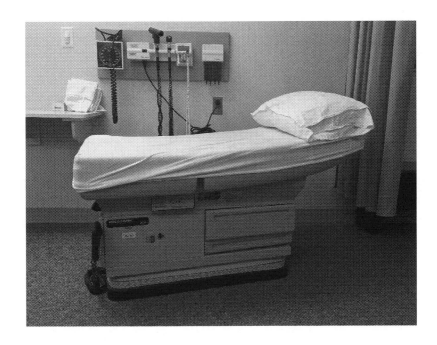

After Syringomyelia

I have a nervous disorder called Chiari Malformation Type One with Syringomyelia. Strange name, isn't it? It is. In fact, it is a rare disorder. In a simple language, the bottom part of my brain called the Cerebellum has weighted down onto the passage at the bottom part of my skull where the spinal cord passes through. It has compressed my spinal cord, disrupting the flow of liquids from my brain flowing through the spinal cord thus causing a cyst. The cyst is compressing the nerves going through the spinal cord to parts of my body. Is it a good graphical description? Are you following me so far? I hope it is not confusing and you can get a grasp of what I am trying to tell you.

As a layman, I think this disorder is mechanical in nature. I can see two blockages – one at the passage for the spinal cord at the bottom of my skull and the other is the cyst in my spinal cord. As you read on, you will see that the surgeon solution to this disorder is focused on the two blockages.

I was diagnosed with this disorder nearly five years ago. I am now in the second year of rehabilitation stage after my last surgery. I am in still in pain, but manageable. At times, I felt almost in vain, but I try hard to cope with the situation. It is not easy. I am trying.

Prior to my surgery I do not have the full technical understanding of my situation to describe it. I can only tell I have a nervous problem. One day, a doctor came to my ward with some students. Looking at their fresh, young faces, I know they are our future doctors on a study tour. I

9

overheard the doctor explained about my situation. He said, "This patient sensory, muscle motor and digestive system are affected". He described my problems in detail, but lying in bed, in pain after surgery, I could not understand it all. I just thought that the three symptoms he mentioned are good enough for me. He was right. I understood it. Now, I am feeling it.

Yes, I am in this state every day. I forgot how many days now because a day, in this sad situation is like a few long days! However, today, some of the symptoms are slowly disappearing. I do feel minor improvement. I think this is due to the rehabilitation sessions I was prescribed to. This is also the reason I am able to start writing. I still find it difficult to sit beyond one hour. My whole body will strain and ache.

After Syringomyelia, almost everything changed! My life orientation and equation changed. My focus changed. For a moment I see all my hopes dashed. All my dreams and efforts seem to fall to naught! My focus is just to get rid of this disorder, to find the cure. I don't care from where the cure would come, but I will find it. Suddenly, I felt helpless. I was depressed. So, how do I get myself out of this rut? What should I do? How can I face all these disabilities? This is the time I should apply all my knowledge to help me make this "forced" transition. I have to practice all the management and motivational theory I gathered so far. I must make "finding the cure" as my number one priority!

My journey to find the cure is long and afar. I tried everything people suggested. I just want to find the cure. I am not totally cured, but anything that can ease my pain is considered "the cure" to me. So, in my hospitalization and later rehabilitation, I was taught many techniques to ease my pain.

One "finding the cure" technique is breathing, abdominal breathing. This seems to work, but one minute is not enough. Maybe ten minutes is more effective. It works sometimes, but not all the time. It is quite confusing to practice. We expand our abdomen, not our chest while inhaling. What? How? You try. See, how difficult it is. If it is difficult even when we are conscious, how can we do it unconsciously?

Another technique taught is mind control. Mind control works, sometimes. We try to visualize all the good memories, love and people we like. I can only try when the pain comes. Again, when the pain is severe, it won't work. Maybe for others, but me, I failed. Nevertheless, I wish to thank all those who have helped me discover and learn these techniques

I have one technique that you can follow if you want. One of the ways to ease my worries is by not knowing too much about my ailment. I just rely on a few statements by the doctors and accept it. "Do not know too much" helps. I heard a few worrying statements made by others about my ailment, but I just hear it once, that's all.

All through my ailment, there are people who are affected by my illness that I would like to compliment. I saw their sacrifices, felt their love and touched by their presence and care. This is the most precious of it all. I remember the psychologist told me "Sickness is ten percent medication, ten percent doctors and eighty percent patient's will". I always try to apply this notion. Yes, it is true. It is my will. So, what I do is set targets. I just set it. I would say "This June, I will be fine again. This December I will be able to go out again".

"Sickness is ten percent medication, ten percent doctors and eighty percent patient's will"

After Syringomyelia, my role as the one going out working for the family was abruptly stopped. I no longer have the ability to go to work. I am the one who used to drive my family around, but now, my wife will have to carry that role. In fact, almost all the chores are now on my wife's shoulder. It is not a small feat for her. I know being a mother and a housewife is the most demanding job in the world! On continuing with my profession, maybe I can do something on my own, but that too needs a healthy, fit and capable body.

Now I realized how important the "internal" that eventually produce "inner calm" is and also, children's approach towards life. Children just want to play. I can relate easily with my ailment now. I can quickly switch to music, jokes and thing's kids like. I call this escapism, a way out. I never thought of getting old. I don't feel old. I may look old, but I am young inside. Watching a Nadal-Djokovic tennis game is still enjoyable to me.

As late as five years ago, I can still hit a good, backhand passing shot! I imagine tennis. I played it in my mind. It is part of mind control and a good recovery process. I still listen to Dio, Metallica and Linkin Park as an excursion. In fact, I listen to all genre of music. I didn't set rules. I have a play list I played to get me to sleep with pain.

After Syringomyelia, how I see life changed! I used to see life as a race, a battle to be won, wealth to be gained, but now, the urge is still there, but I know that I am just a planner and executor and I am not the one "determining" the result! Proof is I was having a good job and that good job is not producing any result now! The race stops. No battles anymore. My attitude towards people changed too. I thought everyone is individualistic and racists, but after my illness, I was shown all the goodness in a lot of people, even strangers! I was wrong in many aspects about human relations. I have learned a great deal.

I am also grateful to God that my pain is much reduced when I lie down. I think in a lying down position, muscle motors are not working as much thus the lesser pain. So far, I still have the pleasure of sleeping. I may feel the pain for a few minutes, but it will slowly subside. However, there are times the pain persists. In fact, there are times the pain is unbearable. It is in moments like this that no music helps. I do have my drugs, but at times, despite the drug the pain is unbearable. When this happens, I just cry. I cry and "talk" to God. I say "God take this pain away please. I can't stand it. Please, I am in pain. I know you love me". Once in a while I could not breathe when I lie down to sleep. I would then just sit up and wait.

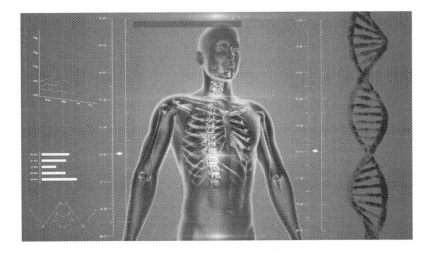

The Early Symptoms

I feel numbness of my hands. I thought, from my reading that it might be Diabetes. However, I did not have that thirst symptom. So, I just erased it from my mind. I didn't believe so. Also, I am beginning to feel some minor gripping pain over my body. Whatever, at that time, it was manageable. So, life goes on. As usual, I was back to the office and friends. After a few weeks, I thought to myself "If it is not Diabetes, what is it?" As much as I tried to erase it, my conscience keeps on asking. "It may be something serious. I must find out" I thought silently in my mind. I was beginning to worry. "What then is this minor gripping pain?" my mind wonders.

Initial Check at a Private Hospital

One of the first places I went to check my numbness was at a private hospital. I needed to verify if it was Diabetes or what! I am just following my conscience.

It is a new hospital very close to our house. It takes just five minutes to go to, a breather. After a simple registration, I was assigned to a specialist. He is a mild, middle-aged Chinese physician. Initially we had a casual conversation about my job and also a bit about my lifestyle. I just told him the basics – non-smoking, engineering field, tennis and cycling. "It's good. You play tennis!" he commended. "Overall you look fine, but tell me what's bothering you" he asked, as he smiled and briefly assessing my physique, probably. I described my numbness and the gripping pain on my chest. He then asked me a few other questions. His first diagnose was that I may have a problem with my heart probably from his understanding of the "gripping pain" of my chest. "See, we need to do a test on you. She will show you the place and I will join you shortly"

I was then assigned to another room accompanied by a nurse for an ECG test. My BP was checked and recorded. "Here is a treadmill. We will do an ECG test. A static ECG where you just lie down is not as complete as this" she explained. "I will have to wire up the probes on you first" she said, as she points to the small unit with a screen. "You just need to walk normally on the treadmill" she explained further. "The doctor will join us a bit later to see the results and explain to you his findings" the nurse said, as she set up the probes to my chest and key in the setting at the dials on the treadmill. I was then given the ECG test.

A few minutes later the doctor came. "How is everything? Are you OK sir?" he asked, as he looks at the screen and the printouts. He spends quite some time looking at it. "Yes" I said. "I will have to tilt the treadmill a little bit to see if you can respond to the extra pressure" the doctor said as he changed the settings. "We increase just a bit first. Later we will gradually increase, OK sir?" he explained. I continue walking normally and I didn't feel much difficulty. My breathing is normal, nothing unusual so far. After around twenty minutes and a few tilt settings, the treadmill was lowered again to the normal position. "We have your records. Do come back to the room after this" the doctor said.

In his room, the doctor flipped through the readings again. He glanced at it in detail. "Your heart is fine. Your response to the test is acceptable for now" he said, as he concludes his findings. "I have decided to assign you to another specialist" the doctor said. "We need to check if you have any problems with your oesophagus and stomach" he adds. Again, we leave him for another room. However, all the changes were quite smooth as there isn't much waiting time.

In this next room, the physician is another young Chinese man. "Do you understand English sir? If not, I can speak Malay to you" he said politely, probably sizing me as an "old" Malay man. I just smiled and he continued in English. "We had a short discussion with the physician you met earlier and has decided to put you to another test" he said. "You may have some problem with your throat and stomach. It is called Gerd. Your stomach content may have return to your oesophagus." he tries to explain in a simple layman terms. He then showed a few drawing from a file nearby as he explained about Gerd. "Gerd? What the hell is that" I quietly asked myself. The name is a bit strange, I thought! "Next, please follow this nurse to a small lab. We will do some visual inspection of your throat. She will explain the procedure" the doctor advised.

I was quickly given a robe and sent to a small changing room. After changing, I was seated on an inclining chair. "We will insert this tiny tube into your throat" the technician said. I couldn't recall if I was sedated or not, but the process was quite simple. I woke up and it was done. "Let's go back to the doctor" the nurse instructs. We then walked back to the doctor's room, just a few meters away. I was anxious to know if I have Gerd or whatever. I felt good because at least the chest pain is not because of my heart. I am quite relieved.

The doctor looked at his computer screen and said "From our visual inspection, you may have a minor form of re-flux where some content of your stomach return to your oesophagus. It is just minor. No worries" the doctor affirmed. "We will give you some medication" he adds. "Also, we have saved your visual inspection on a CD. You can look at it at home" the doctor said. It was soon over and we proceeded to the pharmacy. I then produced my insurance card and got my medicine. I left the hospital without major anxiety. At least I now know that my heart is fine and the Gerd is minor.

My wife was quite happy with the findings. She was happy with the hospital too. "It's quiet, efficient and clean" she said. "Now, let's try their cafeteria. I am hungry. It looks nice!" she adds, excitedly. We spend a few minutes at that clean cafeteria. It was also a good time to brief my wife of the two tests and findings. Overall, I am satisfied, but the numbness and gripping pain is still there. My conscience is still asking what it is.

So, it is not Diabetes, the heart nor the oesophagus. What is it? So, the search for the answer continues.

A few days later, I called one of my close friends asking him for some advice. "I know one man who can check it for you" he said, over the phone. "I will come over and take you to see him. His place is quite near. Maybe you have heard of his name" he adds. Listening to his name, I recalled hearing it. His name is quite familiar and among my circles of friends, it was regularly mentioned. However, I have never met him personally. I then told my wife of my intent to see this practitioner.

The Man Who Could "See" Things

I was told that this pious man has a "unique" ability to diagnose illness through his special knowledge. He leads a simple and religious life all the time. He didn't charge any fees and those who want to pay, do it voluntarily. Based on this background, my trust level is increased due to the "sincerity" aspect of his services. I have many friends who had seek his services and some cured.

As a person living in a culture deep in ancestral history and religion, seeking traditional healers is a normal practice. After all, it is a known fact that there are many traditional healers around. If it were not a normal practice, these healers would have been long disappeared from our society, but it isn't the case. It is a simple logic. So, I think, it is wise to see him to verify and affirm the doctor physical findings. I am just interested to see if, through his "gifted" knowledge, he could do something through the spiritual side. That is all to it. My intent was clear.

I am aware that there are people who would accuse me of seeking "deity" help which goes against my faith. I think everyone has their own perception or assumption of things. I leave it to them. I think I am not an ignorant and foolish person to put my faith in jeopardy. How could they say that if all our elders were in fact religiously strong? I know our elders lived a more pure life than these naysayers! What makes them think that our elders can be that ignorant? They would have known that these healers are religiously deviated and not seek their help for their sickness.

I was told of his simple method that only uses a few verses of the Quran and water. From my research, readings and consultation with many educated and religious scholar, I am convinced that this method is acceptable in my religion. It is not a deviation. It is far from seeking "deity" intervention. I know it depends on the healer's "connection" with God due to his strict observance and remembrance of God! This traditional method was even described in many religious scriptures and book.

In fact, when I was small, my father used to seek this kind of traditional practitioners. It is not that we didn't believe in hospitals and physicians, but it is just an alternative form of medication. We use both these faculties – physical and traditional sciences. My father works as a hospital assistant all his life! Don't tell me he didn't believe in physical sciences! One of my brothers is a physician! So, did he complain about me seeking these practitioners? No, he didn't stop me.

I was sent to this traditional practitioner by my friends. Talking about friends, I am lucky to have many good, sincere, selfless friends. So, two of them came, in their car. The drive was short, but if I were to drive on my own, I may not find it. The area is quite dense and heavily populated.

This traditional practitioner only works on designated days, at night. On other days, he has religious classes he attends. Actually, he has a day job. I didn't ask what. He works out of a rented terrace house. The house is quite empty with just some furniture and one glass display cabinet. He displayed a few herbs he sold in the cabinet. On the floor, there are a few crates of mineral water bottles. He has three assistants to help him. I heard these boys are voluntary helpers. They were partly caretakers of this simple "clinic". One of them is a student, following this practitioner.

I was told the wait may be long as his patients have differing situations and some may require a bit more time. When we arrived, there were around twenty or so people. At that time, my numbness has affected my limbs too. So, my seating has to be comfortable. It was quite a long wait, almost two hours! I felt strained and tired. We were probably number ten in the wait list. He didn't use any numbering system, but his assistant knew our turns and will politely call us in when our turn arrives.

I was finally ushered into his room. Before that, we took one of the mineral water from the crates. It is a simple empty room. There was nothing on the walls and no furniture at all. There is a mat and he is seated on the mat, near the wall. I can see a small book rest in front of him. That's all. His assistant sat beside him. He smiled, greeted us and offered a handshake. He was dressed in a full, white shirt and loose trousers with a turban-like headgear. He looks calm and pious, but smiled continuously. His voice was clear, but soft in tone.

"This is our room. I hope you are comfortable" he said, as he sat us on the mat. "So, he told you about me?" he asked, as he glanced at my friend. "Yes, he told me about you" I said. "Do you have a long wait just now? I am sorry for that" he apologizes. "I usually start after our last night prayers, around nine. I think you already knew I work only three nights in a week. I have other work on other days" he explained his schedule and at the same time, trying to set us into his small room and make us feel comfortable. He looked at his small notebook to verify my name as I had called him earlier. He nods as he flipped his notebook. "OK, I see you have one bottle of water too. Good, then we are ready" he said as he closed his notebook.

He started by silently reciting some verses. I couldn't hear him clearly, but they are verses from the Quran. He closed his eyes and opened it, glanced at me and looked down. He keeps on making silent supplication. All the while, he looked down and gently moves his body back and forth as though focusing on his thoughts. I think he is "focusing" on his spiritual strength to "access" my ailment, probably reading some inherent "signs" from my body.

His conclusion came in just a few minutes later. "You have a problem with your gall bladder and the back of your neck" he said, nodding his head in affirmation. "You must take care of your food intake" he quips, as he looked at me and glancing at my friend. What he said next took me by surprise. "You come from a big family and your father is a martial art's teacher, right?" he politely asked as he looks at me and later, gazed at the book rest. "Yes my family is big and my father did teach some Malay traditional martial arts long time ago" I said, at the same time wondering how he came to know my background! I didn't tell him. I didn't tell my friends either!

At the same time, he did mention the "back of my neck". Of course when I met him I haven't done any MRI let alone knowing that the cause of my ailment is at the back of my neck, but how come he knew it then? "Is this what my friend meant by his unique style of diagnosis?" I quietly talk to myself. I am a bit surprised in the beginning, but not shocked. I recalled that there are others with this capability.

"Your problem is related to some ancestral-linked practices" he said. "Usually, those practicing martial arts do learn some rituals from the descendants or they simply inherit it" he explains. "Normally, those inflicted didn't realize it at all. Of course, they didn't ask for it in the first place, right" he adds, trying to relay to me the basis of his assumptions. "They, our ancestors practicing martial arts do wear armour to protect their body. They are warriors, you know?" he further clarified. "What? Wearing armour?" I asked myself. The gripping pain I felt is in fact, like I am wearing armour! At times I feel like wearing some heavy armour. Was what he said about the armour and what I felt, a coincidence? Am I feeling this armour-like gripping pain because it stems from the ancestors self-defence rituals? How could it be? I sort of feel that there is a correlation – armour and gripping pain. I was surprised at his revelations.

As he talks, his hands made a few movements like cutting and piercing open something. He may be trying to delve deeper in his diagnosis and assessment. While making all those movements, he regularly turns to his assistant as though "transferring" some signs I couldn't understand. He seems to "talk" to his assistant. "We only know we are inflicted when we got strange sickness or disorder" he said.

The session was quite brief. He then holds the bottle for a while recites some verse and passes it to me. "This water is for you to drink. Drink it three times a day, OK? God permits, you will be cured!" he said convincingly.

So, I got my first diagnosis. It is not merely physical numbness, but another element involved – spiritual, unseen, ancestry-related ailment. Did I believe it then? My answer is yes. Why? First, he is pious and he doesn't fix a charge. That weighs heavily on my convincing scale. Secondly, he is able to tell things I didn't tell him like my family and my father. It definitely makes anyone impressed. I am impressed! Aren't you?

It was indeed an experience and eye-opener. I thought I am knowledgeable. This guy makes me humble! I tell myself to never underestimate anyone.

After a few weeks, I met him again. As I sat there in front of him, he looked at me, smiled and said "Oh, it's you again. Nice to meet you" He then recites a few verses, gazed down and said "If you get worse, go and see the doctor and have your neck scan. Your problem is there" he said. I think he "sees" my cyst then and knows that physically it is a cyst, but the unseen may be responsible for leaving it there! It is also a sign that, he is responsibly telling me that he is unable to treat it. He has tried diagnosing, which now I know was correct and his treatment may not be suitable.

I left his place rather disappointed, but later realized that his knowledge may not be encompassing all diseases and he is not God, the all-knowing and controller. My faith intervenes and stopped me from making wrong assumptions about the man. He has tried and knew that there are things beyond his knowledge and capability. However, I believe in an old saying "There is a cure for everything except death" The cure may not be with him, but I think his diagnosis was convincing. The way he points to my neck and his conclusion on my father's rituals and how I feel, the heavy armour "pain", makes sense!

"There is a cure for everything except death"

My Off Shore Stint

A few weeks later, came a requirement for me to go off shore. I need an off shore safety passport. As much as I hate it, it is a requirement I need to comply. It is a three-day course at the end of which, we are qualified to go off shore. Earlier, I have passed the medical, blood sugar test included.

One of the training modules is the helicopter underwater escape training, HUET. In the class, we were trained to familiarize with the equipment associated with HUET. A lot of equipment was shown and its operation demonstrated. The whole exercise is for us to be able to get out of trouble in case the helicopter crash into the sea. In the event of it happening, a few seconds is all that we have to engage our emergency breathing apparatus, unfasten our seat belt, open the nearest window, struggle out and off to the surface. We will do it in the twenty feet-deep pool, not that salty sea though. The "good" part is we will be submerged three times in three different settings. One of it is, the helicopter will be turned upside down and submerged.

So, all the equipment was moved around the class for us to feel and try. One of it is a small valve assembly used to fill up our emergency airbag and when underwater, to switch from the normal air to emergency air. Finally, this little valve assembly reached me and I tried to press the mechanical switch button. It was hard. I couldn't press it the first time until I could hear the snapping sound. I tried the second time and I managed to press it. I tried it again and I managed to press it. I tried a few times, just to confirm it and I succeeded. I was a bit worried initially, but after a few times, I felt fine.

My hands were a bit numb, but the strength, the grip is still there. I was relieved! So, I began to think that in the real situation underwater I will survive. I know that I have an important mission and this is my job. Again, at the pool, I played around and familiarize myself with the valve and managed to press it.

I passed the HUET and other training and I was grateful to God. In the next few days, I prepared the paperwork, look at the drawings, checked the schedule, roster, coordinate the tools and equipment, spare lists and the list of all personnel I have for the mission. In no time, I was in the plane heading for the off shore base. Again, in my mind I asked God to give me the health I need for this short stint off shore.

I was fine managing what I should, day in day out with all the normal pressure of off shore work until one morning I find it difficult getting up. I tried and finally managed to sit up. I was a bit worried as I need to finish off my duty there. I finally managed to walk to the galley for breakfast and then, the briefing. Luckily, it was just one day before I am scheduled to leave the site.

The MRI That Confirms the Cyst

In a few days, I was back in the office and went for another test for my numbness. This time I went to a small district private hospital. I went through the MRI and it was confirmed that there is a cyst in my spinal cord, somewhere at cervical three to cervical seven of my spine. The cyst compresses all the nerves in the spinal cord causing all signals pertaining to sensory, muscle motors and digestive system affected. That is the cause of all the bodily pain, numbness and uncontrolled bowels. I was told that I needed a surgery. I was sad. I was scared. I felt helpless. I was then referred to another bigger district private hospital near the city, for the surgery.

Procedure to Remove the Cyst

Two days later, I went to the proposed hospital with my wife. It was a bigger and more equipped hospital. We were asked to see the surgeon to discuss the intended surgery. I told my wife that I am scared. She tried to comfort me. She gave me some encouragement. She looks composed, but I can sense that she is worried. The wait was long. I am still coping with the reality that I am diagnosed with a nervous ailment and I needed a surgery. I almost cried. It was indeed a long thirty minutes.

The surgeon looks assuring. He smiled a lot. He was cordial. I tried to remain calm. It was hard. He then flipped through my file, his notes, the MRI film and explained what needs to be done and the surgery process. He said the cause of the cyst was due to Chiari Malformation that means my Cerebellum seems to have weighted down and blocked the passage at the base of my skull where my spinal cord leaves the brain. The solution is to enlarge the passage so as to allow more space for the spinal cord that will eventually allow the brain liquid to flow down smoothly. Sounds simple enough, but it is my skull that they will bore and enlarge. Just the thought of it sent chills down my bones.

The surgeon then showed us some slides of those who have a more complicated situation than I am in. One slide showed the cyst was right at cervical one, nearest to the brain. I would imagine how difficult the surgery would be. Another slide showed a much more expanded and elongated cyst than mine. We were then advised to decide on the surgery.

In the car heading home, I can see my hopes dashed, dreams shattered. I am still shocked and afraid. I am still coping with reality and a bit in the denial mode. How can it be me? Why me? I was confused. At the same time, I found that little strength left in me. I slowly assure myself that it is not the end of the world. I will try to look for other ways of treatment other than surgery. I will. I try to persuade myself to be patient. One thing that lingers in my mind is about the chances of surviving the surgery or can the surgery make me feel better!

"Is there light at the end of the tunnel?"

Seeking Options and Alternative Treatment

Ask anyone who is sick and they will tell you one thing – they just want to be cured. They will do anything. They will go anywhere just for the cure, they want to be healthy again. That is all that matters. It rhymes with what Metallica sings - Nothing Else Matters. Now, why suddenly I think about Metallica? Well, it is one of my favourite metal bands. Way back in 1993, Enter Sandman was like national anthem to me!

Back to the issue of looking for a cure, money is not a question. They will pay. It is the same with me. It is like a drowning person gasping for breath will catch anything thrown at them!

So, the search begins.

Acupuncture

The next day, I went for an acupuncture treatment at a Chinese-run hospital. It is new to us. It is also a new hassle. The hospital is in the middle of the city. The traffic is almost jammed all the time and I don't have anyone else to drive me except my wife. She is not used to driving in the city. She has to do it. I know she was scared, but she gave her best.

At the registration, I was like the only non-Chinese, but I didn't get any strange stares. It was a receptive atmosphere. People are nice. The staffs were all helpful. I was told this hospital was funded by a few

Chinese philanthropists. For the poor, service is free. The acupuncturist is a Chinese from China, a specialist in his field. He was quite young and composed. I was then greeted by a young Indian lady, his assistant.

See what we have here? We have a Malay man, in a Chinese-run private hospital, assigned to a Chinese from China acupuncturist, assisted by a young Indian lady nurse. Strange, but unique isn't it? This is the beauty of my country. We are a peaceful country and our people are tolerant and respect each other. We blend well. It has been like this for years. I love it. I am proud of it.

Now, have I told you how we communicate? This is the best part. I speak Malay to the Indian lady and she translated it and relayed my words in Chinese to the acupuncturist. We passed through the diagnosis quite easily and in a clear manner. The acupuncturist explained his procedure. I was a bit nervous and starting to see needles sticking into my body. What a feeling!

In a few minutes, the needles were inserted in one by one. It wasn't that painful, but I felt some minor irritation. That was after all, my first experience with acupuncture treatment. I was lying on my stomach and pretended to be dead. I can't move. It lasted for twenty minutes.

After that, we continue for another ten sessions. I wasn't feeling much different though. The numbness, the pain, the weakness and imbalance still persists. I was in fact advised that the healing may take months and it is a slow process. We finally stop the treatment after two weeks.

All the while during my acupuncture treatment, it is not just me that is "sacrificing". My wife has to sit outside waiting for the session every day. Waiting can be tiring and demanding. I know the place. I have seen it. It is not the best of places although the seat is comfortable. I usually give her a little treat after my session. We will go to one little cafe at the adjacent building in the hospital.

One day when we were at the cafe, we saw a woman in a wheelchair at one of the tables accompanied by two women. She looks sad, moody and depressed. She didn't talk much as the other two women. She was in the hospital robe probably one of the inpatient. Soon, they were ready to leave. She was pushed out of the cafe. I heard the woman who was pushing her, said something. She was speaking Chinese and I couldn't understand, but from her gestures it sounds like some words of encouragement and persuasion. The woman in the wheelchair suddenly starts crying. At first it was just normal, but later it became louder. As she left the cafe further she began to scream. It was loud. Everyone at the small cafe was shocked and left bewildered.

I wondered what makes her cry like that. "We don't know what she went through. She may have a chronic disease" my wife said, after seeing me a bit puzzled. "She may even have to face a surgery, who knows?" she adds. I pity the woman. From her cries, I know she is deeply worried and distressed. Soon, her screams fade away and we stayed there for a while catching up with our croissant and coffee after that short interruption.

We then left the cafe for our car, but my mind keeps thinking of that screaming woman. "Why is she screaming?" my mind wonders. I know she must be facing one big dilemma. She wouldn't be screaming like that if her ailment is a normal one. It is just one of the many tragic situations in a hospital. There are many more stories like her we never know.

The cafe is also at the lobby. So, we could see the many Honda, Mercedes, BMW and even Jaguar passing through dropping off patients, some walking, some in wheelchairs. I could only reflect that not everyone is lucky. We can be driving Honda Mercedes and BMW out there, but one day someone else may be driving it for us. We may not be going shopping and having lunch at some plush restaurants anymore. It may be our turn to be driven to a hospital. It can happen to us, any time!

This is the reality of life. I used to drive in front of this particular hospital. I never thought that I would be entering it one day.

Meeting My Surgeon for the Surgery

As the pain persists, I decided to see another surgeon at another hospital. I was told that the hospital has a very experienced neuro surgeon and the hospital specialized in neurosurgery and neurology. This is a public, government hospital. It is a national level hospital and is huge! It was also recommended by my sister-in-law who is a doctor herself.

After a visit, we managed to see the surgeon. He is a mild person. He looks relaxed. After a short greeting, he went right to the issue. First, he asked me to explain my overall situation. I talked about the bodily pain, prickling pain on the hands, numbness, burning sensation, itchiness, the gripping feeling of the chest. I used the analogy that as though I am wearing armour over my body. I felt burdened. That was how I feel.

He then explained the procedure he would take. He will bore my skull to expand the passage so as to ease the spinal cord passing through the passage. A titanium ring will be planted and circumvent the passage. He said, this is the first procedure to ease the pressure on the spinal cord and releases the compression of the cyst on the nerves. He did not elaborate further, but his explanation with a model and screen images was quite clear. He then explained that from the MRI and the position of my lower brains, it is Chiari Malformation, a kind of malformation from early birth. He did, however try to determine if there were any other potential causes by asking if I had a nasty fall before. I said, as far as I could recall, no.

At the end of the session, he looked at me and said in a firm tone to decide on a potential date for surgery. He said, "Think about it, but do not think too long". He then added, "Please come again soon. We are ready for you".

By this time my conscience is clearer. I needed a surgery. However, I still try to avoid a surgery because I know from most people, in any surgery, our basic structure may be affected and some damage can be permanent. I was worried because the boring is done right next to my lower brains. It sounds scary, isn't it? Again, I told myself to look for alternatives.

Homeopathy

I then, through the advice from some close friends, tried homeopathy. I must thank a dear friend, who selflessly, came to my house and send me to the homeopathy centre. He held my hands and walked me up the stairs. He sent me to the centre a few times. He even waited for my treatment. What a wonderful person he was. He has since left us all.

Homeopathy is another unique treatment. I did some research about homeopathy. I didn't really understand the theory behind it, but I conclude that it is a non-intrusive, non-drug treatment. I don't understand what those little white sweet balls did. I don't know how homeopathy could treat me, but I was told even Queen Elizabeth prefers homeopathy. She is a staunch believer in homeopathy probably due to the non-drug treatment.

As a technical man, I know my problem is mechanical in nature. It is about presence of cyst in my spinal cord. I don't know how by administering tiny white balls as medication can move the cyst down. I was a bit sceptical and reluctant, but I persevered anyway. One of the reasons I tried is because of the friend suggesting it. He is a very close and sincere friend of mine. I know he will never hurt or disappoint me. I trust him! Also, as I said earlier, a sick man will try anything just to be cured.

Again, after a month and many sessions, there was no improvement. So, we quit the treatment. At the same time, the numbness, the prickling, the pain persists. I am like wearing armour over me. It felt burdensome. I didn't succumb and give up. I keep on thinking about alternatives. "How can that cyst flow down?" my mind keeps wondering looking for a solution.

Chinese Sports Masseuse

As I was contemplating my next potential treatment in the next few days, a friend of mine called. Apparently he heard about my disorder from friends. He brought me to a Chinese masseuse. He was kind enough to drive me some hundred and fifty kilometres down south. As ever, I am surprised of people's kindness and help. He wasn't a close friend, but we went to college together, some twenty years ago. It was a Saturday. There goes his family day. I was grateful to God. In time of hardship, there isn't any short of help that I got. I think God is giving me this sickness to make me a humble person.

I know I was pushy, impatient and arrogant at times. Furthermore, in our daily work demand and pressure, we tend to be ignorant and arrogant. It is almost inevitable. We were all caught in the daily three hour traffic grind. We have endless meetings, deadline and irritating and annoying client. I think everyone is like me. I don't know.

"I had a nasty landing from my skydiving. I hurt my hips and knee" he said, when we talked over the phone. "He is a Chinese masseuse and he is good. I had a few sessions with him and it is improving. He also specializes in sports injury" he adds. He suggests that I go try this treatment. I think it makes sense too as my spine may be the reason the cyst formed at my cervical bones area. I think the masseuse could check my spine and see if it is the reason the cyst is there. I was just guessing, but hopeful to hear the diagnostics of this masseuse.

It was a smooth drive down south that Saturday morning. In no time we were already at the clinic. The clinic is in a modest shop house in a small city. It has a signboard in Chinese and in between I could see the word "Chinese traditional massage" and "sports injury". "This is it" I thought to myself hoping to hear some good news and probably a solution. It was quite a wait as there are a few patients ahead of us.

The masseuse was seated in a small cubicle and we got seated in front of his small table. I explained my situation and he then referred to his medical journal, I think. It is a thick, big book written in Chinese. He spends some time flipping the pages. He seems meticulous. He asked a few questions as he keeps on reading his journal. Finally, he looked at his journal, looked up at me and said my problem couldn't be solved by massage. He was kind enough to show me that particular page from where he derives his conclusion. I couldn't read it anyway, but I trust his judgment. He said, he could only prepare a paste made of herbs and I should place it at the back of my neck, where the cyst is. "This is what I can do for you sir" he said, closing his reference manual.

It was over in an hour and off we went back home. I was thankful to this friend of mine.

I think seeking other options before going to the hospital is not wrong. I know of many traditional masseuses, traditional medicine practitioners whom I heard had advised to avoid surgery. "Not all ailment needs surgery" some of them said. "Surgery will definitely cause some permanent damage" I heard another comment. "We go to the cause not the symptoms" yet, another view. "They give you drugs and painkillers. It just solves the symptoms not the cause. You end up taking drugs all your life and the disease didn't go away" another strong view from another practitioner!

I have heard a lot of views from many practitioners. Almost all of them suggest avoiding surgery! "Of course, if you had an accident and your bones are broken, we can't do anything, but some bodily pains and muscle strains can easily be solved traditionally" one traditional practitioner said. "Do you know that there are cases where growth suddenly disappears?" asked one practitioner. Some of the questions are outright straightforward. "Long before all these medical sciences were found, how do you think our ancestors treat illness? They treat it traditionally, using herbs, using acupuncture, massages and even by just supplications!" claimed one man I met a few years ago.

I had also from my reading learned about traditional Chinese medication. I think all the comments from these practitioners make sense. Don't you think so?

I think the debate between traditional medicine and modern medicine is healthy. Today, in a few hospitals, there are traditional medicine department catering for those seeking alternative medicine. So, it is not fair to totally discard traditional medicine or alternative medicine in all forms. I know there are sceptics out there, but there are diseases that physical sciences can't cure! As I explored the various techniques and methods available, I am convinced of the argument that not all ailment needs surgery.

In Chinese medicine as an example, they can sense your internal organs problem just by touching your wrists. What about that man who can "see" my gall bladder and says I have a problem with it? What about that guy who knew my background just by "observing" me? What about the thousands of herbs that are now commercially available everywhere?

I think the world of medication and treatment is vast and many have been explored! In fact, these traditional medicines still exist today. It is a sign that these methods have been tried and tested for thousands of years, longer than modern medical sciences. The very fact they are still around is a testimony that it works!

I have even tried foot reflexology! Do you know that all organs have their designated touch points at your feet? Amazing right? I have always been fascinated with traditional medicine. I give you another scenario. What can medical science do to hysteria? You have probably heard of a group of students suddenly inflicted with hysteria or obsessed by evil spirits. What can medical sciences do? There are also cases where babies cry all night long especially when staying in a new home. They may "see" something our physical eye couldn't. What can a physician do? Drug the baby?

I am against those who belittled traditional medicine. I think they have their reason and I respect that. After all, it was I who is in pain. They can say whatever they want, but finally, I have to decide. I have to try to find the cure!

So, my next step is modern medication. I am into it, never discarded it. It was just that I was trying to avoid surgery, if possible.

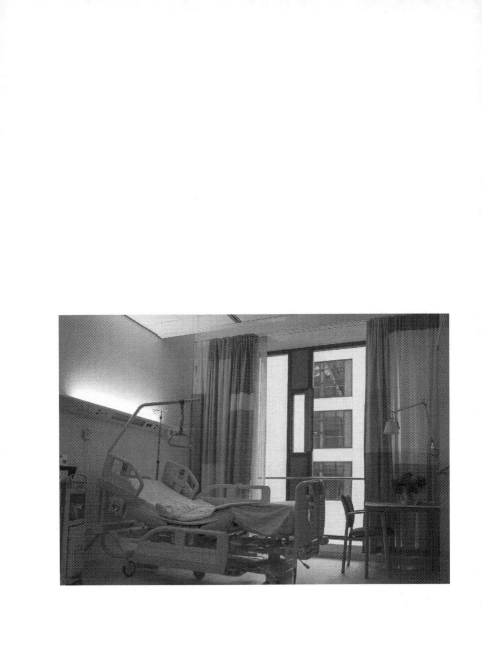

1ˢᵗ Hospitalization

Finally, after two and the half months seeing the spiritual practitioner, surgeon, acupuncture, homeopathy and a Chinese masseuse, I surrendered myself in. The bodily pain persists and began to worsen a bit.

I went for the appointment and unlike other appointments, this time I said, "Put me in the ward. I am ready for the surgery". We came with a bag and clothes. We had earlier informed the surgeon that we are coming and already knew that we will be admitted. At that time I could still walk, but rather slow. I felt weak due to the signals not reaching my muscle motors, I gathered. After a short meeting with the surgeon, my wife went for the registration. I was then given a wheelchair and taken away to the wards. I felt nervous, worried and lonely. Along the walkways, I saw other patients, some bandaged, some with tubes dangling from their faces and even children. It wasn't a pleasant sight. So, I said "Everything is going to be fine. Everything will be fine". I know I am not feeling well. I must go through this. How I wish things could be easier.

I had the surgery after a two-day wait. I think the surgeon knew the urgency and had given me priority. A young anaesthetist came over and briefed me about the surgery, the precautions and the risk. He read it to me and asked me to sign the document as consent. He said "I will be there for the whole duration of the surgery. Don't worry sir. We will take care of you"

I was then dressed in the surgery garb. In a few minutes, they transferred me on to a stretcher and off I went to the operation theatre. My wife was with me walking along my stretcher. I don't know what was going through her mind. This is serious enough for her not to worry. At the operation theatre, another short briefing was given. I was worried. A bit scared. However, it was quite comforting seeing all these young and fit-looking men and women at the receiving area. All dressed in light blue surgical uniform and head covers. They were all courteous, some greeted me and there were a lot of smiles. A few of them gave me encouragement and consoled me. I felt relieved. I know I will be in good hands. It was a warm and receptive atmosphere.

I am still worried, but I prayed"God, if this is my last day, please forgive all my sin and let me die as a faithful person. Help me through this. I leave it all to you".

Next is the transfer to the operation table. I was then given the anaesthesia and in seconds I was gone.

I woke up a few hours later. I was told it was a seven hour surgery. A few hours at the operation room holding area, I was then moved to the ward again. It was over. I recovered quite fast. Now, I get to see my love again. I can see and hear again. I passed the test. I didn't feel much pain either, but now I have titanium at the base of my skull. I hope the procedure went well without complications and will soon lead to the cyst being flushed down. I was hopeful, always hopeful.

I was discharged two weeks after surgery. We were told to come for another MRI in a month time. After the first surgery, I could still walk. I was fine initially, but after a week, the pre-surgery bodily pain came back. As before, my body is weak, muscle strained, I wobble when I walk and that "wearing armour" feeling remains.

I think the surgery is successful. I know the surgeon has expanded the passage and placed the titanium, but it doesn't work, as yet. However, I do not want to stir any misconception on the surgery. As a patient, I am the only one who could feel the difference.

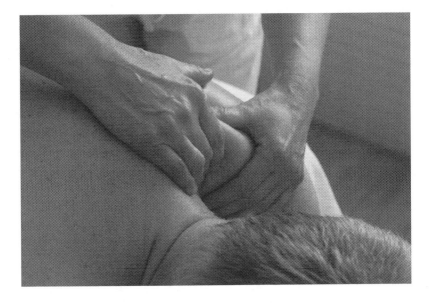

After 1ˢᵗ Hospitalization

I guess, after this first surgery was the time when I was really confused. In one hand, I have those who urged me to pursue the medical side of treatment and at the same time, there are those, both relatives and friends who asked me to seek alternative treatment.

Looking back, I sort of regret it. I don't know if I was right or wrong. One thing I know, all along this time, I want to find the cure. As I said earlier, ask anyone who is sick, they will all do the same thing. Do anything, anywhere just to be cured. One thing unique about my country is we have many types of alternative, complementary treatment.

In the next few months, we went through the gamut of medication, healing and therapy. We just go anywhere. We just hope that, somewhere, we will find the cure. We prayed a lot. We got many suggestions from family and friends. Along the way, we got a great deal of help from many, kind and beautiful people. I was thankful. I was grateful. Some are strangers, but they helped. They gave more than a friend could. They sacrificed.

Spiritual and Physical Islamic Treatment

One of the first practitioners we met was a famous spiritual medication practitioner, Professor Dr. Haron. He has a centre and it is well known that in order to see him, one has to queue to get a number. He has been practicing spiritual medication for more than thirty years. I talked to an old friend of my

41

intent to see Dr. Haron. He cautioned me that the queue to get the number is tedious. I was told the counter to get the number opened at six o'clock in the morning. It was earlier opened at eight o'clock, but was changed because most of the time, people are already queuing as early as six o'clock.

Just imagine how well-received this centre is. People seeking his treatment came from all over the country. He didn't have a fixed charge, but accepts payment in the form of charity. A charity box is placed at the waiting hall.

I was lucky that this old friend of mine offered himself to get the appointment number for me. He said" Just come tomorrow morning around eight o'clock and I will pass your number". I was touched by his kindness. So, the next day we came at eight.

The road, leading to the centre was crowded with cars and people. We have to park our car from quite a distant and I have to walk, slowly. We reached the centre and there were people everywhere, patients and those accompanying them, in the waiting hall and at the compound. I looked around and saw my friend. He came to me, smiled, but he looked groggy. His eyes are red. He looks tired and weary. He gave me the tiny slip. I asked him" What time did you come here? You must be very tired". He said "I came at midnight". I said "Midnight? Where did you queue?" He just smiles and said "Never mind. You are the patient. I don't think you should be the one queuing"

Later, he told me he waited all night long, sitting on a chair and in his car, catching sleep whenever he could. No wonder he looks tired and groggy. This is true sacrifice. I felt grateful to God for sending to me kind and sincere people to aid me in my times of need. I never know how I can repay him.

I looked at the number and sensed that it would be another two or three hours before I would be called in. It is a long wait because a nerve impaired patient like me, need a comfortable chair to ease me from strain and muscle ache. I was offered a chair by someone as I told them I could not sit on the floor. It is a mix of people sitting on chairs, on the floor and some, just standing. I think there are almost a hundred people in the hall. It was a long, strenuous wait for me.

Finally, my number was called. I stood up and walked into the room. I was not accompanied as only patients were allowed in. He has a few assistants by his side, ready to aid patients to the seat. He was sitting on a chair and I could see two empty chairs in front of him. I looked at his calm, "glowing" and pious face and felt easy. He is quite old, but his face doesn't reflect his age at all. He was always smiling and at ease with everyone. He greeted me with a broad smile and seated me. I was with another patient on my side. "We try to speed up the treatment by calling two patients at the same time. I know outside there are many in pain and sick, waiting" he said, with a gentle smile.

He asked me about my problem. I told him about my nervous problem. His treatment is quite unique. It is through supplication and reading some verses of our Quran. He didn't use any equipment. He just placed his hands on my forehead, at my back and continuously reading supplications and verses of the Quran. He seeks God's help to heal me. He is just the intermediary between me and God. He read the verses which are related to healing. I later learned that there are a few verses in the Quran specifically for healing and used for healing.

The process was quite fast, around five minutes. I was then passed over to his assistant, all pious and religious people. I was later interviewed by his assistant and was then given a bottle of water for me to drink with some instruction, when and how much. I left the centre and hoped that I will be cured. I don't know. I can only hope.

I wish to share that, I did seek Islamic medication for a reason. Prof Dr Haron specializes in healing black magic. To put it simply, a person who practices black magic inflicts evil spirit on to others due to revenge, hate or jealousy. Out of curiosity, I suspect that I may be one of the victims of black magic. I was advised to seek those who can check if I am inflicted with any spirit. It is also a known fact from practitioners of Islamic healing that most infliction is towards the nervous system. I was told there are many ways and forms of infliction and depending on the types of infliction, the diagnostic and healing differs.

So, welcome to the world of "spiritual" healing. This field is an entirely new world. It is full of mystery and intrigue. As much as we try to ignore and avoid, witchcraft and evil spirits do exist. It is part of our society. Yes, people do resort to evil deeds due to revenge, hate and jealousy. In this kind of treatment, the diagnostics and explanation may be beyond our normal apprehension. I was told to just listen. I didn't expect to comprehend in full anyway, but I hope that some solution may come out of this treatment.

I just said "If indeed there are evil spirits in me, just chase it away and restore my health". It is just that simple. My goal is cure. I will try and venture into any kind of treatment and healing. Again, I seek these treatment based on the conclusion of most practitioners that evil spirits attacks the nervous system more often than other parts. My intent is to check if I am indeed inflicted.

1st MRI after 1st Surgery

Next, around this time, five weeks after discharged, I went for the MRI to ascertain the size and location of the cyst. Apparently, despite the surgery to ease the spinal cord passage, the cyst did not reduce in size and subside. I remembered the surgeon told us that the surgery done is one of the procedures. They may, I gathered, resort to other procedures.

So, with the MRI result, we had another appointment with the surgeon. It was in this appointment that the surgeon informed us of the next procedure they will perform. It was again mechanical to me. They will insert a tiny tube or shunt into my spinal cord to suck the cyst liquid out of the spinal cord. It is an invasive approach now. The suction would be natural, through differential pressure between the pressure inside and outside the spinal cord. As an engineer, I could understand the concept because in instrumentation and control, many flow measurements were done from measuring differential pressure. It is easily understood.

Never mind the engineering terms. Let's get back to the procedure. A portion of my cervical bone will have to be removed in order to insert the tube into the spinal cord. This time around, after my first surgery, I am not as scared as before. I just listened to the explanation calmly. Then, the surgeon said "You must come for a surgery on this date. We will order the shunt for you". He showed a date, which is around a month from that day.

Another decision has to be made. Again, I went through the same confusion. In one hand, I have the medical side of treatment and at the same time, I have alternative treatment.

A few weeks passed by, the pain persists. I calmly console myself that the cure may not be with me yet. As ever, my goal is just to be cured. I remember a good advice. "We are not the one who cures. It is beyond our control, but we can do things within our control that is to find the treatment. Do not try to worry about things beyond your control" A profound advice. I forgot who told me. You know, when we are sick, people do come forward with words of comfort and advice.

Far-Infra-Red Treatment

In my search, I began to remember that my friend had a sauna. I knew about it but never tried it. I began to do some research about the far-infra-red thermal system. FIR is an invisible heat ray that penetrates the skin. From my reading, it has a few health benefits like detoxification, cardiovascular health and healing. I gathered since my problem has got to do with sensory, why not I try it.

It is basically a wooden box containment where we sit inside for some duration and expose ourselves to the FIR generated. I went for around ten sessions with the FIR treatment. I am just experimenting. I was hoping the FIR could improve my blood circulation which can eventually ease my neuropathic pain. It was just my self-made theory.

Again, after a few sessions, there wasn't much improvement. I then stop the treatment. I also learned that, our morning and late afternoon sunshine has FIR. So, even though it doesn't cure my pain, I had at least learned a new treatment. I had since reading about FIR been exposing myself to FIR around thirty minutes almost every morning.

The Massaging "Teacher"

In one of my visit to my hometown, I was told by a cousin to look for this traditional Malay masseuse. He is actually a retired teacher.

He is not well-known but I was told that a few well-known figures had sought his treatment. I thought that since the cyst is still there after the 1ˢᵗ surgery, it may be caused by my spine being crooked. So, I need someone knowledgeable enough to have a look at my spine. After all, I don't have anything to lose. I am just seeking a second opinion.

I was advised that I need to go through three sessions with the masseuse. It is reasonable as I have heard of this type of requirement before. So, I told my wife about this masseuse. "Yes, let us go and see him" she said, positively. "Let us go early in the morning and come back before noon as I need to send our son to school" she adds. I then called my cousin for the direction to the masseuse house and we are ready to go.

The next day we left early in the morning for the first of the three sessions. My wife drives the car. It was a smooth ninety minute drive and the area is not strange as I have been there before. It is a quite an old kind of housing estate from the façade of the terrace houses. It must have been built in the eighties I guess, but overall, it was a nice and clean neighbourhood.

As it was a working day, also a schooling day, we were probably the first to come. "Please come in" the masseuse greeted us, as he ushered us in. "Give me a few minutes. I need to prepare my grandchild here. The mother will come and fetch this baby" he said, as he packed some of the baby's things into a small bag. "I just take care of this baby while the mother went out just now". In a few minutes the mother came and took the baby. We are now set for the session.

"Come sit here" he instructs, showing us the mat and a small pillow on the floor of his living room. "It looks like your movement is restricted" he said, as he saw the way I tried to sit down on the mat. I finally managed to sit with my leg straight with the help of my wife. My wife told him about my disorder, the surgery and my general situation, my numbness, imbalance and so forth. He listens intently as he looks at my overall posture.

"Please lie down here. Slowly" he said. He then starts to touch and press various parts of my legs, starting from the knee. "If I press here can you feel something there?" he asked, as he starts to press various parts of my legs. "Can you feel anything?" he asked as he starts pressing more points. In fact, yes I feel some sort of twitching at other points of my legs and hip when he presses at every point on my legs. He seems to know the "wiring circuit' of my legs.

"From the way your feet sways out to the left and right in your lying position, I know your hips and your spine is not aligned" he explained. "It also looks like one leg is shorter" he adds. He then holds my feet and pushed it inwards and asked "Do you fell some twitch at your knees and thigh?" I could feel it. He was right. It was true for both my legs. He keeps on pressing and analysing the points on my legs. His focus was just on my legs. He then holds my knees and said "Here, this is weak. This is one of the problems" He pressed my knee and push my knee cap a bit as he tried to feel the overall "strength" of my knee, I guess.

He didn't do anything else after that. He has given me a general analysis and conclusion. At least my general apprehension is answered. My spine is crooked. So, I just get back to my sitting position, stand up and get prepared to leave. We know we have to come back the next day. It was quite a brief session.

The next day, again we left early in the morning for the second session. It was another smooth ninety minute drive. Again, my wife has to drive. I know it is tiring. It is a hundred and fifty kilometres drive. It is not near! I sympathize with her but I have no choice. She may never complain but I know she is tired. It is her sacrifice for me, her husband. She has to worry about me and the kid at home going to school. I know she has to iron the school uniform and prepare lunch too. She needs all the time she could save. She has to rush back. It must be depressing and tiring!

We arrived as before, probably the first client too. This second session is the same as before. He still focused on the legs. He did some light massage at the knees and thighs. He did lift my legs and check for the overall flexibility and probably the range of motion. "Most of our problems are with the bones and our posture, the way we sit, walk" he said. "Here, I can feel that it is week" he said, as he pressed my knees. "You must drink milk and take a lot of green vegetables. It will strengthen your bones" he adds, as he looks at my wife. "Give him milk. I suggest goat milk" he adds. Here, we have goat milk. You can buy anywhere but I just prepare this for my clients" he said, showing us a few boxes on a table nearby. "Goat milk is good for the bones" he affirms. We thought that it might be a good idea to drink it. I think I will buy it in our last session. So, it was another brief session. We then rushed back home for our son.

For the last session, my wife couldn't make it as she has to send our son for the co-curriculum activity. So, I called my friend to see if he can help me. As ever, this friend never refused. "I will drive you down tomorrow. Don't worry" he happily agreed. This is the guy that helped sent me to my homeopathy session. I am glad to be surrounded with selfless, sincere buddies. In fact, there are others like him too. I considered these friends as "religious" friends, friends of the mosque, people who has simple and humble "souls". It is not that others are not good but these are people who do things to please God, not me. I am sure of this!

The next day, as usual, he came with his car and drove me down. It is again, hundred and fifty kilometres down, fuel and tolls paid for. He really serves me. I am pleased. He is more than family to me. After all, in pain, I couldn't ask for more.

In the third session, apart from lying down, the masseuse asked me to lie down on my stomach. "From day one I can see your movement is slow and restricted. Now, do you think you can lie on your stomach?" he asked, as he looks at my overall slow and stiff stance. "Just try, slowly" he advised. With the help of my friend, I finally managed to lie on my stomach something I have not done in months. It wasn't easy. It is uncomfortable and strenuous. He then adjusts my head onto the pillow and I could see he stood up, probably trying to have a full view of my back. He then touches my spine gently. He did some presses at the lower back and slowly up my backbone. It is just light touches and nothing else. He then did some deep, hard presses at my buttocks and massages my hips. "Your spine and hips are not aligned well. Your spine is crooked" he said, as he did some more presses at my lumbar bones. "I can't massage you now since your body is still stiff" he adds.

I was then asked to sit. "You can't even move freely. I don't think I can do any massage on you now" he confirms, as he looks at my friend.

"It takes time to correct the backbone" he adds. "For now, drink the goat milk and take many green vegetables. It helps strengthen your bone" he said, persuasively. I then bought a few boxes of goat milk, gave him an envelope and prepared our move back. I was a bit disappointed that he did not "straighten" my backbone, but at the same time, I think he was right that I may not be conducive enough to get any massage yet. My body is still stiff. I think he knows better. So, that wraps up our three-day sessions with this particular masseuse.

The fact remains the same. The "wearing armour" gripping, the pain, the numbness, stiffness is still with me. Am I supposed to give in and give up?

The Martial Art Sifu and Traditional Healer

I was introduced to this practitioner by my sister. She happens to have a friend who was treated by this practitioner. He stays in an area known with many kinds on spiritual and traditional healers. I have personally never been there and seek any healers from that area. In my first trip there, I was accompanied by a friend. We went to his simple, modest clinic. It was quite a long wait. There were a few patients ahead of us.

I was called in by his assistant. He looks young and has a "glowing", pious and calm look. I took my seat and got myself ready. Our initial meeting was quite informal. He looks at me, analysing I guess and said "I am sorry for the wait. We have many kinds of patients coming with various situations". It looks like he is mumbling. He looks at his roster, his Android, cleared his table and said "Yes, please tell me how you feel". He added "Here we practice traditional medicine and also, Islamic medicine. We also do *bekam* if necessary". So, I just told him I had cyst in my spinal cord and that causes my body to be in pain, numbness and weak. Again, he looked at me in a rather sharp gaze as if he wants to say something.

After a short interview, and telling about some of the patients being treated there, he called his assistant to take me to another room. He proposed that I am treated with *bekam* or wet cupping therapy. I know *bekam* is well known among us in our country. It is more of a prevention and treatment for general health. It involves a process of drawing blood through suction cups and small vacuum pump. A practitioner usually knows the points where to draw the blood depending on the types of situation.

We then moved to the next room. He said "My assistant will do the *bekam* for you. I will show him the points and he will do the rest. In your case, today, we will do at three points. Don't worry". He joked "He is my right hand man, quite experienced. I trained him personally. I will be in my room and will come back". The assistant took out his cups and pump, prepared some cotton and cloth and sat me on the floor. He sat behind me. He told me the three points he will draw blood from. He said one point will be at the back of my head and two at my back near my shoulder blade.

Using a tiny needle, he started to punch a few holes in my skin, which wasn't that painful and quickly place the cup onto that area. Using a vacuum pump, he pumps the air underneath the cup causing vacuum that eventually suck the blood out. He followed the same steps with the other two points and leaves the cup there for some thirty minutes.

When he was about to lift the cup and collect the blood, he called the practitioner in. He then collects the blood off the cup and showed it to the practitioner for diagnostic and analysis. The practitioner or I rather call him the *Sifu*, just nods his head and didn't say anything. I will tell you why I call him *Sifu* later. He then asked the assistant to clean me up. I put on my shirt and was ushered again to the practitioner room. He then talks about his services there, some of his clients, types of cases and some of the herbs he provides. He then asked me to come again in a week time.

Before we left he looked at me rather deeply. I didn't think much then, shook his hands and left. Payment there is an option. He did not specify any rates. In fact, he asks me to give whatever amount to his assistant.

I came a week later with my wife. It was quite a wait too. We finally got our turn. I greeted him and sat at his table. He looks at his roster, his Android as though to confirm if it is my turn and said "Oh it's you. I remember. Welcome back. How are you?" I said I am fine. He then said something that still rings my mind even now. He looked at me and said "I have seen many bloods from many *bekam* sessions through the years, but yours is different". He seems serious making that statement. He added "Usually the blood collected is in a jelly form but it remains in that form only for a few minutes. It will normally liquefy, but yours is different". I am a bit startled with his analysis. How could it be that way? Have I got something else I didn't know? He said "Your blood remains as a jelly for one whole day". He said even his assistant was shocked.

I was again shocked if what he had analysed was true and new to him. I just sat there not knowing how to react. He looked down emptily at his table then stared at me as though he wants to reveal something. I waited. My wife looked at me. Lastly, he said "For the next session, come over to my house. It is much proper to do it at my house. I also have some water to give you". He then joked "I don't invite all my patients to my house, but you are special". He smiled and gave us his home address. It was already late and we left his clinic.

Our next meeting at his house was on a Saturday. We came with our own plain water as requested by him. We were ushered in and conveniently seated at the living room. He greeted us and asks us to wait. His wife was also with us.

We managed to look around his beautiful and cosy living room. At one corner lies a glass display panel. We can see photos and memorabilia of him. Apparently, he is more than just a traditional medicine practitioner. He is a leader for a huge traditional martial art and self-defence group. It is not easy to be in martial arts let alone being the leader. He must be a fit, agile and athletic guy. Besides that, he leads the local youth group. He is also one of the mentors for a drug rehabilitation organization. I also came to know that he did appear in many local television programs. Indeed, he is more than I thought. As I said, he is qualified to be called *Sifu*! On top of all his achievements he is a pious, religious and knowledgeable person. I am impressed.

After a while, he appeared again. We moved to another area of the living room. He started our treatment session with a short supplication. He then left for, I guess, optional prayer because I could see his face was a bit wet when he came back. He then sat in front of us and talked a bit about his history. He was actually a child healer. He said "I am doing this not because I wanted to do it. I think it was hereditary from my grandparents and ancestors" He told us a bit about how at a very young age, he could see the unseen and cured people of illness. To me, this is nothing strange. I believed that when we were young, our soul is pure and the probability that we can see the unseen is high. I think his story is not strange. I can accept it.

So, my next interest is to know his diagnosis. I want to know his conclusion. He came nearer to me and said "Your pain is concentrated at these four points." He put his finger at my chest, my stomach, my heart and my back. He asked "Right?" I nod in agreement. He adds "There is disturbance within your body. This is a bit delicate. It is bedevilment from someone". He went on to say "It has been going on for quite some time. What I will do is I will prepare some water for you to bathe with. I will try to cleanse you"

He looked at me, smiled and said "You must be working in a big company and holds a good managerial position. You are a big person. People like you are prone to this kind of infliction" I didn't say anything, but inside, I thought "Just now, he showed me all the points where my pain are severe. He was right. I didn't tell him about it. How could he know it? Now, he seems to know about me being a manager. Again, how could he know about that? I didn't tell him about my job either!" I was curious. I felt a bit strange, but I quickly recalled his story about being a child healer. Whatever that goes through my thought, I tend to accept the fact that he knows what he is doing. He has knowledge that is beyond my apprehension. After all, he is pious. He may be able to see "spiritual beings" my bare eyes couldn't see.

He prepared his water and blended it with some herbal ingredients. He gave instructions on how to cleanse myself with the water. He said "Try this first. Hopefully you will feel better. Come again in a week's time" We took all the plastic bottles and left. For a week, we did as told. We met him a few more times and he tried different mixed of substance to be used together with the water. I think he was trying different "medicine" to chase that evil spirits that is disturbing me. In fact, in one of the days he did say "It looks like the source of this infliction is from a "hard" source. It is tough to fight it"

I think he was right saying it. It is not my expertise and I can't dispute it. By then I am beginning to be exposed to the mystic world of witchcraft, I think. I know it takes an extraordinary people to deal with this mystic world. I did have some argument with my physician friends who refute traditional medicine as a myth. I accepted that point as he is physician, but I replied by saying that their medicine knowledge could not solve "spiritual" disturbance. They tend to agree although reluctantly. I just want a cure. If it is spiritual I must get a spiritual solution. That is all to it.

The Recitation and Supplication Treatment

We move on and seek another famous practitioner. I am beginning to believe my ailment may be due to some spiritual infliction. I think there may be a probability. So, the next practitioner is as expected, non-medical. It is again, spiritual. I found this practitioner through the internet after reading about his practice in the local paper. We first went to his house, but a notice showed that they have moved to a new centre in the city.

We then drove to the city and found his centre. It is in a crowded area with school, offices and shops. After parking our car, which was quite far, I have to walk slowly to the centre. With my condition, the walk was quite strenuous. The centre is on the ground floor of a new and beautiful building. It looks impressive. It resembles a private medical clinic. It is air-conditioned, with a counter and comfortable chairs for the patients. We went in only to find that the appointment number counter was closed for the day. We booked ourselves for the next day. We paid the fees and left immediately as I was tired.

We came early the next day, parked our car and were seated at the waiting area. The crowd is quite large, around fifty people. We were finally ushered to an area behind the counter. It is spacious and has around six sizeable cubicles. Each cubicle is manned by a practitioner. I was lucky that day. I was able to meet the owner of the centre, the lead practitioner.

I took my seat. The man has a big piece of the Quran on the table in front of him. He doesn't look calm and friendly. I guess he may be a bit stressed. He asked me about my situation. I told him about the cyst in my spinal cord the overall pain and numbness of my body. He then moves his hands over the Quran and selects one of the many tabs on the pages. He flipped to one of the marked pages and glance at the verse. He then took a small form, filled it up and passed it to me. He said "Please read the verses I noted here a few times each day. I have written the times there on the form. Just follow it" He said "Bring the form to the counter and they will give you a few more instructions". He then stood up and shakes my hand. I was surprised. Is that all?

I left him and went to the counter. The man looked at my form, punched something into the computer and said "That's it sir. Thank you". I was a bit puzzled. As we walked out of the centre, I complained about the very short diagnosis and "treatment" I got inside. My wife said "Yes. It was quite fast! What happened?" I just shook my head in disbelief. We left the place, wondering. I tell myself "I will recite those verses as prescribed. I leave it to God. That's all"

The Aura Healing Water Therapy

As I said earlier, my search for the cure is between the physical and the spiritual. I may be inflicted based on one of the practitioner diagnostics. I do have supporters and detractors of my experiment with the spiritual practitioners. It is irrelevant to me. I am in pain. They do not know what I am going through. I am still in pain. The search must go on.

My next attempt is with a medical doctor that has produced a certain kind of treated water. Dr. Nordin is a medical doctor, a renowned wellness guru and water therapy specialist. He was the medical officer for our national sports team. Late in his career, he was struck by blood cancer or lymphoma and can only live for a few more months. As he underwent severe suffering due to the side-effects from the treatment and medication, he felt inspired by God to use water as a solution. Water from this special filtration system helped him recover from the cancer within only a few months. Feeling responsible to share this breakthrough with others, he worked to propagate The Aura Healing Rx-Water therapy. I happened to know about this doctor new Rx-Water through a friend. At first we tried to look for this Rx-Water in the open market. We couldn't find it. We asked around and was later introduced to one of the doctor many distributors. We bought a carton of twelve bottles from the distributor. We were also advised to have an appointment with the doctor himself. We looked for the office from the internet, made a few calls and secured an appointment.

It was not far from our place. This doctor is quite successful looking at his four-story centre. He is also a well-known figure. He appeared countless times on television and his product is well received nationwide. On the first floor lobby is mostly a display area and a distribution centre where his distributors purchase the stock. It was quite busy, but the place is spacious. There are few tables and chairs for small meetings and discussion. We took a lift to the fourth floor where his clinic is. I was seated and he quickly starts the session.

I was a bit sceptical as my understanding of my ailment is mechanical – the need to suck out the cyst. I thought "How, by drinking treated water can the cyst be pushed down?" I proceed with the session anyway. I described my ailment and the sequence of events leading to me meeting him. He took down notes as I spoke to him. His assistant a nurse stood by the table.

He then instructed the nurse to prepare the water for me. The nurse then came back with one bottle of clear water and a few small droppers for us to add to the water. He said "These are salt droplets. Each has a different concentration. You need to add the correct number of drops to a certain volume of the Rx-Water" It has a special time and quantity of droplets for us to mix and drink.

It was a short and brief session. I was satisfied because the way he explained the effects of water to our well-being was quite comprehensive. He has a very extensive knowledge probably because he researched and worked hard to find the cure to his cancer from water. I told myself "Let's try this treatment. Who knows what will happen. After all, there are many testimonials from his distributors about the benefits of Rx-Water" I am well aware of distributors selling benefits of their products, but as an engineer, I am impressed with his explanation.

Basically, water is important to the prevention and preservation of our cells and organs. I was hoping, by drinking this treated water, my blood circulation and cells in my brains and spinal cord could benefit and ease the flow down of the cyst. Again, this is just my theory.

He even let me apply his pain management technique by using sound and visual effects. He has a small laptop which played a file that emits some "healing" music and an animated, moving graphics on the screen. I tried. Well, it was not that effective to me. I do not want to blame the technique though. I believe there is science and ample amount of research behind the creation of all this healing techniques.

I know our pain is processed by our brains and certain area of our brain computes different sets of pain sensor signals. I recalled a statement made by a friend. He said "Your problem is about nerves and all nervous activity originates from your brain. It is a delicate disease. So, you have to control your thinking" I think he is right. Probably with a correct mind control my pain may be managed and controlled. It makes sense, isn't it? Mind control? My thinking is still about that cyst. I think as long as the cyst blocks my nerves, I will be in pain. I thought, never mind, I let the treatment takes its course. After all, I am not the one healing, but the treatment will heal me when God permits!

Our experiment with the Rx-Water treatment lasted approximately a month. Physically, I didn't feel any improvement. So, what should I do? After the Rx-water session, our search seems to accelerate. We still have the two options –physical or spiritual. At that particular time, we did not know which is right. I thought we may never know until we find the cure!

Detecting the Presence of Evil Disturbance

My next venture brought me to an Indonesian-descent spiritual healer. He is known for chasing away evil spirits from patients bedevilled with evil spirits. He has appeared in a few television programs. Why did I go there? I really don't know. I was in pain. I need a cure. I think that is all that I can say. I just want his diagnostic to affirm the previous healer assessment. As usual, these healers usually work from a centre. It was packed when we came. I got an appointment number, but the wait was quite long. One thing different here is the healing is done openly. He sat at one side of a small hall and everyone, patients and spectators can see his method of treatment. It is very simple. He just touches your foot with a tiny seed. If a patient is possessed by a spirit, you can hear them scream or shout in pain. For those who are not inflicted by evil spirits, they do not react. Do you find it hard to believe? I saw it right in front of my eyes. I saw a few positive and negative cases.

In fact, from the looks of the patients, we can guess if they are inflicted. What I gathered from asking around the people there, people afflicted usually has a frown, freckled look with empty gaze. They display a common facial expression. They look sad and lonely. I think his method is amazing. It is not new to me though. I have seen previous practitioner performed what he did. So, I just watched his treatment, one after the other. Then, it was my turn.

He looked at me and smile. He said "Sit here please. How are you, son? Do you come alone? I will place this tiny seed at the sole of your feet. Just relax" Like the others, I sat in a long position with my legs straight out in front of me, facing him. He holds my feet for a while before pressing the seed at my sole. I didn't feel anything. He then put it on my left foot. I didn't feel anything either. I think I am through. It's a negative. I am not possessed.

He looked at me and said "Thank God, you are fine son. I didn't see any internal disturbance" He then quipped "I saw you among the crowds just now and I knew you looked fine" So, I thanked him and moved away.

Now I am confused. Am I possessed or not? One practitioner says I am and now he says I am not. I feel a bit relieved though. At least I have tried and went through another assessment. Regardless, the pain is still with me. We drove back and talked it over to my wife. She said "That is his assessment. We can try other practitioners. We cannot give up"

An Audience with the "King"

I then seek assessment from another practitioner. This particular person is also pious and religious. King is a nickname as he is known to be a King or conqueror over evil spirits. He is well known for chasing away evil spirits. I was first brought to his house, a modest two story link house in the suburb, close to my place. I was told his involvement in his current practice was also through chance. He did not study anything, but just inherited it.

His hall is quite unique. At the centre of the hall was sort of a display area, filled with sticks or probably wand with some magical properties. I saw maybe fifty pieces plus some knives, daggers and strange looking sticks. I don't know. This man is known to the local as a "ghost buster". His specialty is helping patients inflicted with evil spirits by chasing away the spirits.

He greeted us as we are seated on the sofa. He is in the early forties, looks healthy and fit. He doesn't look much like a healer though. He is in jeans and t-shirt, very casual. I was told that he is also a committee member of his local mosque, situated in front of his house.

As we talked, he could sense that we were a bit curious at the things we saw in his hall. He said "Look, these are things I managed to retrieve from my patients, objects used by those who wanted to inflict them with evil. So sad, our people still resort to this dirty kind of work" He adds "It is not easy to cure those bewitched. The spirits do come back and haunt us. It can be demanding and tiring. It can come in the middle of the night. Our defence must be strong, better than them. Anyway, don't worry these objects are not as magical as it used to be. Basically, I have defused them. It is safe" He quipped "If not I wouldn't keep it in my house. I have children of my own"

I was then asked to come again the next day. Apparently, he has an appointment somewhere. Furthermore, we just called and went to his house without knowing his other engagement.

We came the next day. He immediately starts his session. He asked me to sit long with my feet facing him. He has a small piece of pencil-like wooden object. "I will have to check you first" he said. He placed the wood at my sole randomly at a few points. He then placed it at my other foot. He nods his head as if acknowledging something. He then looked up at me and said "This thing can be tricky. It may reside inside someone else. It can come and go. It may be just an ancestral infliction". He said "How far is your wife's family home? I need to do the same to your in-laws, just to check". Also, he requests to do a check at my house. "I need to see the interiors and surroundings of your house. After that, let us drive to your in-laws. We do it today"

At my house, he entered for a while and said "I feel a bit jittery." He did not elaborate. We offered him a drink, talked for a while and left for my in-law's house. We drove back in our car. He was kind enough to drive. It is quite a distance about an hour and a half drive.

My in-law was ready for us as we had called her earlier. As before, he entered to gauge the overall situation. He then stood at the living room and recites some Holy verses. He then sat down on the floor and got down to business. He gently placed the wood at my in-law's feet. He looked at me and nods. All the while his lips move, reciting something. His method is short and simple. In a matter of minutes he is done.

As a courtesy and out of respect he told my in-law that he was there just to check if the "thing" that may have inflicted me resides there. He told my in-law "Please forgive me for causing you some discomfort. This is my way of treatment auntie. Thank you" I asked him how the check went on. He breathed a sigh of relief and said "Looks like everything is fine. I didn't see anything alarming". We had a few drinks and off we went back home. Again, he drove. "You are the patient. I serve you today" he jokes.

The Traditional Healing "Diplomat"

Until now, we have consulted seven practitioners, mostly traditional. We thought we have seen it all only to be introduced to another practitioner. One of my former officemate came for a visit. He just found out that I am having a nerve ailment. He is an engineer. He said "You know some of our ailments are not all the time physical. It may be caused by some other element" I said "Yes probably. We have been trying some Islamic and traditional treatment too". He then said "I know one good practitioner. His style is a bit unique. I think you should see him. I met him a few months ago for my problems" He pulled out his mobile and transferred to me the number. "I will call him first for you" he adds.

According to my friend, this man is actually an ex-officer in the foreign ministry. He has served in many countries. He was even conferred with a Datuk ship, a special title from a Sultan for his services. He has since retired. He too became a healer by chance. He just did it on an ad hoc basis on his free time usually through words of mouth only from friends. He is low-profile as he is not into healing, full-time. So, we managed to get an appointment with him quite easily.

A short drive brought us to his gated-community housing area. He lives in a bungalow. He was watching TV when we arrived. We were invited in. His wife was there too. He looks quite old, but healthy. He speaks English well, warm and still has that diplomatic demeanour in him. It was a receptive atmosphere. I feel good, despite the pain I feel.

He then starts to talk a bit about his background. "Actually, I didn't do this full-time. In fact, I am new to this" he said with a grin. "I am a retired government servant. I served in our foreign mission offices. I have been all over" he said while filling us drinks his wife served. He lowered down the TV volume and continued our conversation.

He said "I was in Mecca performing my *Umrah*. After my *Isya'* prayers, I just sat in the mosque, resting for a while". While he was resting, he said, suddenly someone came to him and gave him the prayer beads or *misbaha*. The man then taught him the methods to use the prayer beads to cure patients. To some, this may sound weird, but I believe our knowledge about the unseen is too little for us to make any judgment. I should leave it to the practitioner to decide. He is the one experiencing it. He is the one who knows the "effects" when he used it. I am just a patient seeking his help if he could cure me. Of course he has no powers to cure me, but through his methods, his supplication, he may help. I am not there to question his methods. I am in pain. I need to find a way to solve my problem.

Next, he told me "If I were you, I would not be able to come. Your pain is terrible. You are a strong man". I was a bit surprised. How could he know that I am in terrible pain? We have not even discussed my pain. Indeed, I am in terrible pain that night. He even showed me the points where my pain is the most severe. He was right! I was taken aback. I looked at my wife. She seems startled. He then took a few bottles of water, gathered it in front of him and dipped the *misbaha* into it for a few seconds. He then took it out and said "You should use this water to bathe with it" He asked me to do it a few times a day. I forgot how many times now.

He then asks us to come back later and bring along water from three ablution ponds from three mosques. He told us to go to old mosques and get a bottle from these mosques. It is not a strange request as I have known these practices since I was a kid. I know some traditional medicine practitioner uses this method. It is a blend of religious and traditional method. I don't know the origins of this practice, but I believe our elders must have their reference before practicing it. It is again, not my right to judge them.

So the next few days we went to a few old, famous mosques to get the water.

We came back to meet him with three bottles of water from three mosques. He did the same thing. He dipped the *misbaha* into each bottle, uttered a few verses and supplicated. Again, he asked me to bathe with it. We were then asked to come again and this time, with water from just one mosque and one type of lime. The name of the lime he mentioned is quite strange. I haven't heard of it. I said I will try to find that type of lime and come back.

We have no problem looking for water from the mosque, but the lime, we have to think. I suddenly remember one friend whom I know is special. He has helped me before. I called him one afternoon and asked him if he could help me find that lime. This friend of mine knew I am in pain and a bit disabled. In fact, he came to visit me before. I asked him where he was. He said he is at home. He said "Don't worry. I know that lime and will bring it for you".

In less than an hour, he called and said "The lime is in your mailbox. I don't want to call you down because I know you can't move that well". I said "Where are you now? Where did you find that lime" He said, "I am still around your house. Just now, I just took my bike to Chow Kit". I said "What? Chow Kit?" I felt a bit embarrassed for troubling him. I know his house is almost twice the distance between my house and Chow Kit. Furthermore, he took a bike in the middle of the hot sun! He did it in an hour! I was grateful for his kind gesture. I am indebted.

It is this kind of people and event that makes me feel delighted to share with all of you. He sacrificed his free time riding in the hot sun, passed through traffic and went to one of the busiest market in the city to get me the lime I need. I am neither his relative nor a close friend. He is just a friend to my friend. I just knew him for a few weeks. This world is still full of kind and sincere people. I am glad God sent him to me. I learned about kindness, sacrifice and sincerity from him alone all in one afternoon. I don't think I can be like him. I am humbled. I wouldn't have known him if I am not sick. I know God inflicted me with this ailment with a hidden blessing and to show me His mercy through this man. God, I am elated!

I did mention that he is special. Do you want to know why I said that? Prior to my first surgery, I did try acupuncture and homeopathy, remember? Actually, after the two treatments, I was suggested to meet one religious teacher up north. He is a pious man and known among the religious circle. He practiced one traditional treatment called *bekam* or wet cupping therapy. He was on a religious tour up north some three hundred and fifty kilometres away, a three and a half hours drive. Just thinking of it makes me weary.

My friend who suggested that I meet this practitioner called him and set a date. After the call my friend said "Don't worry. We will drive you there" I said "Who else is going? Do you have a car?" He said "I will arrange with someone. We will use our car. You just sit at the back. Relax". We arranged to leave the next morning at seven o'clock.

The next morning I waited at my porch. Then, a Volvo came. It stopped right in front of my gate. I saw my friend, this "special" person and his friend came out. They both greeted me and look ready and happy. They were all fresh and smiling. I then said goodbye to my wife and one of them took my bag. I brought spare clothes as I expected to spend overnight at any hotel there. I planned to cover all expense, fuel toll and all. I felt obligated to pay looking at their willingness to assist me. They opened the car door, the booth. I was carefully brought to my seat. They are all selfless. They treated me with care. I felt like a VIP. I don't know them that well, but they have one common trait. They are all pious. I know they are doing all this to please God, not me. I know they are convinced not mere believing in the rewards of the Hereafter.

I am glad I am surrounded by good, pious and sincere souls in my time of need. Sometimes in life, we tend to think that religious people are self-restrained, isolated, rigid and unhappy people. I think you would agree, right? It is a common perception. We tend to avoid them. We have a certain mind-set towards them. God was I wrong.

I was also gifted by God to "be brought back" on the right track after being a little naughty, clumsy, muddled and a bit deviated when I was younger. I don't consider myself a pious person, but I am a student, learning religion all the time. I started to frequent mosques and mix with "guided" people. So, I have a lot of good people that slowly influenced me to change. It wasn't easy though. I remembered and advice from a buddy. He said "Our faith is so weak that in the mosque we remember God. Outside, we forget about God. We are situational. We are easily influenced by our surroundings!" I think you would agree. Well, never mind about that. Take it as a piece of advice, a profound one.

So, all of us got into the car and off we went. The driver is this "special" person. He volunteered. The first thing I thought about was fuel. I said "Don't forget about fuel. I will fill it up" The driver said "Oh we already filled up the tank. It is full now". I thought never mind, but I must buy them breakfast. I didn't expect them to have taken their breakfast. It is too early in the morning.

We drove on and as we entered the highway, we pass through the first toll gate. There, we picked up the ticket and it has to be paid when we exited. It wasn't that much, but considering the distance, I guess it is quite substantial. I tried to pass the driver a big note for the toll, but he said "Keep it first with you" I insist but he said "I will let you know when we need it". Then, I make a suggestion "Please stop somewhere. We need to have our breakfast. To those who are familiar, show us all to a good restaurant" They said "We will do".

Apparently they know a good restaurant, but it is off the highway. We need to exit the highway and move to a small town nearby. I thought this would be a proper time I pass the money. As the car stopped and even before I got my purse, the driver paid the toll. Again, I tried to give him the note he smiled and said "Never mind. It's OK. We pay". I didn't get to fill the tank and now, they paid the toll! When can I get to pay? I thought to myself.

In a few minutes, we reach the restaurant, a small one. The town is small too. It was early in the morning and most people are just about to go on doing their daily chores. We were told that this small restaurant has one of the best *Nasi Lemak*, a local well-known dish. It was a bit crowded with people buying and taking breakfast. I was again, treated with care and served. After eating and looking at the papers, I stood up to pay at the counter. My friend pat my back and said "Sit down. Don't worry. It is on me". Now, I didn't get to buy them breakfast either!

We then moved on to the highway and off towards the north. It was quite a smooth three and a half hours drive. As usual, I am always feeling the discomfort of cramps, pain and strain not to mention the numbness. I tried to grapple with it. It wasn't easy, but manageable. I still hope to pay the final exit toll charges.

We finally reached the toll exit gate. I quickly passed the note. The driver was reluctant to take my note, but this time I pleaded "Please let me pay. You have been so kind to me. Take this please" He relented and took the note. It was another twenty minutes' drive until we reach the destination. It was already around noon.

I was treated at a small house beside a mosque there. It was brief, but there is a short wait. The practitioner has a few patients too. We then took a short nap and rested. I thought everyone was tired and proposed to book a hotel and check in. We have a short discussion and they all suggested we drive back. I said "What? Aren't you all tired? It's another four hours driving" They said "Don't worry about us. We are healthy. You are not well. I think your wife will be worried. We will drive you back".

We then took our lunch and got into the car again. In no time, we reach the highway and it is back on that long stretch again, southbound. I was really tired on top of the strain and pain. I just lie back and slept. I think they stopped once at the rest area, but I was too weak to wake up.

I finally reached home. I forgot who paid for fuel and toll. I told my wife "These people are really good people. They treat me like their parents. All of them were nice, courteous and caring. I don't have words to describe them" May God is pleased with them and grants them Heaven.

Looking back, I know the special person is not that wealthy. I know where he works. I don't know whose car was that. I never know until today because they didn't tell me when I asked then. One thing I am sure is I am humbled. They have shown me what devotion, hospitality and on top of it all, what religion is. It is all about loving. Yes, religion is about loving. It is about compassion.

A Short Visit Overseas

In between all the visits seeking cure, despite the declining health, I did manage to try doing some business. I have always done some sort of freelance work related to oil and gas with my friends.

It is about one little proposal for a secondary oil project, overseas. I was approached by a friend who has a "connection" with the owner of a secondary oil concession area. They were looking for potential investor to help them produce oil from that area. On my part, I managed to get one businessman as a potential investor in the venture. After a few meetings, we decided to bring the businessman for a short site visit. The businessman then planned an all-expense-paid trip for me to view the site. However, the business trip didn't materialize on that date due to some technical matters between the investor and the owner.

Since the trip was planned and booked, the businessman proceeded with the trip anyway. He said he is familiar with that area and has other businesses too. So, we made that short 4-day trip. So, to me it is like a holiday. I was accompanied by my friend. So, being a bit unhealthy, he is kind enough to aid me with all my needs. At that time I could still walk normally except for the "wearing amour" feeling and minor pain. Overall, it's manageable.

We were picked up at the airport by an MPV and efficiently sent to our hotel, which is plush by the country's standard. We have a day free before our next excursion to a nearby city. "I heard you have some ailment" the businessman said. "Do you know that in this country, there are a lot of religious and pious people who may be able to help you" he adds. "The place we are going to tomorrow is quite well known. Let me see what treatment they could offer. In the meantime enjoy this holiday" he jokes.

The businessman has good connection with the provincial leaders and one "Sultan". The next few days brought me to the descendants of the well-known "Nine Saints". We got to meet the "Sultan" of that province, personally at his humble palace and even had dinner with him and his advisers. We then visited the mosques and graves of their ancestors. We were then brought to a place of meditation where these "Nine Saints" would spend hours daily and at time months isolating themselves from the world, to meditate. It was an enlightening experience.

The whole area is filled with mystical stories and wonderful history. We visited a few historical and holy sites. In a nearby city, we visited a mosque said to be built by "Angels"! It was said by the locals that construction starts at night and completed before dawn. It has a few pillars and each dedicated to a certain "Saint". The mosque has endless lines of visitors from all over. It is always filled with people coming for prayers or just visiting and savouring the peace and tranquillity of the mosque. Beside the mosque pulpit is a small structure, a prayer compartment for the Kings. Its design is unique. It has a mixed design from various religions! I guess this was all part of the progression from various religions in that area.

Our guide, a local gave us a good explanation about the mystical world of the place, the mosques, the ancestral graves and the place of meditation. I remember asking him about the rostrum nearby the palace "This area is not fenced. Anyone can enter it, right?" He just smiled and said "Yes, there are many who tried to enter and destroy the rostrum and nearby artefacts. There are a few rival warlords claiming "ownership" of this place" He then revealed that the warlord trying to enter the area was kicked out by invisible "powers" and ended up being "flown away" a few hundred meters from the place!

He may sound weird, but I have been to the palace and the ceremonial rostrum and I can see many "valuable" artefacts. So, no one in the right frame of mind would leave the rostrum open without a fence! Yes, it is guarded by some invisible powers, so he said.

For a moment, I forgot that I have a nervous ailment. I was too busy absorbing all the mystical places and its "powers". The trip was good, the food was delicious and cheap, the guide and the MPV plus the hotel are all excellent! I don't think I can grasp everything about that mystical place, but I believe in the existence of supernatural forces. I may not comprehend it all but sometimes, we can think logically! How can a rostrum will all the valuable artefacts be left without a fence and not a single guard?

All in all, I love the place. I hope to be there again when I gain my health. It's fine even if the deal does not materialize. It doesn't matter much to me. In fact, from the number of old colonial wells mentioned and the capital and operation expenditure of developing the wells, storage and sales to the nearby refinery, it is indeed a good proposition. The daily net inflow is quite lucrative.

I always believe that there will always be another opportunity, somewhere, later! At least I know that physically I may not be fit, but that ten billion cells up there are still functioning. That is good enough for me. Who says I am crippled?

2nd MRI after 1st Surgery

My 2nd MRI is roughly five months after the 1st surgery and four months after the 1st post-surgery MRI. Again, we have to drive all the way to the huge hospital. It is forty kilometres away, but we have to pass through part of the city and that makes it an almost two hour journey. I have to withstand the constant pain and endure the traffic at the same time. Also, the one driving is my wife. She has to hassle through the morning city snarl on almost the whole stretch of the journey. Another difficulty is parking at the hospital that is almost all the time, full. She has to drop me off at the foyer and go park the car outside the hospital compound. Then, she has to walk all the way to the hospital entrance and up a ramp to the foyer. It is far. It is troublesome I know.

I am glad to have a very patient wife. She has been my chauffeur, my "servant" and nurse the last eight months or so. In fact, this is above her responsibilities of commuting to and from school to send my youngest to school every day. She has to get her friends to replace her wherever she has to take me somewhere. It wasn't easy for her. This is a priceless gift from God. I can't imagine going through all this without her.

For the MRI, I usually register at the MRI clinic and there will be some waiting time. I was told this hospital has to accommodate patients from surrounding hospitals too, for the MRI. I will have to change my clothes and I need my wife to assist me. She will have to be with me in the changing room. I couldn't bend easily and even my hands are numb to feel my trousers and shirt buttons. My balance is affected because the balance is concentrated at the bottom of my brain, the area where the surgery to enlarge the passage was done. It is expected because our surgeon did highlight about the loss of balance. In fact, it was there, even before the surgery.

I had a few MRI before, but I never really talk about it. It is just one long wait inside a small tunnel. Luckily it is not that dark. You can't move so as not to interfere with the scanning and mapping of the scan area. So, I just "play dead" and close my eyes. You have an option though whether to plug your ears and listen to some music or just lie there hearing the occasional sound of the scanning. So, you are not actually "dead" in that tunnel. Maybe if it is totally dark and quiet, you will feel like you are inside a grave. Do you want it? You are actually in a "partially dark grave with piped in music". Not that bad, right? So, that's how I describe the MRI experience.

A week later, we were shown the result. The cyst is still there. No wonder, I didn't feel much improvement. In fact, after the 1st surgery, the surgeon had already suggested to us to come back. I remembered his advice. "You must come on this date" as he showed a date a month after that. He added "We will order the shunt for you". We didn't come for the surgery. I am not sure why I procrastinate then. Probably I was still exploring other avenues.

It has been almost four months now after the first instruction to come for the surgery. Again, in this appointment, the surgeon gave us another new date for surgery. It is around a few weeks after this appointment. The surgeon reminded me "You must admit a day before the date of the surgery. We have the shunt for you.

Again, yet again, I didn't come. Looking back, I think, this delays may have caused my disorder to worsen. At that time however, my mind was still focused on looking at other alternatives. In short, I was trying to avoid surgery.

In fact, just a few weeks ago, two years after failing to come for the 2nd surgery, my brother and I had a little disagreement. Actually, we were discussing on some issues via SMS.

In the SMS, he ventured into my health problem. He said "You know we talked a lot about you" he remarked. "Your problems could have been saved and you would be better now if you didn't delay the 2nd surgery" he said in a rather annoying tone. I didn't expect him to make such a comment. I was shocked, but tried to remain calm. He is my elder brother. I don't want to be rude. Then, he starts to make this irritating conclusion. "You are too obsessed with other treatments. You didn't listen to your brother's advice and the surgeon!" This was roughly what I recalled he said. Keyword is "obsessed".

I think he found out about my delays from the neurosurgery clinic. My sister-in-law and my eldest brother are both physicians and they had served in that hospital before. They probably have some relationship even though both my sister-in-law and brother had retired ten years ago. Yes, I believe my siblings did talk about me. They are concerned and have the right to be disappointed in me. I can't blame them. They are right. I shouldn't have delayed.

The next one month after this appointment, I didn't do much.

I thought to myself that if I could get my spine straight and correctly aligned, there is a possibility that the cyst may flow down naturally. I am thinking based on my logic. You see when we are sick we think a lot about it. After all, I haven't tried massage. I know there are many traditional masseuses around. I also thought about my bodily pain, the itchiness and burning pain. How I could reduce it. I haven't tried applying any kind of medicine or lotion yet. My mind keeps on thinking.

As much as I believe in modern medicine, I know I haven't explored other treatment. I know, out there somewhere, I will find the cure. I was always hopeful. I want to avoid surgery if I could. I know inserting a shunt into the spinal cord will definitely cause permanent damage to some if not all the nerves.

I also know that, out there, there will always be people to help me. My mind goes on the search mode again. I realized then that traditional medicine is not time-consuming. Some of it lasts only for a few days. Some of the session was just a day, only for analysis. My thinking was just to go, try and if it works, it works. If not, just move on. I also keep all options open be it modern, traditional or Islamic.

Traditional Sauna and Massage at the Orphan Shelter

I then tried a short sauna and massage treatment. This man has a small treatment centre where he focused on sauna and massage. His place was quite old. He has a few assistants and some orphan he takes care of. He was known to treat drug addicts and "rehabilitate" them through physical and religious treatment. When I say physical, I don't know much, but I saw a few sauna cubicles, some massage chair and some bed and sauna mattresses. I guess that was what his physical approach would be.

On the religious side, he talked a bit about it. He said "I have a few orphan and drug-addicts now staying here. For the drug addicts they were usually sent in by someone or I bring them here. I will give them shelter and food, according to what I can afford". He told me the best way to treat drug-addicts is to give them love. He said we must be like their parents. I was a bit surprised when he said love, but I realized while I was there, he called everyone there *"sayang" Sayang* in Malay language means love. I also realized that the few "patients" there seem obedient. They talked to him in a casual way, like in a family.

He adds "I try to bring these boys to the mosque for the daily prayers and follow the religious programs there. However, we have to treat them using the sauna and massage first. Some needs a longer time to rehabilitate. I have some who left too. Once they can take care of themselves, I persuade them to learn about religion". When we came, he brought with him packed lunch for the boys. He said "I used to have many patients and some stayed longer as my assistant. Now I am getting older and furthermore I just lost my wife and a son in a road accident last year"

He then showed me around his small centre or more like a shelter. I can see some of it was not well maintained. He said "I pity these boys. I am not as strong as before, but this is all I could afford. I try to come here once in a while. Otherwise, my assistant will keep this house for the boys" He is more of a volunteer and he does it out of his religious obligation.

He first put me through his traditional sauna. He still uses a fire stove and some herbs in a boiling pot for the heat. It is a simple cubicle with the stove beside a wall. The wall has an opening to channel in the steam and heat from the pot. It is really traditional. He said "Just sit there for a while, OK? Sorry, my sauna is not a modern one, but good enough for the effect. I hope you don't mind. You will sweat, but try to endure for thirty minutes" He then adds "After that I will give you a short massage" He then set a timer outside and moved away. I was left there, alone in the heat.

He did elaborate earlier that most ailments are due to poor blood circulation. Sauna will open our pores to release toxin and generally improve blood circulation. It also helps overall muscle relaxation.

After the sauna, I was seated to cool off. He gave me a clean towel. In the meantime, he spends some time with his patients at the hall, probably having his late lunch. He then asked me to lie down in bed and he did his massage along my shoulders and my bottom back. He said "I will try to align your spine. Sometimes the way we sit and walk changed our spine position. It may be the reason you feel all this pain" After the twenty minutes massage, I was given another towel and put on a chair back massager. He then gave me warm water and a spoon of honey. He said "If you have time, come again tomorrow. It is not an easy process you know".

I came twice after that. In both sessions I went through the same routine, sauna and massage. On the third day, after the session, he gave me herbal drink. He even gave me a bottle of herbal drink for my consumption at home.

A few days later he called and said he wants to visit me. I think he "*sayang*" me and want to see how I am doing. He came with some of his obedient patients and a new friend. He then introduced his new friend to me. He told me "My friend here knows someone around your area here who knows some treatment for your itchiness. He will bring that person here" We then have a few drinks. Before he left, he gave me a rather strange advice. He said "One of the ways to cure your ailment is to pay your *Zakat* or obligatory alms. Check if you have missed any over the years and pay" I said "Yes, I will".

With this man, I learned another lesson. At this age of everyone going around feeding their greed and fulfilling their lusts, there is still selfless being that goes down to the downtrodden, care for them, feed them and love them. They do all that by sacrificing their own wealth and health. This is noble. I am nothing compared to this man. Again, I was deeply humbled.

I never stopped thinking about him and his little shelter.

Our Medicine is Close to Us

My next experiment is with my itchiness. It is unbearable. So, when someone proposed a treatment, I immediately agreed.

The man came with a friend. He is a teacher at a local religious school. He said "I heard you have some problem with your skin" I said "Yes. My whole upper body is itchy. This is because of my nerve problem". He didn't ask me further. He requested for a bowl of water and a small knife. He brought with him a few pieces of Aloe Vera leaves. He said "I will prepare you a simple lotion made up this Aloe Vera leaves and two more items. One is limestone and the other is that tiny mound of an insect nest usually found on wood or iron structure. I am sure we can find it around here".

He then walked out to my porch looking for it and immediately saw it at one of my window frame. He carefully scrapped it and collects the mound. He then quipped "You know, what I learned in traditional medicine is, most of our "medicine" is found around us. God is merciful. God doesn't like to trouble us. God made it all easy for us" He said "If we go into the jungles, even garden, we can find almost all medicine for our illness. We need to learn about it. It is there. We can find herbs, fruits and even roots that have medicinal values. Our ancestors know about all this, but most of us did not learn from them" He joked that we are more interested in engineering accountancy and sciences. Yes, he was right.

In fact, once I had kidney stones. I was hospitalized and the treatment was through, I think, shock wave. I lay down on my stomach and a certain round object touches my stomach and it emits a certain kind of electric shock. After around twenty minutes or so, the stones were fragmented and it flushed out through my urine system. It was quite a simple procedure. Unfortunately, there was recurrence after that. I went for another treatment. A year later, I had another kidney stone pain. I drank lots of water for a few days. The pain was still there, but lesser.

So, I asked around for any traditional treatment. I even called my mother-in-law. I am sure she must know someone who has a traditional remedy to treat kidney stones. After all she lives in the village all her life. My mother-in-law said "Yes, there is one old man here who has a remedy. You have to come back and see him" I was delighted. So, over the weekend I drove back and immediately went to his house. I happened to know him. He is a distant uncle. He was sitting at his porch when I arrived. I greeted him and told him about my stones. He said "Yes, I know. Your mother called me yesterday"

He went inside, came back from behind his house with a little knife. I thought he is going somewhere because he was in his shirt and sandals. He usually wears a singlet. I asked "Where will you get the herbs uncle?

Is it far? Let me take you there". He said "No. It is all here. No worries son. I need to look for a few types of leaves here" To my surprise he started looking for it just in front of his house, at his compound garden. It is just grass there and a few shrubs. It wasn't even a big area! Believe me, his compound is just the size of a badminton court! That was interesting.

I followed him around his compound for a while as he bent down and picked those tiny leaves, grass and uprooted some tiny trees. I couldn't differentiate it because to me it is just grass! He said "I will prepare six sets of these leaves. Give me some time" In no time he had it all, placed in a tiny basket. "I need to get some other leaves later. You can come back later" he advised. He said "In the meantime, let me remove the soil for you and separate it into six sets. You need to wash it and when you go back, boil it with a glass of water. Just drink it three times a day. You have six sets, so it is good for two days". I left and came back in the evening. He had the six sets ready for me, wrapped in small newspaper cuttings. It was so simple and crude.

Do you know what? That was the last time I had kidney stones! It has been fifteen years, stones-free. Amazing isn't it? Yes, the man was right! Indeed, most of our "medicine" is found around us. God is merciful. God doesn't like to trouble us. God made it all easy for us. I am convinced. I believe in this notion. I saw it right in front of my eyes.

"Most of our medicine is found around us. God is merciful. God doesn't like to trouble us. God made it all easy for us"

So, back to the man that came to treat my itchiness. He cuts the Aloe Vera leaves and squeezed out the gel. He placed the gel inside a bowl. He then pours in the mound and a little limestone into the bowl. He mixed it into a lotion. He said "Take off your shirt and let me apply it right now". He used a little brush and applied it all over my body. He asked me to let it dry and leave it for one or two hours. He said "This mixture is good for three sessions. Do it again tonight". It felt cool on my skin. However, after three applications, the itchiness persists. At that time I didn't know that the itchiness I felt was internal. I was just trying to cure it.

Looking back, even though it doesn't cure my itchiness, I am beginning to be more confident of finding the whole cure. I know the "medicine" is around me. It is near! At the same time, I must admit that my ailment is mechanical. I know the key is removing the cyst. Once the cyst is removed, my nerves won't be compressed and signals to my whole body will never be blocked. I will have to try to remove the cyst, if possible, not through surgery.

The search continues.

Traditional Malay Massage at the Plantation

This time, through the man that owns the shelter, I was introduced to one caretaker of a local mosque. The mosque is only a few kilometres away from my house. He gave me his number and I called the man. On the phone, he said "I will come over to your house to meet you. There we can talk about your treatment." I said "I can go to your place" He said "I was informed about your situation. It's fine. I will come over" "Is tomorrow fine with you?" he seems happy to help. I said "It's up to you sir. I am here and I am not going anywhere". We then set a time to meet.

The next day, around ten o'clock in the morning, he came. He came with a friend. He looks quite old, but very active and agile. I was told he runs a food catering business. He asked me "Have you tried traditional massage and Islamic healing? I said "Yes. A few" He said "I think our friend here has a suggestion" He then introduced his friend and joked "This man is the pillar of our mosque". His friend just smiled. What he meant was his friend is more than a regular at the mosque. He spends a lot of his time at the mosque meditating, reading and he is fasting most of the time. His friend didn't say anything. He seems reserved. "Tell him about your suggestion" he urged his friend.

"I know a man who is quite good at massage and also a healer for those inflicted with evil spirits. Maybe we can let him analyse your situation. I can drive you there" his friend said. I thought for a while and nodded in agreement. He said "I will call the healer tonight and if he is fine, we can go tomorrow" I then offered to use my car. They agreed. We planned to leave early the next morning.

The next morning both of them came. It was raining quite heavily. So, I said "Why not we wait for the rain to stop? After that, we can make a move" The place is two hundred kilometres away, down south. It may take three hours because part of the journey is through secondary roads. It is a plantation scheme. The healer is one of the many settlers that the government chose to work at the plantation. The friend, who eventually volunteered to drive, then said "It's raining here, but on the highway is not raining now". I asked "How do you know?" He just looked down and said "I know. No worries. Let's go"

We started rather immediately. It was raining all the way, but at the toll gate entering the highway, it looks dry. It's not raining! I was surprised and amazed at his "prediction". He then took the ticket and we got onto the highway. As we got moving, he said "Our journey will be a dry one except at the exit to the old secondary road. It will rain again there" He made another prediction. This guy is unique.

In the car, I started to ask about his background. He was reserved at my house, but in the car, he wasn't that reluctant to talk. He started by saying that he is a retired radio man with our elite commando unit. "I was a communication officer in the commando unit" he said. After retiring, he runs a small company dealing with communication equipment. He also spends most of his time at the mosque. He said "I am either at the mosque or at the office. I only get out to the town to fetch my wife from work at the bus station. This is my routine"

He looks jovial talking about his past experience. "I spend a lot of time in the jungle, sometimes for months in many secret operations" he adds. "I am used to hardship. I am now retired, but my regiment is still that of an army man". I looked at him and asked "I heard you fast a lot" He said "Fasting is good to our body and soul. Fasting helps suppressed our lust and desires" He then joked "Would you lust over a woman when you are hungry? No, isn't it?" He then became a bit serious and philosophical. "All the world problems could be solved if people can control their lust and desires" he uttered.

He said "I almost never got sick" He adds "Our elders encouraged us to fast. It is good for our health, but most importantly for our soul!" I think he was right. He looks healthy for his age. He did not only say it, but he practiced it.

He then talks about his friends in various positions some has become officers in big communication companies. He still remembers the progression from Morse codes to analogue and now digital. He knows his subject well. He even talked about how to thwart a radar communication system. He explained the technicalities in detail. It was very interesting. I am impressed. He opens my mind to international espionage. He said "If you don't understand communication system, you can't be a spy!" He jokes "In the technology world, the US and Russians are nothing compared to the Germans" He did elaborate, but I forgot the details.

It was a long drive, but his stories make me feel relaxed. He is one hell of a guy!

We finally reached the exit to the secondary roads. Guess what? It started to rain! Yes, it rains. His prediction was right on the dot, again! I said in my heart "This is one hell of a guy!" So, from the exit, it is another one hour drive.

He then talks about religion. He stressed a lot on fasting. He encouraged me to fast. He said "I fast almost every day. I have been doing it for years, even when I was in the army" He then adds "Our strength lies within, internal, inside us. To feel strong, we must train our internal desires. We can't remove them, but control them, curb them" One of his key advice is this "When you are fasting, your connection with God is strong. You will feel a special bond. You will feel close to Him" He said just praying is not enough. We need to do more of the voluntary not just the compulsory. It was a stimulating conversation. I rarely meet this kind of person in my engineering world and industry.

I almost forgot the long winding road listening to his stories and advice.

It was a very different setting. The plantation is a huge area with lines and lines of palm trees, miles and miles on both sides of the road. The road is quiet and quite deserted. Once in a while, we passed by few lorry with loads of palm oil fruit bunches. It is green all the way. What a contrast from our city atmosphere. Suddenly life seems easy. We finally reach the house in the plantation.

It is an old wooden house nestled between the rows of palm trees. He has quite a big compound and I can see a tractor and lorry parked there. He was there at home waiting for us as we had called him earlier. We were invited towards the back of his home. He said "Welcome. You must be tired. It's a long way. Come in please. Please take a seat" as he showed us to an old set of wooden furniture. He went into the kitchen and informed his wife of our visit. He came back and said "Usually at this time I'll be at the plantation but today, I have a special guest from the city"

He is well built and looked strong, despite his age. I guess his years working in the plantations make him rugged and strong. He looked at me and said "I am not so much of a healer. I just try to help people when I could" He is actually the Imam of the mosque nearby. It was a Friday morning when we came. So, we need to leave as soon as possible as he needs to read the sermon and led the prayer of the mosque congregation. We are aware of that.

After a few drinks, he brought out a floor mat and a pillow. He said humbly "I will try to do what I can within my knowledge. First, I need to work on your shoulders and legs. Tell me which part hurts when I touch you" He massaged my shoulders for a while. He then asks me to lie down as he wants to work on my legs. He cautioned "Some of the parts I touched will be painful. Just bear with me.

I will try to check your veins. You will feel a bit relieved after my massage" He massaged the whole length of my legs from the thighs, knees, calf and every finger of my feet. It was painful. Every part was painful. He even pulled every finger of my feet. It was painful, but not all the fingers he pulled were painful though. In fact, before he pulled, he already knew which is painful and which is not! He was right. He said "I am loosening your muscles and veins. Everything is stiff" He said "We can let blood flow and hopefully reduce your numbness by working on the leg" He spends twenty minutes just on my legs. It was painful, but I felt a bit relieved.

Then he asked me to sit and he touched my lower back. His diagnostic and conclusion are about the same. He said "If your spine is well aligned, your overall health will improve" He did press part of my lower back and it was quite painful. He said "The way we sit can cause the spine to misaligned" He works on my lower back for a few minutes and proceeds to my shoulders. He then gave me a glass of water to drink. He asked me to be patient when in sickness and in pain. "I hope you will get well soon" he adds.

In the end, I was satisfied. I felt relieved, but my concern remains the same. Will the cyst be reduced or flow down? I didn't ask about the spiritual side of my ailment, but I recalled that while massaging my foot he did say "This is a bit strong. I am unable to deal with it" He may be right because a few healers I met before did indicate the presence of some kinds of internal evil infliction. I know this kind of infliction is tricky and difficult to prove. Anyway, I kept my option open. I need the cure. It can be through physical, traditional, spiritual or Islamic.

On the way back, again with that "one hell of a guy" new friend of mine, we talked more about the power of self-restrain, the power of fasting. He asked "How do you think people can be kicked at the groins, chopped at the neck and can withstand?" He said martial arts practitioner does possess a certain level of psychic powers from mind control. We too can possess the power to immune and protect ourselves from any kind of hit, even bullets he adds. He said, through fasting, we can gain psychic and spiritual powers. We can be saved and shielded, he adds.

It was interesting. I have ventured into another world, I think. It is a bit bizarre, but yes, it exists. People do withstand a kick in the groin. I don't think that is done through physical defence. No, it can't be. The pain must be excruciatingly painful! Just thinking about it sent chills to our bones, right? I don't think any amount of physical training can protect the muscles in the groin from the pain of a kick. I am convinced it has to be something spiritual or psychic. What do you think? Can you take a kick to the groin? Do you dare give yourself a try?

A trip down for a massage treatment brought me to meet more people. I learned a few things from these humble, simple souls. Again, these people aren't my family or relatives, but they sacrificed their time for me. May God repay them and grant them a peaceful bountiful life. I am glad I am surrounded by these kind and selfless people. This is what the world needs. We have enough hate, anger, violence, killings and wars. Imagine a beautiful world where people give selflessly. This is all about loving. This is what religion taught us. I saw religious acts of servitude, care, respect and concern being practiced right in front of me. I am touched by these people.

My heart is filled with joy yet again. Yes, I am in pain, but I am not in vain. Even if I couldn't find the cure, my pain is relieved temporarily. My burden is lessened from these sacred acts of religion. Thank God for sending these people to teach me love and life.

The Royal Masseuse.

One day I got a call from my neighbour when we were staying in a condominium. He is Chinese. He said he knew about my problems from my tennis buddies there. He quickly proposed a Chinese traditional masseuse. He said "I will call him for you. I sent my relative there too. He is good. He is a Royal masseuse" I said "What? Royal?" He said "He had massaged one of our Sultans and had since becoming the Sultan's in-house masseuse. Apparently, the Sultan had a nasty fall from his horse and had hurt his neck" This is news to me! Indeed, he must have some special talent and the Sultan likes his service. My ex-neighbour added "You know if the Sultan wants to summon him, the Sultan will send a car to fetch him to the palace". Yes, a Royal masseuse! Sounds interesting, right? I will get the service of a Royal masseuse too!

He then said "I will accompany you there. Just wait at your house and we can go together. I need to explain to him your problem in Chinese language because his Malay is not that good" Another kind gesture from an old friend. Indeed, I am surrounded by good people. Thank God!

A few days later he fetched me and we went to this Royal masseuse. The centre is not far away from my house, in a terrace shop lot, on the ground floor. We were quickly registered and my ex-neighbour met the practitioner. He explained my problem briefly in Chinese. I was then given a number and asked to wait.

In the meantime, I looked around the centre. The waiting area consists of a few seats and there is a television set showing a Chinese program. There is a table and magazines on it, which are all in Chinese. Most of the signage's and posters are in Chinese characters. It has a few wall posters showing the human body in Chinese description. For a moment I thought I am in a foreign land!

At the centre of the hall, on the wall is a display panel showing many photos of the practitioner. Among the many photos is of course, a prominently placed photo of the Royal masseuse and the Sultan. He also has other photos of community services he is involved in and many karaoke championship photos. My Royal masseuse is an avid karaoke singer and probably a talented one. He won a few trophies too all displayed in the panel.

So, I just have to bear the Chinese program on TV and the few patients, who on that day are all Chinese. I got a chance to do some catching up with my condominium neighbour. It has been six years since we moved to a new home. We haven't met for some time. He said "I have told him your problems. See what he can do to help you"

He then looked at me and said "Did you play tennis after you moved out? I hope you find a good court to play there" I said "I played at a few places, make new tennis buddies, but the condominium courts is still the best because the players there are young and good" I enjoyed playing there because most of my buddies there are ten years my junior and we play a power game. A few of them are State tennis players when they were in school. We also have one "imported" guy who is a coach and another, a coach with USTA License! So, you can imagine our level of play. I have to up my game too. I also got to learn many tennis tips and tricks. My ex-neighbour then joked "There goes one good tennis player from our condominium team"

While I was staying there, I played almost every day. It was fun staying there; the clubhouse, the pool and all. My former office was also nearby. Basically, in twenty minutes I can switch from my office attire to my tennis gear, Nike sneakers and wielding my Wilson Hammer. The temptation to play is irresistible. Why not? I can see the courts and the blue pool right from my eleventh floor unit. Can you resist? If I am not at the tennis court I will be in the pool! I can even choose to serve, volley and smash in the evening or at night. I was one hell of a fit guy there.

I have to move because of my job. The new company is in the city. I couldn't stand the daily ninety minutes commute in the morning and again, an hour drive in the evening. It is tiring and expensive too.

Let's get back to the Royal masseuse. The wait wasn't long and I was called into a small cubicle. There are around four small cubicles in the centre. It has a small cupboard, a few more diagrams and pictures of the human body description in Chinese characters, a floor mat and a pillow.

My first session was mostly his overall assessment of my situation. He speaks to me in poor Malay and some broken English. He said "You have to remove your clothes and will have to lie on your stomach. I need to work on your spine" He also showed me a small bottle containing some herb lotion. He said the herb lotion will be wiped at some points of my body after the massage.

He jokes "I will have to touch your neck a bit. Don't worry, the Titanium you have at your skull is a strong material. They build airplanes using titanium, you know? It won't break!" He then commented "From the way you walk and looking at you now, your spine is a bit crooked. He then explained that strengthening and aligning the spine is not an easy task. He reminds me that it may take a few weeks. He has to do it bit by bit, part by part. He showed the overall spine diagram on the wall as he explains his method to me. He then started using his "magic hands" along my spine. He is firm, but careful in his finger presses and touch. He knows his stuff.

As he massages me, he explains the relations between each bone and areas of the body. It was not a painful session, maybe not yet I gathered. At the same time, he talks a lot. He is talkative, but an interesting person.

He talks about his relationship with the Sultan. "The Sultan is firm and generous. He said I have magic hands. I massaged his neck when he fell from his horse once before. After that, I was called to massage him and his Prince many times." he spoke using his limited Malay vocabulary with some broken English and use his hands a lot to express himself. I think I got what he meant. He adds "The Sultan likes my magic hands. If he needs me, he will send a car to fetch me to the palace, but the palace is so far away! It is very tiring and I have to cancel many appointments here" I know the palace is around five hundred kilometres away, on the East Coast. It is easily a five hour journey. No wonder he grumbled. He said "I am given a chalet to stay near the palace, but I usually come back on the same day. I am an old man. I must sleep at home! I miss my love, here" He also talks about his son studying traditional massage in China. He talks about how expensive it is and how he missed his son. He opens a lot to me. He then talks about some of his patients. I see him as a friendly guy. He likes to joke too. It is just that I couldn't grasp all that he wants to say! I simply smile and nod as a courtesy.

I spent around ten sessions with him. It was also expensive. The whole session lasted around a month. After a month, I couldn't feel any difference. I am still in pain, the numbness is still there, my muscles are still weak and I could not walk better than before I came. I decided to stop that treatment. I was hoping his "magic hands" could align and straighten my spine. It doesn't happen. I am a bit disappointed especially after spending a lot on his service. I just tell myself "Never mind. It is just not the cure I am looking for. I must let it pass and move on"

It was indeed strenuous for a man in my situation to go there every three days or so, being massaged for twenty or thirty minutes and finally, this. My wife was a bit frustrated as she didn't see any improvement. "I am the one taking care of you. I see you every day. I don't see any improvement at all" she said in a rather upset mood. She said "Let us think of some other treatment. For now let us forget about this massage"

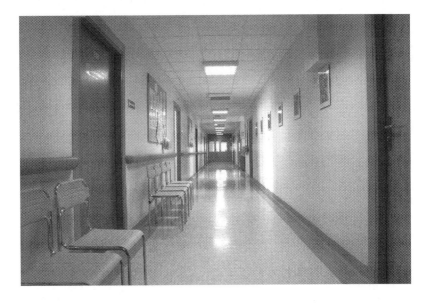

2nd Hospitalization

It has been almost eight months since I was discharged after the 1st surgery. In the eight months, I met many practitioners and healers and went through many types of treatment. Slowly and surely, it became obvious to me that all that I tried was not effective. I just tell myself it wasn't the cure I was looking for.

Now, looking back, I realized that I had defied the surgeon advice. I may have taken too long to decide. At that time, I was in pain. I didn't think about time. In fact, you can see that every single week I seek new treatment from different practitioner. I kept on telling myself "Go. Try everything. The cure is somewhere out there" I was persistent in my search for the cure and so does my wife. We talked about it a lot. Every time when I intend to try a new treatment, she never objected. She always encouraged me. She was always on my side. I know she wants me cured as bad as I am.

My concern then was just to seek alternative treatment to cure me of the disorder. I was just trying. It isn't wrong, isn't it? I also got different kinds of opinions and advice from relatives and friends. One of the most common opinions is that surgery may cause permanent damage.

Generally, after the 1st surgery, my condition slowly got worse. It is a gradually slow process. I can still walk, but the way I walk becomes abnormal due to increase in motor muscle weakness, imbalance and numbness of both my legs, the left leg being a bit worse. On the body pain, the "wearing armour" pressure and gripping on my upper body increased slightly. I also felt an increase in the burning sensation pain, muscle cramp pain and itchiness. Basically, gradually over the eight months, it gets worse. The numbness and tingling "needles and pin" pain also increased.

Finally, I made my decision to go for the 2nd surgery. I thought it was time to get a shunt inserted. It is apparent that enlarging the spinal cord passage at the bottom my skull did not relieve the external pressure on the spinal cord. In short, the cyst is still there compressing on my nerves.

We made an appointment at the neurosurgery department again. We got to meet the surgeon again. He didn't ask why I took too long to come back. He was as calm and composed as before. He greeted me with a smile. He said "How are you now? It is good to see you again. We have ordered the shunt a few months ago. We are ready for you"

He then started to explain the procedure he would perform on me. As I said earlier, they focused on the two blockages. They will now perform the second procedure to remove the cyst, mechanically. "We will insert a shunt into your spinal cord. We need to stick it into the cyst or bubble and from the differential pressure inside and outside the spinal cord the liquid will gradually flow out. That is our plan" the surgeon said as he showed us the scan image of the cyst on the computer screen. He adds "A portion of one of your cervical bones will be cut for us to insert the shunt. Do not worry. The portion that we cut is not an important part of you cervical bone. It won't affect your ability to support your head"

He also brought a model of the spine and showed me the location of the point. It was a thorough and professional explanation. I was impressed.

We were then asked to register at the admission counter. My wife went to the counter and I was given a wheelchair. The surgeon asked the nurse in attendance to arrange for my admission. The nurse made a few calls and said "Someone from the ward will come down and send you to the ward. For now, wait for your wife to come back"

I was a bit relaxed now compared to the first surgery. I can visualize the sequence of event. I can still "hear" the sounds of the medicine trolley, the surgical trolley and the food trolley. I can even differentiate the different sounds for which trolley! I was a bit scared, but more informed than before. I know I will be in the same ward and most of the nurses and hospital assistants already recognized me. I can "see" their faces. I will be in good hands, I know.

A few minutes later, a hospital assistant from the ward came to meet me. He looked at me, smiled and said happily "It is you again, sir! You remember me". I said "Sure, I remember you. How is everyone else at 7G?" He said "Everyone is still there. Not many changes" He then pushed the wheelchair and my wife walk along beside us. He recognized my wife too.

I was quickly moved onto the bed. A nurse came with two sets of the green patients "uniform". I am now in their hands. I can't say and do much. Next is to wait until the time for surgery. Back to the same routine, the drips and the pills, the daily morning rounds by the doctors and the noisy "change of guards" at 7 am, 2 pm and 9 pm. Also, the not-so-tasty food, the cleaners and the daily BP check.

My wife asked "Do you need the hand phone?" I said "Yes, just keep it on and put at my side" I am still on my Nokia E72 while most have gone to touchscreen Androids! I was a bit "lost" the last one year with all the pain and treatment. I couldn't be bothered about gadgets. My wife already has a Samsung Galaxy. I thought I will switch to Androids after my surgery. For the moment, I was contented with the E72 for the few SMS I am going to send, some pictures I saved and some Scorpions, Dio, Metallica mp3s I had stored. It wasn't something that I can show off though.

One of the things unique about me than other patients is I am in the ward, bare body. My sensory has deteriorated to the extent that nothing can touch my skin. I felt excruciating pain. Initially, I tried to wear the shirt, but it was unbearable. In fact, even before the admission, I already felt the difficulty with the pain when I wear clothes. So, I seek permission from the nurses to exempt me from wearing the shirt. I still feel the burning sensation and muscle cramps pain, but manageable. The Pain Score is not as high as when I am with a shirt. So, I was in the ward bare body for the whole duration there.

As I have already settled down in the ward, my wife then makes her move back as she has to take care of my three kids at home. For the day, she had the kid's lunch and trips to school taken care of by our cousin who happened to stay nearby. I am grateful to my cousin. I know we will need a lot of her help in the coming days. I am also grateful for the sacrifices of my wife. It will be a daily one and a half hours drive between the hospital and the house, between taking care of me and the house chores. It is indeed a heavy task for her for anyone, in fact. I can only hope that she can endure and persevere. I glanced around the ward for a clock as I have lost count on the time. It's eleven o'clock. I was tired and just closed my eyes.

I was informed that a few tests would be conducted before my surgery. My surgery was conducted four days later. I forgot how long the surgery was. According to my wife, it was a seven-hour surgery and like before, I recovered quite fast from the surgery. She said "There are patients who went in earlier than you and they are still in the operation room ICU" I am glad it was over. I passed another physical and emotional test.

I was moved back to 7G the same day and the anaesthesia wears off quite fast too. I was, however, just lying down in bed. I felt sore and a bit paralyzed. I am not actually, but my movement is restricted. In no time, I was able to see my wife again. I don't know how she went through and cope with all that. Seeing her is therapy. It is, every single time.

I spent another two weeks at the ward. In the ward, the usual faces, the young nurses and doctors greeted me. It was a pleasant stay overall. It is around this time that a few people from the pain management team start to make their rounds. I was given a few drugs to help ease my bodily pain. There were also visit by the in-house rehabilitation team. They were task to rehabilitate my urinary function and functional rehabilitation, to make me sit and probably stand.

The bladder test is what I dreaded most. It is painful. What they do is they insert a tiny tube into my urethra up to the bladder. The urine is collected and measured. They do it a few times at certain intervals. They sort of measure the volume released and ensured that a certain amount remain in the bladder. They need to ensure the emptying of my bladder functions normally. Sounds simple enough right? No! It sounds simple, but physically that is one thing I wouldn't put myself through voluntarily even if you pay me! No! The procedure to insert the tube, despite the tube being tiny and a gel used to facilitate entry, is extremely painful. To me, it is unbearable. The whole process from insertion to the draining and pulling the tube out lasted for a few minutes. It is a long few minutes! So, when I was there, every time I hear the sound of a surgical trolley, I will pray "Not this bed please, not me please. Go somewhere else!" Do you know what? This "horrific" test is done three times a day. I wish I could get off my bed and run away! No, really not that pain again.

The functional rehabilitation was not that bad though. The therapist was careful to start with the easiest and minimal of tasks like lifting our fingers and hands. They then move on towards lifting of the whole arm. I remembered one pleasant "instruction" I heard from one therapist. She said "You should learn to lift your arms. You need that to perform your prayers" What a surprise! Her name tag shows that she is a Christian. How can she be thinking about my prayers? I was delighted at her gesture and courtesy. "We are a harmonious society" I thought to myself.

Indeed, there is a lot of respect and tolerance among us, despite our differing religion and race. Who says we are racists? If there were some minor frictions, it is expected, but really isolated and very rare. I can count with my fingers! We have been like this, at peace for as long as I could remember. Beautiful! Our forefathers have delicately set our constitution and system of governance on a shared responsibility, contribution and respect among the races. I call it, simply, a sound alliance.

Let us get back to my situation. At this stage, it was obvious that my muscle motors have weakened, my bodily pain has worsened and urinary function was affected. In fact, prior to surgery, these symptoms are already there. I couldn't feel much difference probably because I forgot the intensity before.

As I was recovering, recuperating and transiting to rehabilitation, it was decided that I am moved to another location. Apparently, the rehabilitation department has its own separate ward. One of the doctors told me nicely "Sir, we will move you to our wards. It is only for rehabilitation. It is not as big, as new and comfortable as your room here" I replied "It is fine with me" She smiled, looked at me again and said "Really sir, it is not as comfortable as your room here" she reiterates. "It is not in the same compound as this new hospital complex, but very near. We will probably move you there tomorrow" she adds.

I then asked her "Can I continue to stay here? I like it here" She pondered for a while and said "Yes, actually you can but to transfer you daily twice to and fro will be hard on you. We rather have you warded there" I guess I have to relent. I just hope it is not too bad.

Hospital Rehabilitation Ward

In the morning the next day, a nurse came over and advised us to clear the room. She said "We will move you in an hour time. Kindly pack your belongings" My wife packed everything in two bags and we waited. I can't help thinking about the new ward. From the way the doctor explained, I got the feeling that it wouldn't be a nice place, as comfortable as I expect. My mind wanders. Whatever, I am going to miss the room. At the same time, I know I am in the rehabilitation stage and it wouldn't be a long stay there.

We are all packed and I am still on the bed. I couldn't move that well. The nurse came back again and said "I will bring a wheelchair for you sir. We will move you to the ground floor and transport will bring you to the ward" I then asked my wife to follow us in our car. I don't know where the place is. I just hope she will find out from the nurse later.

A few minutes later, a nurse came with a file and said "Let me push you downstairs" We went down the lift, out from the wards area to the open common area and turned right to a waiting area. It is also the first time in three weeks I will be able to feel the heat and rays of the sun. What a breather! It's a new world. At the side of the waiting area, there are many people, some visitors, some waiting for taxis and nurses going to and from the big cafeteria nearby.

I am suddenly out in an open public area, but this time in a wheelchair. For a moment I did enjoy the air, the people and the noise. My mind, by the way, still wanders, where I am going? The nurse told me to wait while she stands beside me. "An ambulance will come here and take us there. It is only a short drive, less than five minutes"

As I sat there "minus my limbs", I thought to myself "All these people will never know how difficult it is not to be able to walk. I was like them before. I was too busy to even think about it" I began to remember all those times I could walk and do all the things I want and yet, at times, I complain and grumbled about little things, little difficulties. I was ungrateful at times. Now, the ability to walk, the strength from my limbs, my feet, the pleasures I had was being taken away from me. There is nothing I can do about. I felt helpless, disabled and sad. It is a sad reality. I may lose my ability to walk forever. A sense of negativity seems to creep in. My mind is suddenly thinking about my wife, my family and my future. I was in a different world. I forgot I was at the waiting area.

I was suddenly shocked by a voice from behind me "The ambulance is here. Let us go sir" She held me to a standing position. I realize I could stand, but the strain is too painful. She quickly folds the wheelchair, lift it onto the ambulance and strap it to position. She came back to me and leads me to the seat in the ambulance. She jumped in, pulled the door an off we went.

In less than five minutes we were already at the wards. It is just across the road, a little to the right. It is actually one of the few old buildings of the old hospital. When I say old, I really mean old! It looks like a 2nd world-war army barrack, linked by covered walkways. There are around eight single-story barracks each as long as a hundred feet. The walkway cuts through the rows of barrack perpendicularly, in the middle. So, we have some fifty feet of usable space in the barrack to the left and right of the walkway. I can also see that some of the barracks are totally abandoned, locked and closed. It is probably fifty years old maybe more. I was like "Is this it? No!" I thought to myself "How long I am here? I don't think I can survive one day here!" I glanced around the "barrack" and asked "Where is my room, my bed?" It is as though I am back in the sixties. I felt depressed just looking at the place.

The ambulance stopped at one of the barracks. In a few minutes, my wife arrived. I was then helped to alight from the ambulance and walked to the entrance. As we walked towards the building, I looked at my wife and said "This place is terrible. It is old" She cautioned me "Lower you voice please. It is not nice if these people hear what you uttered. Just relax and take it easy".

As we approach the door, a beautiful young nurse greeted us "Yes sir. Please come in. We have the bed readied for you" I gave a forced smile and replied "Thank you" She then gave me a short briefing on the ground rules of the ward. It is a bit rare that I am given any ground rules. As I listened along, the key points stressed are the way food is served and the closure of the back door at night. "Your breakfast, lunch and dinner will be served at that small hall across the walkway there" she said as she showed us the hall. She adds "We do not serve your food in bed as in the other ward. It is different here" She then reminded us about the times they close the back door. So, everything was set. I then got onto bed.

The ward is quite small. It has four rows of beds with three beds in a row. There is one table at the entrance and two security guards are seated. The nurse's station and doctors room occupies half of the hall. I looked around and see that most of the patients here are not as sick as those at 7G. I can see most of them sitting on bed and talking to each other. It is a different atmosphere here! A few of them smiled at me and greeted me. I then begin to realize that these are patients in their recovery stage just like me. I didn't see any IV line hanging at their beds either. This ward is also clean, despite its old interior façade. I also see all the fans are turned on.

As I was adapting myself to the situation mentally and physically, a nurse came over and said "We do not have air-conditioning here. Sorry" She then tells my wife "Here, we are different. We want patients to try to walk or push their own wheelchair to the small hall for food. This is part of rehabilitation. We also have two exercise sessions in a day. The gym is a bit far, but we also want patients to make their way there on their own" The nurse added "So, do not spoil him, try not to help him, OK? If you know he really can't stand and walk, use the wheelchair" On the back door, she said "The back door leads to a bathroom, washroom and toilet, but at night, use the toilet inside"

I also realized the nurses and doctors here are all friendly. They don't look as tensed and stressed as those in 7G. Probably we are beyond the critical state where nursing and special care is required. I thought to myself "It is not bad after all! I'll be fine here"

I then looked around to find a suitable place for my wife to sleep. I asked her "Where can you sleep. Go ask the nurse" She was then shown two chairs where she can sleep. That is all they have here. It is another sacrifice she will have to make. She took the chairs and placed it beside my bed. Unlike 7G where there is a visitor area with few comfortable seats, a television, a few reclining chairs or a small sofa bench in my room, they only have chairs here. It would be a long night for my wife. I thought of buying one folding, reclining chair for her. However, who is going to buy it? I don't think my wife knows that area well.

I finally settled in and took a short nap. I was tired and strained with all the moving. My wife then told me "I want to look around this new place. Need to know where the canteen is. I will be right back. You take a rest".

I was, however, still not able to put on my shirt. My skin is hypersensitive. It is painful when I put on a shirt. In fact, I couldn't even stand the fan. So, I just put on my shirt without buttoning it. I am like that most of the time. I informed the nurse and they allowed me to dress that way. One of the nurses told me "Here, we will also try to rehabilitate your skin. We have a few desensitizing method you can try. The therapist will teach you" We also get a few visits from the therapist here. In fact, they were the ones rehabilitating us, not the nurses.

I woke up a few hours later. It was almost lunchtime. "Lunch is ready. Try to make your way to the hall on your own" the nurse instructs. I then got onto my wheelchair and my wife pushed me. Again, I sensed something different here. The food smells good! I can smell it as I entered the small hall! It looks delicious too. That is also the first time in two weeks I am tempted to eat, I have my appetite back. I thought "This is much better than 7G. It looks like home-cooked!" My wife was happy too. "I think this will make you forget about this old place" she quipped. Yes, she was right. At least patients here are more cheerful, the nurses and therapist look friendly and even the doctors are nice. Now, the food is also good!

It was indeed a great lunch! For a sick and depressed man like me, it was good so far. What a change it was. It is different from 7G for sure. I like it! We spend the next few minutes watching TV and got to know a few more patients there. A few minutes later, the food janitor came to collect the trays. "The food was delicious. Thank you very much" I made a remark as he passed by. He is also a cheerful person. He smiled and sings as he collects the trays, clean the tables and pantry.

He looked at me and said "Did you just come in?" I said "Yes. This morning" "Did you say the food was good?" he asked. "It is actually a different caterer than the main hospital. We cooked for fewer patients" he explained. He then joked "Do not go to sleep after your stomach is full, OK? You have your afternoon exercise session afterwards" He seems to know the "ground rules" here too.

After getting to know the background of some of the patients, I realized I am not as bad as I thought. Some of them are in a much worse condition than me.

I met a young man, just thirty-two and broke both his legs in a motorcycle accident. He is wheelchair-ridden and has spent six months in the hospital and a month at this rehabilitation ward. Yet, he looks cheerful. Always with his tiny earphone plugged and playing games on his Android. I wonder how he must have felt. At thirty-two I was at my peak, working and earning money. I already have two kids at that age. In his situation, I doubt he would face an easy life.

There is also a young boy, aged thirteen and semi paralyzed. He had a nasty fall at a swimming pool. His spine is injured and has a support around his chest. He is accompanied by his mother and father. His mother looks weary and tired probably she lacks sleep. I talked to the father who is an engineer. Looking at their style, composure and clothes, they seem to be a well-to-do family. They have been there for a few weeks. "I have been taking many leave to be with my son. Work has been stacking up at the office" he frets a bit. I was told that both of them slept at the ward to be with their boy.

Across the ward, there is a woman, a stroke patient. She has four growing up kids. One of her sisters, a student at a local nursing college has to quit her studies to work and takes care of her. She has lost her job as helper at a restaurant due to her stroke. To add to her predicament, her husband is in fact, a disabled person. I can't imagine how difficult their life is. However, among the patients, according to the nurse, she is the most determined to go through the rehabilitation exercises and programs. She is one strong woman. In the ward, she is the most friendly and likeable. She smiled a lot, despite her difficulties.

Another patient I saw is a young man, resigned to a wheelchair because of stroke. He is a bit overweight and his head always slops to the sides and saliva seems to drool out of his mouth. He can't seem to move his arms too. The good part is this man is always accompanied and aided by a handsome young man, his younger brother. It is rather rare to see brothers aiding each other in hospitals. We usually see wives aiding husbands and parents with their children and vice-versa, right? It is heart-warming to see this handsome young man helping his physically-impaired brother.

Every morning he would lift his brother off the bed onto the wheelchair and pushed him to the bathroom. In the bathroom, it has to be a demanding task to unclothe, bathe, dry and put on his brother's clothes. He would then push his brother for meals and then to the gym, not forgetting a little towel to wipe off that drooling saliva! He did all that with tender care, love and a happy face. He smiles a lot and he would always talk to his brother. I observe all that and I thought to myself that the brotherly bond exhibited is rare and remarkable!

One of the many patients is one middle-aged woman and her husband. The husband is the caretaker. However, the "bond" is rather loose as they seem to quarrel a lot. I can see that the wife is always grumbling probably due to her pain, stress and depression. She is wheelchair-ridden and there is a chest support over her chest. She makes a lot of demands, called her husband almost all the time an even scolded him. It wasn't a pleasant sight to be in. I think the nurses are immune to their friction and simply ignored that couple. I didn't see the nurses interfere or try to defuse the situation.

On the other hand, the husband seems like an obedient servant! He is always present, trying his best to fulfil her requests and make her comfortable. I can see his seriousness and effort. He rarely rests, always at her side, always being asked to do a lot of things. I think this one couple is an exception. All the other patients are quite calm and happy.

Looking at all these patients, I tell myself that I am nothing compared to all these people. I should be more calm and grateful. At least I have my wife and family. I should stop complaining over little things, I thought. I learned a lot in that one day alone. It is about sacrifices, love and determination. I don't think I can be as patient as that young man who has lost both his legs. How I wish I could help the woman with that disabled husband and her children. May God grants me the strength of that young man and gave me the determination of that woman.

After two days at the rehabilitation ward, and trying to adapt to the changes, my wife came with a new story. Actually she was displeased at this ward, but she didn't say it earlier. When we came she already felt that the place is old. She said "The aura of this place is not conducive as a rehabilitation ward! It would be difficult for patients to recover"

Now, she came with this new finding. "This place is haunted. I have been talking to the sweepers working here. They have seen "things" around this place." she looks anxious as she talked about it. "Is it true?" I asked in disbelief "Yes, these sweepers worked on night shifts. They have seen horrific creatures at night!" she frowns talking about it.

She then adds "Do you know why the nurses locked the back door?" I said "No. Is it because of the sightings?" She looks scared, but finally she revealed "Did you see the building thirty meters behind this ward? Do you know what it is? It is actually a mortuary!" So, I was a bit shocked to hear about it. No wonder the nurse locked the back door! "You can ask the sweepers if you want to know more" she suggests.

"I think we should park our car at the main car park in front" she said as she moved towards the car behind the ward. "I'll be right back OK?" We have been parking the car behind our ward, near the mortuary the last two days!

After hearing about the sightings, I thought to myself the people hear are friendly, nurses and doctors are always smiling and positive and the food is good. Now, we have this building behind us! It is not any building though. It is a mortuary, home for the dead! It sounds a bit disturbing. Yes I do believe in spirits, in ghost. I know these things exist. I am just worried about my wife because she is the one running around here, going to the canteen at night for her dinner, doing all the chores for us. At times, she would leave for home, looking after the kids and come back here, sometimes in the evening.

So now I have something to think about. I hope there is no "uninvited guest" appearing at night in my ward! I would be horrified!

I was actually depressed at the ward. Although I tried to adapt to the situation, my emotional and physical self is not coping well. I could see that in the normal morning test conducted by the nurses, my BP shot to 140, beyond my normal rate at 7G of around 125. My wife realized that and she keeps on telling me "Your BP is high here. You are not like this at 7G!" She was right I guess.

Here at the rehabilitation ward, we were required to attend the exercise sessions at a gym nearby. There are a few physical-therapist and occupational-therapist to facilitate our rehabilitation. It usually starts at nine o'clock in the morning and two o'clock in the afternoon. Basically the gym caters for a dozen of us. It is not that big, but spacious enough for us. It is well equipped.

For me, my first few days focused on the parallel bars. They park my wheelchair and aided me to start walking in between the parallel bars. I have to walk the ten feet span to and fro. I saw a few exercise bicycles, exercise mats and tables, treadmill, few weights, training stairs and a few tilt tables. The young boy that fell at the pool was put through the tilt-table to rehabilitate his standing posture. Others have specific exercise routines. I don't know the names of some of the equipment there. I also went through a short interview with a therapist in a separate room.

What an experience it was. Suddenly after more than forty years, I am learning to stand and walk again! It was painful as my limbs are numb and stiff! A few steps feel like a hundred meters. It was tiring too. The therapist was so patient with me. She keeps on encouraging me. "Yes you can. You sure can. You want to walk again with your wife, right?" she persuades and encouraged me. She said "I know you can do it. You are a strong man. I know you want to go off shore again!" I guess she has my records and know that I worked in an oil field.

In moments like that, I began to appreciate all the pleasures of being able to stand, walk and run. I recalled the days I could run around the tennis courts. It was mesmerizing. It is emotional when you are deprived of all those "pleasures". I felt a big chunk of my life is taken away! I felt helpless and depressed, but the spirits displayed by the patients around me motivated me. What I see was an expression of determination, grit and hope.

My parallel bar routine is nothing compared to what that boy had to go through at the tilt table. I can see his face grimaces in pain. He even screams at times. The mother was always by his side wiping his tears and holding his hands, giving encouragement. It was a touching scene. To some other patients, they were also taught to read and write and go through simple cognitive test. At least I can read. At least I can identify objects. I am not as bad as them.

In the afternoon, around six o'clock, my wife would push me around the walkway. I can still remember the way she gently pat my back and sings as she moves me in the wheelchair. She pampered me with love and affection. She fondles my hair. She talks about being patient and acceptance of fate. "I will be here for you. I am with you. I will take care of you" she gave me hope. She is the best nurse I could find. I am grateful to God for sending me a loyal, obedient, patient and beautiful wife. I am in heaven.

I may be disabled, but I am loved. That is more than enough for me. It is precious. It is so assuring!

"The best Hospital is Home. The best Nurse is Wife.
The best Medicine is Hope"

In the morning, she will push me in my wheelchair to the bathroom. She will bathe me. It wasn't an easy task. First, I have to be transferred to a special wet wheelchair. She then has to undress me. I will then be moved under the shower. She has to scrub me and cleanse me with soap. It is a tedious process. I will then need to be wiped and dried before dressing me up again. We have to do it all in the wet bathroom. It is slippery. I may fall.

Once at the bed, she will have to gently help me onto bed. At that time, I am still weak and my balance is bad. I may easily trip and fall. That is the last thing I want to happen.

I think I am the most fortunate patient there. Indeed, she is the best nurse. She is more than a nurse. I am grateful to God that, despite of my predicament and possibly a bleak future I have a strong person beside me. Even though I don't know if I would work again, I know she will accept me with this condition. I am in love again. I felt assured.

While at the rehabilitation ward, I was visited by a cousin of mine. "I went to 7G and you were not there. I thought you have been discharged!" he said, looking tired at the same time probably due to the hassle he has to go through. "This place is actually near, but the signs are not clear. I don't know where I parked my car. I already lost direction" he complains.

"Anyway, I didn't know about your hospitalization until I went back to my parents last week. I am sorry. How are you now?" he said as he looked at my wheelchair. "Your condition looks serious. I see now you need a wheelchair" he looks concerned as he speaks. I can sense that he is surprised at my condition. Who wouldn't? He knew I was fine all this while, going places and working as usual. He knows my field and my industry. He didn't expect to see me in this situation. In fact, I do look frail. After two weeks in a ward, anyone would feel the stress and change, physically. I could only lie back and listen to his concern. He was visibly shaken looking at my condition. He is quite a close cousin when we were kids. We haven't met for quite some time though.

He asked "Your wife stays here with you?" I said yes and his question reminds me of her reclining, folding chair! I quickly chipped in "Can you do us a favour? I need to buy a reclining, folding chair for her. She has been sleeping on a chair the last two days. She is not familiar with the area here" Listening to that, he immediately offered himself "I will get the reclining chair for you! I will go now" He left and in a few minutes he came back with the reclining chair! "That was fast" my wife said. "Oh, I find one helpful guy outside and he gave me the directions. It wasn't far" he explained as he set up the chair.

He spends a good half an hour after that catching up on news about me. He was happy to see me. "It is good to see you again. Never mind. This is part of life. It can happen to me too. I know you are a strong man!" he jokes as he holds my hands. I asked "How much is this folding chair?" "No need to ask. This is just one little thing I can do for you!" he said as he shrugs off my question. A few minutes later he left.

I looked at the folding chair and thought my wife will at least have a better sleep now. I know she didn't sleep well on an upright chair. Who could? It wasn't easy for her. It is indeed an adverse condition for her. "I hope I wouldn't be long here. It's a pity to see her like this'" I thought to myself.

I then got another visitor, my brother. He went to 7G too and was directed to this ward. I could still remember his startled look when he first saw me. He didn't say much for the first few minutes. I can see he is taken aback as he glanced at the old ward façade, my bed and the wheelchair. My brother is a businessman. I know his expectations. I don't think he is pleased at what he saw, the ward I mean. I am not pleased either, but as a patient I couldn't do much.

"How are you? I happened to have a business meeting around here. So, I come with my friends" he said as we shook hands. He then introduced me to his friends. I couldn't recall everything but one of them has herb cultivation business. He talks about his herbs and proposed to me to try and consume it later as a remedy. We then talked a bit about business, a bit about my industry, the oil and gas. I had earlier told my brother about some oil field concession. He himself has plans with his business associates to venture into the oil and gas sector. "We need your experience and hope we can work on something" he suggests.

I find it a bit awkward to talk business in a hospital ward, but I tend to forget my disorder for a while when I delve into something close to me, the oil and gas industry. It was interesting. I think it is a good therapy.

We deliberately change our mind to not think about the pain. It works for a while, at least.

The Semi-Paralyzed Young Dad

A few days before we were discharged, I witnessed another tragic story. A young man around thirty was admitted to the ward. His bed is right in front of my bed. Apparently, he had an accident as he was trying to get onto a bus. His body is semi-paralyzed due to a serious spinal injury. He has a neck brace on and could only lie down. His wife accompanied him. I was told he has one kid.

I couldn't communicate with him as he couldn't speak. He could, however, smile back at me when I nodded as a gesture to him. Again, another new lesson I learned. I am not as bad as him. He has been on and off between the ward and rehabilitation for a year. His recovery may take years according to one of the nurse. All I could see while he was in front of me was his wife patiently and gently wiping off his saliva. She seems to be there, sitting beside him, all the time, day and night! It was a sad condition. I was grieved. He has lost his oral capability. However, food was still administered orally not through tubing.

His wife had two photos pasted beside his bed. It was his photo when he was handsome and healthy and the other of him and his boy. "I feel so sad looking at him" my wife told me. "I pity his wife. She didn't sleep at night. She just sat there and cared for her husband. She must be tired, but look, she is still there!" she adds.

As I was pondering about this new patient, I heard the nurse pushing a surgical trolley followed by two doctors. They were heading towards me! I am still not off the urinary system test! As I said earlier, this bladder test is what I dread most. It is painful. Yes, they will insert that tiny tube into my urethra up to the bladder, again. No please! "Good afternoon. How are you today?" the beautiful lady doctor greeted me with a sweet, gentle smile. I just smiled half-heartedly. The other doctor is beautiful too! "We need to do the bladder test again. It is just a follow up. It is part of your rehabilitation"

She then asked my wife to move aside as she pulled the curtain. Guess what happened after that? A few minutes of "hell"! It was painful. I forgot about the new patient for a while. It was just me, the doctor and the pain. It was over in five minutes. The doctor then told me "We will have another test and that's it. Your current reading is satisfactory. We need to re-confirm it" Oh no another one?

We spent around ten days there at the rehabilitation ward. It has all the trauma and drama although it may not be as tragic and serious as those at 7G. I remember each of their faces and their stories. I do admit they are in a worse situation than me. They may not feel my muscle cramp pains, my numbness, the burning sensation neuropathic pains and my weak limbs, but seeing them is enough for me to sympathize with them.

When we left, almost everyone was still there. I went over to the boy's bed and met his father. "Please say something to my boy. Please encourage him" I forgot what I said but I just fondle his head and tell him that he will be fine and that both, mom and dad will be with him. I went around meeting the others too. They were as cheerful as before.

I left with heavy heart thinking of them and at the same time glad and happy to finally leave this place. What's next? I couldn't be bothered for now. I just want to be home. I just want my room! I am glad that my wife wouldn't have to "suffer" further there with the "old" atmosphere and the "sightings" anymore! I know she missed our bedroom at home too!

Goodbye military barracks. Goodbye bladder test. Goodbye mortuary!

The Day That the Ambulance Came

After my second surgery, there wasn't much improvement. Probably, the shunt they inserted did not function as expected. I am just guessing, but as a patient, I am the only person who can sense if there is any improvement. In just a few months my situation worsens. Apart from the continued body pain, muscle motor weaknesses and digestive problems, I am beginning to lose control over my ability to swallow food, even liquid. It got worse each day and finally, I could not swallow any food. I could not even regulate my saliva.

At this time, I was already resigned to my bed and food has to be served at bedside. For my ablution, water in a pail is brought to my bed. I will do my ablution and prayers, sitting on a chair facing the *Qiblat*, the direction I face in my prayers.

Finally I decided to call the ambulance as my body weakens due to the lack in food intake. My wife called the ambulance. Two officers have to ferry me off from bed down the stairs and into the ambulance. Remember, all the continued body pain, muscle motor weaknesses and digestive problems are still with me plus this failure of my oesophagus. Saliva keeps drooling out of my mouth because I couldn't even swallow my saliva. It was so inconvenient.

The trip was however, to the nearest hospital, not the hospital that I had my previous surgery. This is again due to some miscommunication between us and the ambulance. It was a short ride and I was quickly rushed into the emergency room.

Emergency Room of the Public District Hospital

What ensued here next would be one of the most painful memories. The emergency room was so crowded, cramped with a lot of patients, some screaming in pain, some crying, even voices of kids. I can see doctors, nurses everywhere and even onlookers accompanying patients stood around, watching. It has a central open area with a few rooms with slide curtains, at the sides to treat patients. It was chaotic. It was so depressing.

I was alone, in pain. I was worried about my wife. She is somewhere, outside. I don't know where my son is. He accompanied me, but he is nowhere in sight. He is probably doing the registration.

In a few minutes, a soft voice greeted me. She's the doctor assigned to take my case, I guess. The first thing I asked was for a small plastic bag to dispose my saliva.

Next, there was a small interview. It is procedural. I described the whole history, from the early symptoms and the two surgeries I had. The lady doctor was diligently taking notes. She was so calm, oblivious of the chaotic situation around her in the room. I wish I could see her now and thanked her. I forgot her name.

Then, she made a few calls, met a few nurses and for a while, I was left waiting. She asked me to wait because they need to do some test on me. It was expected because this hospital does not have any of my records. She told me that after the tests, she would have to assign me to the proper department.

It was already an hour in the middle of that chaotic room. At the same time, new cases pour in, more noise, more people. It was then too I had the first sight of my wife. I was relieved just looking at her. She looks tired and stressed, but maintained her composure. She is one strong girl. I love her so much. By now, I have my patient tag, my small plastic saliva bag and the most precious of all, my wife.

A few tests were done including X-Ray. With all the tests and the waiting in between, I was already there in that noisy, chaotic room for three hours. It was a long, lonely, painful and sad day. It must be the same for my wife too. However, thinking back, I was surprised at my ability to endure it and face it all. I don't know how to describe it, but more like total surrender. I just let it flow. I just follow!

I was finally pushed out of that noisy room, passed a small walkway and into the ward. The ward looks old. I mean, really old. It looks haunted too probably because of its architecture, interior and façade. I finally got my peace to ease my pain and agony. I am now on a bed, white and clean. It was quiet.

My wife came and said she has to send my son home and she will come back the next morning. Later, a nice young Indian lady doctor came, greeted me, explain my situation and the next procedure she will undertake the next day.

It is time to sleep. I was so tired. My wife went through a lot for me. I do think of her, but I lost track of the time. I dozed off probably at one. I tell God, thank you for this. I was thankful and so relieved.

Transfer to the Public, National-Level Hospital by Ambulance

The next morning, the doctors made their round. I saw a few of them and one of them is a senior, I guess. He gave a short introduction about me. Later, two doctors came and prepared the nasogastric intubation for me. It was quite a short process, a bit uncomfortable. By then, my wife is back. I saw her at the corridor making calls.

It was a rather peaceful morning except for the bed on my left. I overheard their conversation, almost like a quarrel. I think the family was grilling that boy on why he fell and got admitted. Apparently, the reason or I might say, the excuse given was not satisfactorily to the family. So, they grilled him. It went on for hours.

In the meantime, sometime in the afternoon, my brother and sister came for a visit. I was then told that, my sister-in-law, who is a senior doctor, wanted me transferred to the hospital I had my first two surgeries. So, her intent was relayed to the senior doctor in the ward. The intent was discussed and calls were made between my sister-in-law and the doctor-in-charge, probably it went up to the director. In the next few hours, I managed to get some rest.

Around seven o'clock in the evening, they brought in the stretcher and bundled me up onto it. All the while in this hospital, I am a bit different from other patients. I didn't wear the hospital robe. My skin is hyper sensitive and just a touch of anything brought pain and burning sensation to my body. I told the doctors about it. They relented to my request of not wearing my shirt.

So, it's me, without a shirt, the whole body in pain, a tube dangling from my nostrils, secured to the stretcher, lying in an ambulance. On my left hand, I was holding on to that plastic bag for disposing my saliva. A hospital assistant accompanied me and sat by me. It was quite dark and the whole ride was bumpy and painful. It was noisy and the hail of the siren was deafening. It was a strenuous twenty minute journey.

At The Public, National-Level Hospital
Emergency Receiving Area

In no time, I was lifted off the ambulance, shoved into the emergency reception area. Suddenly, it was lights everywhere. My records were passed to a lady officer. She took it away, disappeared for a while and came back. She said "Now you will be under my charge" She teased me a bit "Listen to me OK?" Well, what I can do anyway, I told myself. I was left there for a while waiting for the ward staff to take me in.

While waiting, I saw another ambulance arrived. I can see a frail looking old Chinese woman being carried off the ambulance onto a wheelchair. She was accompanied by a younger woman. The younger woman was asked; "Is this woman your mother, sister?" She said, "No. We are from an old folk home, I am a volunteer there". Listening to her answer melts my heart. I was touched. I saw her glittering, sincere face. She pushed the wheelchair with all the love and care. She fed her drinks, wiped her face and even whispered a few words. She seems to love what she's doing. She was always smiling. It was love, all about love.

All this while, I was so busy working and never thought much about old folk home, let alone, volunteering to work there. I told myself, this world is still hopeful. Love is still around. There are so many good, sincere and caring people around. If you want to see love, here is where you can see it. It was comforting to know. I almost cried of happiness.

All the people around me are not family and friends, but since last night, my whole life depended on them. I learned about humility. I learned about sincerity. I saw love. I know what hospitality meant. It is all about love and care. I learned a valuable lesson.

After a while, I was in a very quiet and cold corridor. It was chilling. We were then in a lift and a few more seconds, I was moved to my bed and tucked under the clean, white cloth. It was quiet. I was relieved, but alone. I wondered where my wife is. Did she know where I am warded? She must be worried.

3rd Hospitalization

I thought for a moment, the emergency room at the previous hospital was horrible. The stay there was considered acceptable except for the old façade and interior. The ambulance rides was a trying one. The receiving area of the emergency downstairs was an experience. "Now, I am here. I really don't know what is next" I thought to myself as I glanced around for my wife. I know she must be tired, stressed and worried. She was supposed to follow the ambulance, but I know she wouldn't be able to catch up with us. Anyway, the painful, bumpy ride and the noise are finally over.

"We will change your clothes in a moment. Just hang on" a nurse informed me. It was already night when I was admitted to the ward. The nurse seems to be alone, sitting at a table or I was at a hidden side of the ward, I am not sure. "I am waiting for the assistant for your clothes" she reminds me. I was a bit uncomfortable probably from the humid air outside and from the ambulance ride. I hoped the nurse could at least give me a simple wipe and a new set of clothes. I am still in the previous hospital clothes.

A few minutes later my wife appeared. She came with one of my son. Actually, she didn't follow my ambulance. She went home, fetched my son and came to the hospital. "It was night and I am afraid to drive alone. So, I went home to fetch him before coming here" she said as she sat at the bedside. She was a bit late as she has to do some registration prior to entering the ward. She looks calm and composed. "So how are you? You are in the same ward as before. They all know you so don't worry. You will be fine" she quips. "You just take a rest. In a few minutes, I will go back home and come back tomorrow". By that time, I was tired and a bit comfortable due to the cooling air-conditioning. I forgot about the new clothes too. I just dose off.

The next morning I was given a little wet wipe, drying and a new set of clothes. One male nurse and an assistant then came and changed the nasogastric intubation tube inserted earlier by the previous hospital. "We need to change the nasogastric intubation tube. First, we will pull it out" he explained. He gently pulls out the tube. It is a minor discomfort. He then pulled out a new tube from its plastic cover and starts to gently insert it into my nostrils. He did a certain kind of measurement prior to it. He needs to ensure the tube reaches my stomach, I think. "You will have your food through this tube from that feeder machine" he said as he showed me a small dispenser.

I am also provided with a vacuum suction tube to dispose my saliva. "Sir, please use this tube to dispose your saliva. Let me put the suction end at your hand. Which one is your stronger arm?" the nurse instructs as he insert the tube to the wall-mounted bed panel and hang a canister near it. "We will change this tube every day or when you want it changed. Just let us know" he said as he left. I was placed at a sector of ward 7G which has roughly six beds and only two occupied.

Waiting for the MRI

Basically, my admission to the hospital this time is because of my inability to swallow. Other symptom has also worsened. My limbs are getting weaker and the upper body pain a bit worse. From my previous hospitalization, I expect that I need another surgery now. Focus is still about reducing or removing the cyst that may have grown bigger, despite the shunt being inserted there. I am just guessing.

In the next few days I will be undergoing tests and a new MRI. For MRI, it will take a few days before it could be conducted. So, I will again be in that "partially dark grave with piped in music". It will be a thirty minute "play dead" session again! I hope from the MRI, the surgeon will do something for me to regain my ability to voluntarily pass liquids into my stomach. I know as I was told before that one of the potential disorders caused by nerves in the cervical area is about swallowing. "I hope this is not permanent. How would it be if it is permanent? Can I live like this with this tube hanging from my nostrils?"

I began to visualize my fate. It was quite a scary thought! Suddenly I am faced with the "grim" reality of life. I do not have the answer. I was sad. I almost cried!

For now, I am lying with half my body exposed, nasogastric intubation tube in my nostrils, an IV line on my left hand and a vacuum suction tube that is linked to the wall-mounted hospital bed head unit, on my right hand. Next, is just waiting and sleeping.

Once in a while, negativity slips in. It was indeed depressing. I tried hard to encourage myself. "I am at your mercy God. I know you love me. I know!" I started to pray. "You have been through this before, right? You will be fine" another thought came. As I look at the empty ceiling, lying there helplessly, I slowly recall all the troubles and ailments I have been through. I don't know how I faced all that. Now, again, I am facing the same thing. "Can I survive this time?" my mind is engrossed in all kinds of eventualities. My mind is mixed with fear and hope.

I began to see those familiar faces again. As usual, they look clean, fresh and happy. They are like family, like brothers and sisters. "Do you have another operation sir? Remember me?" one nurse asked. A few others came by and greeted me. I know their faces, but forgotten some of their names. From their name tags, I began to recall. I looked at these young nurses and I felt a bit relieved. In my last stay, they treated me well. At least I know I am in good hands.

The Oesophagus Test

While waiting for the MRI, they conduct the barium swallow test on me. "We need to do a swallow test on you. We have to go to a clinic downstairs" instructs a nurse. "It is called the barium swallow test. The doctor at the clinic will explain further, OK? We will move you there in a minute" she said and left to the nurse's station. I saw her making a few calls.

A few minutes later, two men, a nurse and a hospital assistant came. "How are you sir?" the nurse asked. "Fine" I said. "Let's go for a stroll outside, get some fresh air outside! You must be bored here, right?" he jokes as he looked at my file. "I am bringing you for a test at a clinic, but first I need to remove some of your tubes here" he said. He unplugs the vacuum suction tube and gave me a small disposable plastic bag. "Use this if you need to spit off your saliva. You need to hold it" he instructs. "I will also disconnect your food tube and seal it" he said as he gently seal the tube and clip it to the side of my clothes. I am left with IV line. "Let's go for a stroll!" he jokes again. "I have not been to this particular clinic for quite some time. I hope I won't get lost" he told his assistant as he moves the stretcher out of 7G.

This guy is quite funny and likeable. He always laughs and makes jokes. He is Malay, but looked like a Chinese. His nickname is Chinese too! A few times I heard he cracks jokes and made fun of the nurses there, but workwise, I see him as reliable and efficient. I can call him any time to ask for anything, he will do it promptly with a smile! He loves his job and it shows! I like him very much. He is young, but quite experienced. I was told that prior to the current hospital he has worked at the busiest and most crowded hospital in the city. I think I can attest to that from the way he carries himself in the ward. He is also one of the "reference" people for the other nurses when they have any queries.

We reached the clinic in ten minutes. We were asked to wait outside for a while as it is a radiation area. I can see that yellow signage. "We need to change to the radiation gown inside. They are preparing it for us" he assured me. The door opens and a lady doctor came to us and greeted me. She then held the door open for us to come in. In the common area, we were each given the radiation vest and she gave us a sort briefing. "Here, we want to test your throat and your ability to allow liquid to pass through. It is called a barium-swallow test. Your throat movement will be scanned, recorded and monitored by a video camera" she said as she showed me the room where another assistant sat with a few TV screens.

"However, first, we need to transfer you onto the table. This table will be tilted into various positions to monitor your throat. You will be strapped to the table. We will give you a coloured liquid for you to drink" she carefully explained the procedure.

Then, I was moved onto the table. In my condition, a simple movement adds to the already painful muscle strains and cramps plus the sensory neuropathic pain. I was finally strapped onto the tilt table. Both the assistants were with me to hold my head and body in position. The doctor came with a glass of blue liquid. "OK, in this position try to drink this liquid" she explained as she signals her assistant to start the video" She then starts to gently feed the liquid into my mouth. I tried to swallow, but I couldn't. In my chest I felt a different sensation.

"Relax and take short rest. We will change position now. Then, we will feed the liquid again" she reminds me. " She then starts to gently feed another set of liquid into my mouth again. It was little, but still I couldn't swallow it. My throat fails to function normally. "If you feel some irritation, it is because the liquid flowed into a different tract, but no worries" the doctor explained. They stopped for a while as the doctor moved into the room to review the video on the monitors.

"Let us continue with a new position" she instructs. My "funny" assistant looked at me and said "Be patient sir. This is so inconvenient for you. Try to hold on. I am here. I will hold and help you" I was again tilted to a new position. Another set of liquid fed. A few minutes later another position. "So far, are you OK sir?" the doctor asked. I just nod. "We will record and submit your video for the surgeon" she tells me. I forgot how many positions, but it was long. It was painful. It was so troublesome. My body aches at each position and my oesophagus was strained.

Finally my assistant tilt me back to a flat position and began unstrapping me. "Thank God it's over sir. I can see you are in pain. It's OK. We can leave this place" he assured me and pats my back. "I am stressed too. It was difficult to keep you in position just now as you slide because your limbs are weak. " he quips.

I was transferred back to the ward stretcher and both my assistant, with the doctor reviewed the recordings. They have a short discussion. I lay back and felt relieved as I am freed from that demanding experience. I was tired. I can just "see" my bed. "Let me remove the radiation gown for you and we can go" my assistant said as he came back from the room. The doctor came to me and said "The test was good and we have your condition recorded. The surgeon will let you know the next plan. Thank you"

"So, our stroll is over. Let's go back to our ward" my assistant jokes as he pushed me back through the corridor. "What other test will I go through?" I thought to myself. "Yes, the MRI" I recalled. The MRI is less tedious than this barium-swallow test. I just have to lie down, "play dead' and in thirty minutes it is over.

The 3rd Surgery

I couldn't recall much about the surgery. Unlike the first two surgeries where I could still stand and walk, I am now bedridden, all wired up. I remembered my wife beside me when the stretcher was pushed. We passed through the same corridor, the lift, part of the link between the wards and admin building and clinic area and right to the surgery clinic. There were two patients ahead of us. We have to wait outside the surgery clinic.

"Oh my God, please make this easy for me. I don't know anything. God, I am helpless, but I am convinced you are there to help me" I prayed and prayed and prayed. I was worried because to me, my inability to swallow is a sign that my situation has worsened. That was why I am there, again. "God, save me from this ailment. I am scared if this disorder worsens" I keep on seeking and asking God.

As before, I am a bit scared, but since this is not the first time, I have gained some confidence. "Those boys and girls inside are good, young, courteous and professional" I assured myself. I saw them before. I was impressed. I even knew the surgeon from his many visits during the rounds. I know I am in good hands!

When I was in the ward, the surgeon has briefly explained that they will re-construct the shunt position and probably insert a longer shunt.

Apparently, the cyst has elongated and a new bubble appears. So, the new shunt is intended to reach the enlarged cyst and the new bubble.

A few minutes outside, our turn came and we were called in. In the receiving area, we went through the normal "safety" briefing, the consent letter, the risk about anaesthesia and so forth. My wife was still with me, signing the consent letter and listening to the briefing. Once in a while she looks at me with a worried look, but tried to smile. I know in a few minutes, I will be sedated and hallucinated, but she will be outside, waiting. I don't know how long she has to wait. Again, I prayed "God, there is no God, but you! Help me through this. Take care of her. I love her"

"We are ready to go into the operation theatre" advised one of the nurses-in-charge. "Bye. You will be fine. Seek God!" was the short message from my wife. She held my hands for a while, smiled and slowly left the receiving area. I heard some of the staff there encouraging me "Everything will be fine uncle. It will be over and you will go back to the wards. We are here. No worries"

In a second, I was again in the "blue" room. I am greeted by some of them. I can see more than ten people, some in surgical masks and some not. Everyone is in their blue surgery garb with aprons busy with their equipment and apparatus. They are setting up the place. The place is familiar, the table, the lights and the many screens. The 'blue" room is ready for me.

I was carefully transferred onto the operation table. The last words I heard from the nurse was "OK sir, breathe normally" She then placed the cup over my nose and immediately everything was quiet. I was "somewhere" for the next few hours!

Suddenly, my blurred vision saw a face. I couldn't recognize who it was. I looked around and saw a cup over my mouth and felt like a tube on my tongue. I am under some sort of a round glass cone. Again, on my right, I saw a figure, a face. I heard some vague sound, but didn't know what it was. Once in a while that person stoops down towards me, saying something. In a few seconds my mind began to notice and recognize the view around me. "I am still alive. Thank you, God. Thank you" was my first initial thought. My eyes are still blurred, but I can see a few faces.

I am also beginning to regain my senses. I can see that there is one dedicated nurse sitting beside me, near my head. She would, once in a while, open the cup over my mouth and wipe off my saliva. I could recall the few times she helps wipe off my liquid. As my vision gets clearer, I could see the nurse's face. It was still silent though. I have not regained my hearing.

The next thing I know, I was back in the ward, at the ICU section right in front of the nurse's station. The surrounding looks familiar. I was still weak and sleepy. In my dizziness, I could recall "seeing" someone beside my bed. That someone is always there every time I managed to open my eyes. After a while, I regained my consciousness. I could feel all the tubes and wires over me. I could see nurses coming over checking on my condition.

Arrived At Midnight Moaning In Pain

After a few days in the ward ICU, I began to realize that almost everyone around me is sedated, unconscious. I am the only one who is conscious! So, I am the only one who can hear and see almost all activities around me. It is normally quiet, but as I learned, life in the ward is unpredictable. At times, you are just exposed to the normal routine – the feeding time, the medication time and so forth. Some other time, you are forced to endure some strange situation or someone else's problem. It is something you can't avoid.

One night, when everyone was asleep around midnight, I heard a hectic noise coming from the corridor. I could hear the sound of radio intercommunication intermingle with voices of a few people. It got louder and louder as it approaches the ward and at the same time a few lights were switched on. "We are from emergency. This patient is for 7G" I heard a voice explaining. "Over there please. Yes, there" a lady nurse instructs. I heard a loud moan. I guess that must be the patient.

The new patient is then stationed beside my bed. I couldn't see much as the curtain was pulled covering the length of my bed, but I can see it moving. There were maybe ten people in the group. I can hear a lot of activity and movement. The patient was moaning in pain. "This is security. Yes, patient is in 7G already" another voice heard.

At the same time the earlier quiet atmosphere is now frantic with sounds of bed being pushed, trolleys positioned, a few equipment being shoved around and voices of more people talking. "Surgeon has treated the wound. She was under anaesthesia just now. It is now in the post-anaesthesia recovery phase. She is in pain" a lady nurse, probably from the emergency clinic, explained. The patient was still moaning in pain. It sounds uncontrollable. She must be in pain now after the aesthetic effect wanes.

"Please withstand the pain, please. We will try to help you. It is already midnight. Try to withstand, OK?" a nurse tried to calm the patient. "You take care of her. Calm her down. Calm her down" another voice heard. "I am in pain. I am in pain. Help me nurse. Help me" the patient moans and pleads. She never stops moaning.

At the same time, the security is still communicating with someone at the main lobby. "Yes, accompany them to 7G" I heard the security commands. Probably, the family members are coming over. I am not sure. The situation is still frantic. I could hear sounds of trolleys being shoved and trays. They were switching equipment as I could hear sounds of beeps and alarms.

"Help me nurse. Help me. So painful" patient continues to moan and cried. "Try to withstand please! I am helping you now. Don't cry" the nurse tires to soothe the patient. The patient keeps on crying. She must be in excruciating pain. As much as I empathize with her, I can't do much. I am left lying there in depression. All the moans and cries are unbearable. I have never been close to anyone in pain, moaning and crying as what happened that night. It was horrible. I wasn't trained in handling trauma either. It was an entirely new encounter!

I hear a lot of discussions between the doctors and nurses attending to this particular patient. I could hear people identifying themselves as doctors, police and even an insurance agent! I think everyone is trying to establish the patient identity and relatives. There was continued radio communication among these responsible agencies. "I am in pain. I am in pain" the moan continues unabated. The nurses are still busy nursing this patient. I glanced at the wall clock and it's half past one! I can't stand it. The moaning never stops. She must be badly hurt.

From the conversation I partially heard and picked up, she had an accident. She was rushed to the hospital by some by passers. I tried to calm myself, but I couldn't. I just hope that the moaning stops. It goes on and on. After a few minutes, I didn't hear the voice of the nurse calming her down anymore. Her moan became slower and slower probably a new painkiller was induced and just kicked in. I am just guessing.

I began to ponder at the amount of strain these nurses and doctors faced in their job. It wasn't easy. I don't think I can do even one percent of what they do! May God reward all of them in the Hereafter, I prayed.

After a while, the lights were switched off again. It was peace again. The patient is sedated, I guess. It was her turn, her fate that night. She may be someone's wife or mother. I am not sure. I looked up at the ceiling, reflecting over what had just happened.

It was amazing how everyone works together to save a life. In the middle of the night, there are those sacrificing their life and time serving us. It may look like just another day at the hospital, but it is also another display of love and compassion. It is about love and hope. It is about giving!

Death around Me

One of the realities of life is death. We will all die one day whether we like it or not, ready or not, believe in God or not. In all the places in the world, hospital would be a place of the highest probability death would occur. It is here that part of one's ability, powers, dexterity and strength is slowly diminished, taken away by "the force above".

When fate comes, even the fittest, the richest, presidents and Kings will face it. It is not a matter of choice. It is also not an option. You will get it when and where you are fated! It can be dengue from just a bite from one tiny mosquito. It can be a freak accident. It can be a transmitted disease through a strange virus. It can be anything, any cause! We are actually helpless. All of us are vulnerable and prone to be affected by any cause, big or small.

In my case, I thought my respiratory system will be fine. I have all the necessary precautions and prevention in place. I play tennis, cycle regularly and I don't smoke. I thought my digestive system is secured. I don't take a lot of carbohydrates, loves vegetables and drinks lots of water. I thought my muscular system is intact forever. I take lots of proteins for my muscle growth and perform exercises regularly for strength and endurance. For my sensory, I spend ample amount of time in the morning sunlight for maximum exposure to far-infra-red rays that is good for overall health and skin care.

I have every precaution and protection in place. For a while I thought I am "immortal"! I have always maintained a good height, weight and BP. I even looked younger than my age. I felt good. I have a good, commendable career, family and life. I never thought of fate that much. I thought I can do anything and everything when I want. Suddenly out of nowhere I got this!

Talking about death, not everyone here will die here. We never know when and where we will die, but here, we are at the verge of death or "toying with death". The threat of death is real and imminent. If it doesn't happen to us it may happen to the person beside us. It was always a possibility. So, if we stay a few days in a hospital, we may not be able to see it, but in a few weeks, we may see it.

I woke up one morning and heard one of the nurses asking during their daily "change of the guards" "How is bed number three? Is he OK this morning?" Bed number three was probably under her care in the last shift. "He is no more with us. His body failed to respond to the treatment last night" a voice answered. "Wasn't he admitted two days ago and seems fine? Are you sure he is no more with us?" the nurse wants a confirmation. "Yes, he is gone!" was the answer. Do you know what? Bed number three is beside my bed! Death is "near". It was him not me!

Yes I remembered a patient admitted a few days before and placed beside me. I didn't see his face, but I know a new patient came in. He was transferred from another hospital. He was quiet from the day he was admitted. I could only hear the beeps from probably a breathing apparatus or ventilator hooked to him.

In another instance, I saw a large crowd converging at one bed, across from my area. It has been like that the last few days, but on that particular day, the crowd was larger. Besides the loved ones and relatives, I saw doctors and nurses around the bed. At times, the curtain was pulled for their intended procedures. At times, it was open to the relatives. After a few minutes, more doctors came and again, the curtain was pulled around the bed. It looks frantic with many people and sounds of beeps and alarms behind the curtain. I know something is not right. I could sense it.

From afar, I could hear voices, but in differing tones and intonation. "Relax, let the doctor handle it" a voice trying to calm someone. There were lots of murmurs and noise from the crowd. It gets louder and louder over time. The curtain was still closed. It was quiet for a while. I don't know what transpired. The noise fades away. I keep on looking at the area. People are still standing around the bed, but the noise has faded.

Suddenly, a loud simultaneous scream and cries came from that place. Everyone gathered there seems to cry in unison. It was loud. It was intense. It was over in a few minutes. Another life was gone. It was silence after that.

I lay there thinking "They have tried their best to save him. That is all they can do. He is gone. His time is up" I asked a nurse nearby about that patient "Old man?" The nurse said "He is an old man. He has not been stable since last week. Injury to the head is usually tough". "He seems to have a big family" I said. "Yes. It is good. There are cases where patients died without family or relatives, just us! It is sad you know? Children nowadays" she laments. "You are lucky too sir. Your wife is always here and you have many visitors!" she compliments me. "Thank God. I am glad to have her" I said.

At the same area, in another bed, there lies another patient. I was told that he is a young man, who was involved in a serious car accident. He has been there earlier than me. He is in a coma all the while. He doesn't have many visitors except for one old woman and a beautiful lady, probably his wife. I couldn't recall much about him, but about that old woman, I remembered. She is the mother.

How did I remember her? I remember her clothes. She will be in the same clothes for two or three days! She never misses being at his son's bedside every visit time. She will be the first to come and last to leave. She sleeps at the visitor area and every opportunity she has, she will come to her son's bed. I overheard that she lives in a village quite far away. So, she doesn't have the means to make that daily trip. She chose to stay for a few days, went back home and come back. I looked at her and I could see what motherly love means.

She was the loyal visitor. Day and night, oblivious of everything around her, she will come to her son's bed. Her son is just there, unable to move and speak. She keeps on coming, to be there for him. Once in a while, I do see the wife, but not as frequent as the mother.

One day, the rather quiet bed had a few visitors, more than usual. It was visiting hours. I didn't suspect anything unusual. The wife was there, but this time the wife was heavy on her mobile, all the time calling and talking to someone. It was rather strange. The crowd around that bed seems restless. I saw a nurse went there for a while and she left. Just a few minutes later, I heard the wife cries, an uncontrollable cry. She was hugged by a woman as she groans and sighs. It was a sad sight. She didn't stop crying.

At that frantic time, I couldn't see the mother. She may be sitting somewhere, hidden. I guess all her waiting and anxiety is finally over. All of a sudden, grieve and sadness fills the air. It was quite fast. I remember seeing the patient condition from my bed. His head is heavily bandaged his arms and legs hang from a few supports. There was a lot of equipment around him. It wasn't a pleasant sight. It was painful even at the sight of it. He may recover, but looking at his condition, it would be a slow and long recovery.

It was another sad day in the ward. The doctors and nurses have done their part, day and night nursing him. It may be something new to me witnessing the demise of a few souls around me but to the nurses, I know they have seen countless death and sorrowful moments.

"Do you want to understand the true meaning of life? Go visit the Hospital. Go visit the grave!"

The next morning, the usual sight of the mother slowly sneaking in to look at her son is missing. She is not there anymore. She won't be coming to 7G again. I won't see that same clothes again. I won't see that special motherly love again. Her son is not there. She may be somewhere praying and wishing for his son a blissful life in Heaven. I know that was what she wants for her son to be – happy here and happier there in the Hereafter. She has given her best to the son, to the last days in the hospital, even if it means by just being there, with the little means she may have. I know she is not rich, just a common village folk. I imagine her worries and anxiety every day she was in 7G.

I still have tears in my eyes, even now, thinking of her. I am so sad!

All Sedated Except Me

In the ward's ICU, in front of the nurse's station, there were around ten beds. It houses post-surgery patients like me. Do you know what? Out of the ten patients, I think, I am probably the only one not in a coma or sedation. I couldn't recall, probably there is one or two other than me, but even with their eyes open, they are not responding to doctors or nurses call.

All of us are heavily wired and monitored. I am hooked to a heart monitor at the back of my bed. The heart monitor has a multicore cable that is attached to a few points on my chest with sticky pads. I also have a BP cuff at my arms and a tiny probe at my fingers, both of this is linked to the heart monitor. The BP cuff inflates and deflates automatically for my BP readings. I still have my nasogastric intubation tube into my nostrils for my food and this tube is connected to a dispenser feeder which has a tiny pump. I am given a suction tube as before, to suck liquids from my mouth. Occasionally, based on my oxygen reading I am fed with oxygen from a tiny tube into my nostrils. Now, what else am I wired with? No, how could I forget this? Yes, I have a catheter, a drainage tube that is placed into my bladder. This tube allows my urine to drain continuously into a plastic bag hanging low by the side of my bed.

Let me talk about the doctors making their rounds. The first thing the doctors do is to wake up the patients. So, how do you wake up sedated patients? They go from bed to bed calling the patients with a loud voice! "Good morning sir, good morning!" the lead doctor calls, almost like yelling. "Do you hear me? Yes? Wake up please!" another command given. "Wake up sir!" the doctor usually calls up the patients a few times. At first, I was surprised at the noise, but later I came to know these patients are sedated. "We must shout because they may not be able to hear" the nurse explains when I asked.

When they reached my bed, I am ready for them. "Good morning. How are you sir? The doctor asks politely with a smile. The doctor will look at my file and also refer to a laptop on a trolley which has my detail records. He will then brief the team about my current status and the next plan. Almost daily, I am the only conscious patient they do not need to "shout". What about the rest of the patients? They are in the world of their own, in hallucination. They may open their eyes, look at you, but couldn't hear or speak.

So, being conscious, I could see and hear a lot of activities in the ward. I don't have much to do. Lying down, semi-paralyzed and wired, what can I do? It wasn't quiet though. I have "music" to entertain me. All day all night what I hear is "teet" " teet" " teet" "doing" "doing" "toot" "teet" " teet" " teet" "doing" "doing" "toot" from the many equipment round us, almost like a rhyme, an orchestra. The sequence of the sounds is like an orchestra! Apart from that, I could hear the buzzing sound from the various pumps round me. The sound is quite irritating, but after a while I just have to bear with it. It becomes "music"!

I look around and felt grateful. I am not as serious as the others. At least I don't have tubes into a hole in my throat. I don't have bandage over my head or limbs. I can see and hear. I am "alive" and conscious! At least, during visiting hours, I know who came.

Just across my bed, in the same ward lies an old man. He was already there when I came in. He is in a coma. Every day, his wife will visit him, but she couldn't do much. He is in a coma, eyes closed all the time. I realized the wife likes to glance at us when she visits her husband. One day she drops by to greet us. "What is wrong with him?" she asked. "Oh, he has a nerve problem, a cyst in his spine. As such, his body is not functioning well" explains my wife.

"He fell at home. He hurts his head. Later, he had a surgery here. See, he has been like this for two weeks!" the wife told us. I think she wants to share her problems. She is alone almost all the time. I guess she is the one able to stay in the ward for her husband. During visiting hours, her children did come. Most of them are in the thirties. So, I guess, her children may all be working. I am just trying to have good thought towards her children. I would expect her children to take turns staying in the ward. I couldn't understand people sometimes!

Poor Indian Patient and His Meal

One of the few things I remembered was one patient in the common ward. From my ICU bed I could see part of the common ward flanking both sides of the nurse's station. It was visiting hours. I could hear the chief nurse scolding someone "Don't do this uncle! This meal is for you, not them. You must eat. It is for your health. Understand?" I couldn't understand the reply from the patient because he speaks a different language. "How many times have I seen you doing this?" she deplores. "This is hospital's food. It's for you alone!" she adds with anger. Again, I hear the patient murmured and grumbled, but could not comprehend what he says. Probably he too didn't understand what the chief nurse is saying.

Later I asked a nurse what the commotion was all about. What I heard saddens me. "The family is poor. So, the wife brought the two kids to eat here!" the nurse explains. "Pity them. We have to scold them. It is not that we are cruel. The patient needs to be taken care of and fed" adds the nurse.

I was saddened. I keep on thinking about that poor family. Yes, among us, in any society in fact, there are those who are unfortunate.

We never know these people. We live in an individualistic world where everyone just cares about their own lives! We rarely meet face-to-face with deprived, destitute people in our society.

I learned my lesson on that day. We have three meals a day and yet we complained! We complain about the taste, the texture and many times, we didn't finish it! We wasted it! Why not we think about the poor and the hungry every time we sit for our meal? Can we all do it?

Doctors Making Their Rounds

One of the main activities in the ward is the doctors "rounds". This "rounds" happen in the morning around eight. Usually, a team of doctors and nurses led by a senior doctor or the surgeon will come to every bed to see the patient. The senior doctor will personally perform a physical check and ask the patient of their condition. He will personally flip through my file and confirms with the responsible nurse regarding procedures, tests and medication. It is quite thorough, but done quickly. The senior doctor or surgeon will then briefly explain to the other doctors of the patient current status and future treatment plan. The young doctors are given the opportunity to ask questions during this "rounds".

In some instances, I did see the other doctors were asked to explain about the patient. If there is any issue or discrepancies, they usually inform the responsible nurse on duty. At times, they resolve the issues there and then. From their discussion, I can briefly understand my current status and basically "where I am heading". It can be a relief when I hear some of their conclusions.

After seeing the daily "rounds", I began to learn the overall intent. It is an exciting experience for me to see all this. We as engineers do have a similar "meeting" when on site. We have our daily safety briefing and technical meeting or sometimes called a "toolbox" meeting. A safety briefing is like the pre-flight safety demonstration before taking off. It is the usual reminder of the safety precautions, safety harness to be worn and emergency procedures. It can be boring because this safety officer talks about the same thing every single day, right? Maybe you have heard a safety briefing. It is the same, repetitive thing. Anyway, unlike the site safety briefing, the pre-flight safety demonstration is a more pleasant experience! Why? Even though it is repetitive, we have a beautiful stewardess to present it! It may be boring, but a bit "stimulating"! Whatever, safety is of utmost importance.

After the safety briefing, comes the "toolbox" meeting. A project manager will explain the overall work plan of the day for each discipline based on the schedule. A scheduler or planning engineer will then explain the details of the work order or job cards. After that, the engineers will each meet with the foreman, technicians and fitters regarding their work scope for the day. I can relate the importance of the "rounds" with my "toolbox" meeting.

I think hospital work is as regimented as engineering. We all have our SOPs, manuals and sequence we all need to abide to. The difference is, they deal with sick patients and we deal with machines! I guess their "mission" is more critical and noble. I salute all of them!

Nurses Change of Shift

It is not all tragic at the hospital. There are, once in a while, rare moments you will remember. After all, lying in bed alone, you have all the time in the world to see, hear and feel anything. You are only interrupted during feeding time, BP and blood check. Other than that you are either sleeping or "daydreaming" even fantasizing! Yes, fantasizing! Do I need to elaborate? Let me leave it to your imagination!

Every day, at three different times, I "witness" the "change of guards". No, I am not talking about the half past eleven, morning ceremony about the Foot Guard Regiments and Bands at Buckingham Palace. This ceremony is at the nurse's station minus the Band. It is significant because of the sudden noise you hear, when a dozen people talk simultaneously! A few minutes later, it is quiet.

At first I couldn't relate the noise to hospital work. It sounds like an argument! Only when I hear what is being discussed did I know that it is an important event of the day. The new shift is being briefed of the status of each patient. One end-of-shift nurse discussed four or five patients under their care to the new oncoming shift.

A few times I overheard this "Bed number three, spinal, surgery on cyst conducted a week ago, no allergy, code..." It is all quite confusing to me, but I guess to them it has been their routine. They are exchanging information on our current status and future plan whether we will undergo certain procedure or tests. I think their job and this "change of guards" is very critical. I can't imagine if they faulted at the briefing! We may get a wrong medication or worse still, missed an important procedure!

Now, I really value hospital work. They, the nurses and hospital assistants deserve my utmost respect. Just think, normally, as early as seven o'clock in the morning what would we be doing? We may still be in bed, on our comfortable six-inch mattress, tucked under our blankets, in our cosy bedroom at home, right? We may be enjoying the last few precious minutes of our sleep, but they are already at work! Just imagine what time they woke up! What about the night shift then? They have to leave their family when we were all with our family, about to rest and sleep together! Indeed, it is a big sacrifice. May God grant them peace, happiness and good life! They deserve the best as a reward to their sacrifices.

All this while, I never thought much about nurses. After staying in the hospital, I begin to appreciate them. They are more than men and women in white working at a hospital. For a moment, my life depends on them. I was left in their care. They cared for me.

Patients Bathing Time

I can recall, how, very early every morning, I will hear sound of trolleys being pushed around. Besides the trolleys, there will be sound of some hectic activities. Then, I hear people talking, giving instructions, and kind of a short briefing of whom will take care of which patients. Usually, when they start their "cleansing session" it is a happy one. In this particular ward, they will play music from a small radio while they go around undressing patients and move them to the bathing stations. Until now, three years later, I can still recall this one song, not actually a song, just a rhyme that went viral, Gwiyomi. Have you heard of this Gwiyomi rhyme? I am sure you had! It is just a few weeks earlier than Gangnam Style! Do you like that one? So, every time I play this rhyme on mp3 or YouTube, I can "see" the ward and "hear" the activities there.

A few minutes after the briefing and Gwiyomi "on air", a nurse and a hospital assistant will approach me. "Good morning sir. How are you? It's bathing time" the nurse will softly instruct me. By then, they are already in their "bathing uniform", plastic boots and plastic apron, with gloves. "Do you have your toothbrush, your soap and shampoo? Tell us where it is. We will get it for you and bring it with us" they asked before we go to the bathroom.

First, they have to carefully remove any IV line or our oxygen apparatus. They will then undress me and wrap me in a large, soft white towel and place me on the "wet stretcher". They even have a nickname for this stretcher! At that time I didn't understand when they said in the briefing "Bed two, three and seven needs a ship. Bed one and four, a wheelchair" Later, I found out. For patients like me who are unable to sit, they use a "ship" to transport and clean me up! For other patients, they move them in a wheelchair. There are those whom they just clean them in bed with water, sponge, soap.

It was well coordinated. It is a "happy" affair too. You will hear them sing along, jokes, gossips as they diligently cared for all of us, from undressing us up until putting on new, clean and dry clothes on us. As they move to the next patient, they will also brief each other a bit about the patient. Yes, they will bathe and clean us. It is part of their job! We will be gently transferred to the "ship" and moved to the bathroom. In the bathroom, they will remove the towel. If we are unable to sit, like in my case, they will slowly lift my head and body to a sitting position. They will then gently brush my teeth. They will shampoo my hair.

Next, they set the shower temperature and will bathe me in a lying down position. They start from the head, down. It wasn't an easy task. After the shower, they will have to change the towel, from the wet one to a clean, dry one, all done while I am lying down. As I said, it was well coordinated. They seem to have a standard operating procedure as I can sense from the sequence of event in the whole process.

Indeed, it is very cold in the morning. I shivered, but looking back, I was happy. Although in pain, their care and patience makes me feel humbled. They are all young, like my children. Of course, there are a few isolated instances where one of the hospital assistant wasn't that careful, but I forgive them. He may be tired or sleepy. Who knows? I couldn't ask for more. They are after all, like me, humans.

Yes, I remember Gwiyomi, the "ship" and the cold morning showers, but above all, I remember their sacrifices. I love every one of them!

Once in a while now, I do play Gwiyomi and I cried inside.

Nurses Gossiping

What I learned is hospital work is one hell of a job! I am not in the industry, but as an outsider looking in, I can feel the demand of the job. As an engineer, the basic difference is they have "humans" and us, "machines" to care. When it comes to people, there are many elements that come into play. It is stressful to cope with the physical, emotional and mental demands of the patients, their bosses and of course, their families.

Unlike my nine-to-five routine when at base office, on top of the physical, emotional and mental demands, they have to adapt to three differing shifts! I was there, I know. I do respect their poise, calm and "cool heads".

So, in that kind of environment, when there is a lull in their activities, it is understandable that they will tend to "escape" out of their "uncomfortable zone" Just like all of us, we will retreat to something pleasant. It can be anything, right? We may want to go talk to our friends, call someone or just, catch up with our Androids. It can also be gossiping! Yes, in bed, lying I did overhear gossips. It's normal, I think. It is a form of escapism. A gossip from someone can be a "welcomed interruption" to the harsh realities of their work! I can't blame them.

So, what did they talk about? I can't remember all but surely, favourite topics are families, partners, love, movies, their colleagues, money and of course, complaints, a lot of it. As I lie down in bed, besides thinking about my predicament, I am "accidentally" lured into their topics! They talked about where they decide to settle down, whether at their partner's hometown or theirs. As I listened, their gossips ventured into the probable time they want to move, the cost involved, what they need, their in-laws and children. They seem to have explored all eventualities, risks and preference. It is interesting!

I thought that is good project planning. I remember, when we discuss a project, we look at the four items – time, resource, schedule and costs! Yes, these nurses applied those theories too! I learned a few tips, but without my Android, I can't note them down! So, do not think that as nurses they will fail in project planning! I think they are good at it! As they gossip, once in a while there will be phone calls and minor request from patients.

Another favourite topic is love. Yes, love. It is about feeling loved, the absence of love and even, old "affairs". I can't understand all because some of their gossips turn into giggles and whispers! It must be something interesting and "stimulating". I am too far to hear! Of course, the other topic is attention!

"Sometimes, they just don't care! I don't know what to do!" one of the complaints I heard. "I don't understand men! I really don't" came another comment.

They even tease some of the male nurses there. They joked and broke into laughter. I think they have been together and tolerant to each other. They talked like brothers and sisters, like friends. It is heartening to know they are happy. Indeed, people are productive when they are happy. I am happy too when I hear them joke and laugh. What an atmosphere! A few of their gossips on love can be startling, some "deep" and others, soothing! I think some of them are not married and "learning" the mating game!

So, what else they retreat into? They talk about beauty. When they ventured into beauty, they will have more "participants". A few others will chip in. As nurses, generally they are clean, tidy and have a pleasant disposition. It is in fact, a requirement of the industry, I guess. So, when they talk about beauty and health, it is their specialty. They know about vitamins, supplements and herbs. No wonder they are all fresh, healthy and attractive! Yes, I must admit this. I think many would agree, right? You have seen nurses. What do you think?

As a patient, nothing is more pleasing than seeing a fresh and attractive face. It is therapy. It helps us to "forget" at least for a few minutes, our pain and discomfort.

Another favourite topic is what else if not their colleagues. This can range from the doctors, to the matron, fellow nurse, the pharmacist, the blood bank team, the cleaners and maintenance team! I think it was all justifiable as it affects their work. In any organization where every person is inter-connected and related, it may be difficult to expect a smooth operation. I can see, despite their complaints and gossips, work runs smoothly. Everyone is quite contented and happy.

I think the "gossip retreats" helps. It is one channel everyone can express their views and released their pressures! It may or may not solve problems, but it is "escapism" from the tough and critical environment of a ward.

I can't say that everything is smooth in the ward though! Once in a while, I do hear some minor disagreement and "quarrel". It is mainly about attitude not so much about procedures, medicine or tests. I don't think everyone is perfect and can keep their heads cool every single hour every single day! Definitely, not me! My toughest work environment is off shore, on a rig. No, I can't keep a "cool head"!

Difficult Patients

In my days in the ward, I have witnessed many situations that the nurses face and their reactions towards them. Some of it stems from difficult patients and their ridiculous demands! While I was in 7G, after being moved from the wards ICU, my bed was placed in an area away from the nurse's station. I am no more in front of the nurses.

There was an old woman near my bed. All night long, she keeps on calling the nurses "nurse, I want to go home. Sister, I want to go home". Imagine every three minutes or so you hear her calling! "Nurse, I want to go home. Sister! Friend! Auntie! I want to go home!" She changed the name she called every single time. Yes, all night long! I couldn't stand her behaviour and the noise. It was irritating! She may have an issue, but I don't know what. Nurses do come every thirty minutes to see and check on her. It was so disturbing. "Please pull this curtain. I don't want to see her" I request. The nurse obliges.

She doesn't only call the nurse every few minutes, her bed sways too. I can hear her bed moving and sways! She even fell off her bed! Every time she falls, the nurse will come and carry her onto the bed and tried to calm her. I think she fell off her bed three or four times. I couldn't sleep that night. It was so inconvenient to me, other patients and the nurse. What a horrible night it was.

In another instance, I heard a voice from somewhere across from my area. It sounds like an argument. Apparently, an old man was making a lot of noise, cursing the nurse with lewd and vulgar words. I think the man was depressed and frustrated. "You are all useless! I am like this, what can you do?" he shouts and complains. "You don't allow me to go to the toilet. Why?" another complain from him. "We will send you. You cannot go on your own. You may fall uncle" a nurse calms him down. It didn't stop his anger. He shouts and screams obscenities! "Why are you spitting?" cried a nurse! He spat on the nurse! "What is this uncle? Why do you spit on me?" retorts the nurse.

The man continues his tirade. He is really outraged for whatever reason. "Just stay in bed please. Do not make noise!" commands the nurse. I think a few nurses went to his bed to control him. "What? Why am I here? I can't be cured you stupid idiot! All of you are useless" he keeps on his barrage of curses and vulgar words! It goes on for almost an hour.

I asked a passing by nurse "What is wrong with that old man?" She calmly said "It is normal here, sir. This is a ward for nerve patients. We are used to it! Never mind. He will tire himself and sleep" I can see how demanding their job is. It requires a lot of patience and a "cool head".

My Wife's Sacrifice

All the while I was hospitalized there is another person, besides the hospital staff that sacrificed a lot – my wife. For the few weeks I was there, I don't know how she sleeps. I was in a few places, at the ward's ICU, the normal ward, the rehabilitation area ward or in a single room.

In the single room, a flat, bed-sofa is provided. So, she is comfortable. I have no worries. When I am in the other places, she has to make do with a few seats and sofa at the visitor waiting room. It is not that convenient and comfortable. I know because I have seen the room. She doesn't have any pillow and has to wear a jacket, as her blanket. She has to "share" the space with strangers. It wasn't that conducive. However, it is quite safe as it is close to the security guard post and usually, other visitors are not allowed in. Only registered caretakers accompanying patients are allowed in beyond the visiting hours.

Besides the uncomfortable sleep, she has to use the general toilet located at a different level. While she takes care of me at the hospital, for her dinner and breakfast, she has to go outside the ward building to the admin building area that is quite a distance. She has to go through a lot of hardship. The hospital is big. So, the walking is quite far! It can be tiring.

Apart from the days and nights at the hospital, she has to deal with home too. She has to commute between the hospital and home almost daily. It is a long ninety minute drive as she has to pass through the city traffic. At home, she has to ensure lunch and dinner for my kids is served. She may cook or not, but one thing for sure, someone has to be there for the kids. We even need to rope in my cousin to send my kids to school when my wife is with me. All this hustling is not easy. She needs to plan and make calls all over. These are additional sacrifice she has to make.

At the hospital, parking is irritating. Almost all the time, the parking area is full. It is normal for her to park the car outside the hospital. She then has to walk from the car, in through the entrance, up a ramp, through the admin lobby and to the ward building. It is far, around three hundred meters! I know it is tiring and she has to do it at least twice a day – coming from the car and going to the car. Also, at night, she has to move the car from outside into the hospital area. She walks a lot every day! Easily, she walks almost one kilometre every day!

I am grateful to God to have a loyal, obedient and patient wife. In the ward, I saw a few patients who do not have visitors, as frequent as me. Some of them do not even have their spouses visiting them. My wife knows some of the caretakers there and she heard stories.

The Recovery Stages

After the 3rd surgery, two weeks at the ward's ICU, I was moved to a different ward. It is in the same neurosurgery ward, but mostly for patients in the recovery stages. I was placed in an area of only four beds. It is here that I felt better, more peaceful than the earlier ward. I am still weak and unable to move. It was also the same day where I am most gratified and excited. It is the first day that I can swallow liquid and food again. This is one gift from God that I took for granted until I lost it.

Just a few minutes before being moved to this ward, a physician from the ENT came to my bed and said "Today, we are going to test your throat to see if we can start administering your food orally. If successful, we will remove the nasogastric intubation tube" On hearing that, I was excited and at the same time worried. What if I couldn't swallow? What will happen if this disorder is permanent? I remember from my reading that some nerves may be permanently damaged.

The physician is a young Malay girl. She is beautiful, calm and courteous. She left me for a while and came back with just a glass of water and a small spoon. She told me "Now, I am going to give you a few drops of water and you try to swallow it, OK? I will try a small portion first and will increase gradually" She then fed me the water and you know what, I managed to swallow it! Yes, I can swallow the first drop! She smiled at me and said "I will give you a bit more now. Just swallow it" She then gave more water and I managed to swallow too. God was I delighted! That is probably the first few drops of water I felt through my tongue and throat in a month! She looks happy too.

"Yes, your throat responded positively. You can now ask for a normal diet for your lunch. I will inform the nurse in-charge" she said with a big smile. She jokes "Please call your wife to bring you your favourite food. Enjoy it!" I said "Sure, I will". What a pleasing experience that was. I was so happy and glad.

I have passed the swallowing disorder test and can expect normal food.

I was still with the nasogastric intubation tube when in the rehabilitation ward. The whole day, I could only see the patient in front of me enjoying her lunch and tea. It was tempting, but I couldn't do much. I still have that tube in my nostrils. Only later that afternoon, a nurse came to remove the nasogastric intubation tube. I felt like a part of my life is back!

On the second day in the rehabilitation ward, I receive a lot of visitors. One of my elder sisters came. As though she knew that I am able to swallow again, she brought one of my favourite dishes – lamb curry! "I know you love lamb curry! This is a special dish I cooked for you" she said. I was so excited! I felt like jumping! Lamb curry is definitely something that I craved for. My wife scooped a portion of it from the pot and placed it in a plate. "Can I have more?" I plead. "No, be patient. Try a little bit first. Just savour the taste again" she advised. I then taste it. It was wonderful. I haven't got anything on my tongue the last two weeks and now I am able to taste my favourite, lamb curry.

Life is precious again. It is meaningful again.

My stay at the rehabilitation ward revolves around, as usual, looking at people around me! What else can I do? I am resigned to lying down and my hands are still weak. My standard character is, I couldn't wear clothes and now, I couldn't stand the fan above! Yes, my skin is hypersensitive to touch – be it my clothes or even the gust from the fan! It was so painful and irritating here as I was used to the air-conditioning in the normal 7G ward. As much as I wish, I couldn't switch it off as it is a common area. We have four beds, two on each side and two ceiling fans in the middle. Do you know what? The fans are turned full blast all day and night! That adds to my misery!

At night, where the pain is unbearable, I have to "design" a makeshift "tent" over me! What I asked my wife to do was to shove in the movable, over bed table over me, somewhere at my chest level and put a blanket over it. I lie underneath the over bed table and the "tent" formed by the blanket over it. It really helps. The gust from that full blast ceiling fan is greatly reduced from tormenting my sensitive skin which caused the burning pain! It was a "creative" design! We tend to be creative when we are in a forced situation. I need badly something to block me from the fan gust! I only thought of it on the second night there. I couldn't sleep the first night.

My wife managed to get three chairs and arranged it as a simple makeshift bed. There are extra pillows and blankets for her. In this ward, caretakers are allowed to sleep beside the patient's bed. As this is a rehabilitation ward, caretakers are encouraged to tend to the patient except for defecation and dressing of wound. We were also attended by the ward nurses, rehabilitation nurses and young trainee nurses.

As I am still frail, my bathing is still using the "ship". Remember that ship at 7G I talked about? The difference is here, it is done after seven o'clock in the morning, minus "Gwiyomi"! Also, my bath is done by one nurse and two trainee nurses. As usual, they will first transfer me by lifting and pulling the blanket under me onto the "ship". I realized that the trainees are not as efficient as the professionals at 7G. Luckily, the nurse is there to facilitate the sequence. I am grateful anyway. At least, I am cleansed.

It wasn't an easy task. It takes the same level of patience and care. My situation is quite simple as I do not have any bandages or IV line. I am different. Instead, they need to adapt and deal with other patient with different condition. It is always a challenge for them.

Talking about rehabilitation nurses, one thing typical to what they do is the dreaded bladder test. They need to rehabilitate your urinary system back to normal. Before transferring me to this rehabilitation ward, they removed the catheter that sucks my urine from the bladder to the bag. It was painful, but quite relieving! I am now free to urinate naturally. Have I told you how painful the bladder test was? I did, right? They did it on me here, twice!

My "Pampered" Neighbour

The bed in front of me is a Chinese woman. She fell from her bicycle while cycling with her "new boyfriend" in a park. What do I mean by her "new boyfriend"? Actually, she is a widow and this guy has been courting her. I am not a busybody, but her mother is warm and sociable. The mom divulged these little "secret" to my wife! She had an internal injury to her head and underwent a surgery. I don't know her exact problems, but from her mother, she has lost her memory and could not speak.

She has been there, just in the rehabilitation ward for two months! Prior to that, she has been in 7G for three months. Overall, five long months! So, what is my three weeks in 7G and two days here? She has, however, two extraordinary "caretaker" – her mother and her "boyfriend". For the few days I was there, what I see was a display of "super extra" care!

Super extra care? Both, the mom and the boyfriend took turns caring for her. Aside from the normal care from the nurses, both of them were there for her almost all the time! The guy would take blankets and pillows to comfort her. On the bed, any conceivable space available, the "boyfriend" will insert a pillow. On top of that, he would slide in extra folded blankets for her, at the sides, beneath her legs. My wife slandered and joked "I think all the pillows and blanket in the cupboard is with her! There is nothing for you!"

Almost all the time, I could see him standing beside the bed, adjusting, modifying and sliding in new blankets and pillows! He would spend all the time talking to her although he knows she could not respond except for her fake smile. Her mom told us "You can say anything to her and she will give you the same smile. She is faking it, I think. Maybe, she doesn't understand what is being said. Pity her. I am so sad".

The guy is actually a very nice guy. He is always jovial, smiling and friendly. All the nurses there like him as he is polite, courteous and like to joke. He told me he is a civil contractor. He looks tan and stern, typical of someone doing a tough job, but once he talks and smile, you can see he is sincere and warm! He is so nice to be with. We talked about cycling and he is a serious cyclist – off road and on road cycling!

I am nothing compared to him. He talks about plotting routes, selecting which mountain to climb, which parks to explore and he is also a tech-geek on cycling. He has three bikes and one of it is ten times more expensive than mine! So now you know? I only have one, a mountain bike with a hybrid tire – for off road and on road. I only ride around my home and had never ventured into mountain bike riding. I just ride ten kilometres at one time. I don't wear all the tight riding gear and shoes. I do have a helmet though. I just do it as a light cardio exercise, just for fitness and fun, no gangs!

"She can't talk. I have been trying to teach her" he grumbles a few times. "I even sang her a few of her favourite songs, but she gave me the same empty smile!" he adds, looking sad. One thing great about this guy is he never let negativity kicked in as he will quickly turn anything into jokes. "When I go to Vietnam or Thailand to cycle, I didn't bring her along. I think you know why" he jokes. "See? You are smiling!" he teased me. Yes, he even cycled internationally with his team.

In the ward, I did see him singing to her, make jokes to her and even "dance" in front of her. He is trying his best to get his "girlfriend" up and cycling again, I guess. He must have missed all the "cycle dates" in the park with her. He seems eager to see his "girlfriend" normal again. Once in a while, he would carry her off the bed and put her on an upright chair. The woman can sit down on a chair, but she must be held on to. He will be there, holding her.

During meals, he will feed her gently and patiently. He will bring special juice and cordials from home for her. He really pampered her. Once in a while he is not at the bed. "Where have you been?" I asked. "I went out of this hospital for a while to fill my oxygen" he said. He actually has to get down the lift and walk around three hundred meters just for a smoke! "I quit long time ago, but now, I pick up cigarettes again!" he complains.

The mother is another character. Her motherly love is evident. She looked concerned and tireless. I rarely see her sit down. She is always doing something for her daughter. She will comb her daughter's hair, stroked her head and whispered at her ears. At times, she would talk to her and kiss her. She would massage her feet. She will do anything to comfort her out of her love for the daughter.

This mother is also caring towards me. Sometimes, she will come over and adjust my pillow and even feeds me when my wife is not around. "Do you need anything?" she always asked. She is smiling all the time, always warm towards me and my wife. When I call her to adjust my bed, she will happily come and do it for me. She will pull my curtain when the suns glare sets in. She cares for me. She loves me. I can feel it. I would be awkward even talking to her if I am not hospitalized, but now, she is like my mom. I talked to her about things I need. I don't feel awkward at all.

The Agitated Guy

Beside her bed is a young Chinese guy, probably in the late twenties. I didn't get to know him. From what I see, he had a head surgery, due to some nerve ailment probably. He looks well into the recovered stage. He could sit on his bed, play games on his smart phone and listening to something from the earphone. I like to see the way he eats. I can see him enjoying every bit of the food. He looked like he has a good appetite eating it and seems to savour it well. He doesn't look like a sick person. He is not sad and dreary. He can immediately switch back to a comfortable leaning position and enjoys his smart phone again. He even adjusts his own bed. He reads too!

"What is wrong with that guy?" I thought to myself. He should be home. He looks healthy enough. However, at times he seems agitated. I can hear him grumbling on his own. I couldn't understand what he grumbles about. Every time a nurse passes by, he would stop them and asks something. "No, not yet" I will hear that from the nurse. Another doctor or hospital assistant that passes by, he will again stop them and say something. "Relax. You are not ready to go home yet, OK?" comes another reply. He will as usual, objects and shows his disbelief! He looks restless, walking past my bed to look out at the window, walk back and forth and back to his bed. He is frustrated over something. This behaviour went on for a few days. He will go through the same routine, stopping anyone and pleading for something. Then, walking back and forth, grumbling.

The nurses seem to ignore him probably because they are fed up with his offensive manners. I also realized that he doesn't have any visitor. Strange, isn't it? One thing I am sure, he is agitated.

My wife was irritated by his constant movement across the small hall. "Why is this guy like this?" she grumbled a few times. "Never mind, just leave him. He had a brain surgery and that's the reason he got annoyed easily I think" I tried to calm her. I guessed he thinks he is fit enough to be discharged, but the doctors said otherwise. After all, he is a young chap, usually short-tempered and anxious.

I don't remember when, but one day he is gone. The bed is suddenly empty for one whole day. He was probably discharged while I was asleep. Whatever his grouses, I wished him luck. I will remember him as "that agitated guy without a visitor". Indeed, life in a ward is never short of drama. I am the spectator, watching from a first-class reclining seat!

All the scenes in the ward are still fresh in my mind even after two years. I gathered that he is just some of the few challenging characters nurses and doctors have to deal with on a daily basis. I don't think I am up to that challenge. I don't have a "cool head". To all nurses, doctors and hospital assistants, I salute you! You are awesome!

My African Hall Mate

The next day, the "agitated" guy's bed is occupied by one "long", black guy. He is an African student studying in the country. I said "long" because he is really tall! He must easily be six feet tall! His legs cannot be straightened on bed. He dangles his legs by the side. From one of his friends, we got to know that he had a traffic accident near his college. One of his friends in the accident died and all his friends want to keep that news away from him. I am not sure why he was admitted in my ward. Probably, 7G is full, I guess.

He is heavily bandaged and "wired". Part of his head and one of his arms is bandaged. I can see an IV line and a tube at his nostrils, for his food. He has a catheter to ease his bladder. One would expect anyone in that condition to be motionless and quiet, but not to this guy. He is restless! He moves a lot like every few seconds he changes position. I saw a few times the nurse would come over to fix back his IV line. He even pulls off his food tube off the dispenser! He may just be trying to get rid of all those "irritating" tubes!

Yes, he is restless. He simply changes position. I can hear the bed shaking and swaying. His caretaker, an Arab student couldn't handle him. He has to call the nurse almost every five minutes! I did imagine what kind of a mess it would be if he got entangled in all those lines, tubes including his urine bag! I prayed it doesn't have to happen.

God was I right! I guess my worries about him being entangled come true, finally. Can you imagine with all those lines and tubes, he fell off the bed. Yes, he fell off the bed! I don't remember where the caretaker was at that time, but I didn't realize it too until I saw a few people rushed to his bed and converge there. It was noisy, chaotic for a while. He was on the floor. They have to carry that poor guy back onto his bed. He seems unaware of what is going on.

They finally have him on his bed, but this time, they put restraints on his free hand. I see he is still restless. He still moves his legs and dangles it off on the side. I am less worried now as his free hand is restrained. At least his IV line and food tube is safe. He was with us for a few days. He has a lot of visitors unlike that "agitated guy". During visiting hours that ward becomes like a wet market. I can hear laughter, Arabic language, Indian language, English and of course, African spoken. He seems like "one famous guy" in college.

One of his visitors, one Indian girl, did come over to my bed. To my surprise, she greeted me in Malay! She has been in the country for three years. Her command of Malay is commendable. "He is a likeable person in our class. Everyone was sad and almost everyone is here" revealed the girl. "Two people volunteered to be his caretaker here every night. He is such a good guy and funny! We missed him already" she adds.

The Unknown "Pleading" Man

Now, who is on my left? I couldn't recall the patient there when I was admitted. What I remember was there is someone there. I could see someone. However, the curtain between him and I was always pulled, blocking my view. One other thing is I barely hear any noise from there probably he has recovered and fine. I just hope so.

Things didn't stay like that for long. The peace from behind the curtain was interrupted a few days after that. An old Chinese man was admitted. I didn't get to know him either. I could only hear two distinct conversations – one from the nurses and the other from the patient. "Tomorrow, you must fast. So, from midnight tonight, you cannot take any food. Understand uncle?" instructs the nurse. After that advice, I heard his wife slowly and politely translating it into Chinese for her husband. Her voice is so soft, so pleasant to hear.

The other words I heard over the next one week was this "Nurse, I am thirsty. Please give me drinks. I am hungry" He keeps on repeating it almost all day, all night. I have to bear with it. He has a hoarse, loud voice.

He has a problem with his stomach. He needs a surgery. I may be wrong, but I think the instruction to fast come too early because after a while he was given food again. One day I overheard a few doctors discussing the planned procedure for that old man. I couldn't recall the detail, but he needs a surgery. So, for surgery, I know two things need to be constituted – the bladder catheter and fasting. On being thirsty and hungry, I am a bit sceptical because he surely has the IV line.

Whatever, the issue here is the constant nagging and pleading for drinks. "Please give me drinks. I am thirsty!" every five minutes. His wife keeps on calming him down, in Chinese. I couldn't understand, but from the intonation and soft words, I guess she is soothing him. I have to bear with that irritating hoarse voice for two days.

One night a male nurse came over to insert the catheter and install the urine bag. Strange enough, he didn't make much noise! I thought he would scream because for me, it was painful. The next day, he was fasting and again, he starts his "request". Usually the nurses will come over and say "Please be patient, you must fast for your surgery to be successful. Be patient!" This time, I didn't hear the nurses saying that.

Physical Rehabilitation Starts

As I recovered from my surgery in the rehabilitation ward, a few rehabilitation nurses began to take the lead in caring for me. Aside from the bladder tests to rehabilitate my urinary function, they slowly start to introduce some basic motion exercise. First, they demonstrated to me how to lift a patient off the bed using a hydraulic patient lift. The lift has a base, a mast and a horizontal boom extension with a spread bar and a sling hook.

First, they put on a body sling on me that covers part of my body and thighs. The body sling is then connected to the sling hook at the end of the spread bar at the end of the boom. I am slowly lifted off my bed using hydraulic force onto a waiting wheelchair. What an experience. I never thought things like this ever exist! Suddenly, I am on a swing! It was quite fun! They then lift me off the wheelchair back onto my bed. They did it twice.

"We will leave this hydraulic lift here for you. If you need to have a stroll in the wheelchair, get one of us to help you with this" the rehabilitation nurse told us. I thought to myself "A lot of effort has been put into rehabilitation. I should appreciate the people and the brains behind all these designs" It may look simple to us but to a paralyzed patient that piece of equipment is heaven! To a caretaker and nurses, it helps save their back from injury!

After the lift demonstration, they taught me how to sit up on the bed starting from a lying position. Here is how they taught me. I find it useful as a spinal patient because my spine is not stressed doing this technique. From a lying position, I am slowly taught to lie on my right side. At the same time, they lift the inclination of my bed a little bit. Then, they ask me to place my left hand onto the mattress, somewhere under my right chest.

Once my hand is on the mattress under the right chest, I am asked to gently push my hands down thus lifting my body off the mattress and at the same time, drop my legs off the side of the bed, down to the floor. It is the weight of my legs that is actually doing the lifting of my upper body off the mattress as my mid body becomes a fulcrum. Remember fulcrum? I am sure you can recall from your high school physics lesson term – the fulcrum. Can you visualize the technique, roughly? Like a seesaw!

So, slowly and gently, they helped me and aided me to go through the sequence from lying on my right, my left hand under my right chest pressing down on the mattress and letting off my legs off the side of my bed. They did this first with the bed inclined up a bit, but then in the next set they leave the bed flat, without inclination. Again, I am put through the same sequence.

After a few "drills", I can finally sit with my legs dangling touching the floor, after three weeks! I felt dizzy, but after a while, it wears off. I felt great! My body was still weak, stiff and strained because my muscle motors were affected, but I feel good. What a milestone!

The next day, from a sitting position, I am taught to stand. First, they taught me some feet and ankle exercise. They ask us to wiggle our fingers and rotate our ankle to loosen up and let blood circulates. After a while, the feet felt loose and limber. The nurse then wraps her hands around my body and slowly lifts me to a standing position. "When I lift you, you try to push yourself up with both your legs, OK?" she instructs. My legs were so painful at first. "Slowly try to stand. You can do it. I know you can" she encouraged me. She continues to hold on my body to a standing position for a few seconds. Then, she let me back to the sitting position to rest.

"I am heavy. How can you lift me up just now?" I asked her. "We have a technique to do it. We already learn all these" she answered with a smile. She did this exercise a few times. "Once you can stand, we can then teach you to move from the bed to your wheelchair, OK?" she suggests. "Let us do it slowly, step by step" she adds. I felt relieved. At least I can wake up to a sitting position. I can see out the window! A big improvement for me!

In this ward, there are many exercise and techniques being taught. My next drill is to stand up from a sitting position. I will usually start with wiggling my fingers and rotating the ankle for a few minutes. The nurse will aid me in the beginning, holding me in a standing position. I will do it a few times. Once I am comfortable, they will just let me rise from the sitting position, unaided, but they will be close to me in case I stumble. I will do it a few times too. It is indeed a slow and tedious process. Every step need to be repeated and patient tends to struggle with each step. For me, with numb limbs, I couldn't "feel" the floor thus reducing my sense of balance. Also, my leg muscle motors are not getting the signals and my reaction is affected.

Yes, looking back, it wasn't an easy process, for me and the nurses. It takes a lot of care, concern and tolerance. I realized these rehabilitation nurses have a different kind of patience. They are also very positive, always encouraging and motivating us.

After a few days, I am able to wake up, sit on the side of the bed and move to my wheelchair! I am still closely monitored though. "You need to go to the toilet soon. Try not to wear your diapers anymore, OK?" the nurse urged me. After my catheter for my bladder was removed, which was another milestone, I am in adult diapers. Talking about diapers, I am so indebted, thankful and gratified by the few instances the nurses have to clean me when I defecate and urinate.

My wife has to take the role a few times too. It is a big sacrifice for her in taking care of me. In fact, the nurses taught her the proper technique to "cleanse" a patient defecating or urinating, doing that while the patient is lying down. They let my wife see how they did it. They let my wife do some of the steps in the "live" demonstration.

The sequence is quite tedious! It starts from pulling the curtain. They need to first lower or raise the bed and then, raise the inclination. They will then get a bowl of warm water, a lot of tissues, wet wipes, towels, few waste plastic bags and a trolley as a worktable. It is in this kind of awkward and private situation that I feel the realities of life, of how helpless, feeble and dependent we are when we are sick! We simply surrender our ego and pride.

You can be an engineer or a boss in the office, but in this condition, you are nobody! I feel tiny.

After what my wife went through cleaning me, I am more patient and forgiving towards her. I am less demanding now. I am humbled! I guess God is making me a better man. Without this disorder and the hospitalization, I may never understand the word "love" and "sacrifice" I would never learn the word "appreciate" if the nurses were not patient, caring and tolerant of my demands. This may sound like a part of hospital life, but to me, it is a school. I am taught about the lessons of life! I learned about the meaning of the phrase "giving to others"! I am able to learn how it feels to be on the receiving end of the selfless and sincere "giving" of the nurses and my wife!

Question I always asked now is can I do the same to my wife if she is hospitalized? Can I be that patient and gentle "caretaker" she needs? How good is my resolve? Can I be better than her?

In line with the nurses advice to stop wearing the diapers, my next few exercises was to move from my bed to the toilet, first in a wheelchair. I tried a few times and managed to enter the toilet. All movement is done under the watchful eye of the nurses and my wife. I finally got to urinate the proper and natural way again. Another milestone for me!

With my sensory, motor nerves and digestives affected, every movement is quite a daunting task. It is slow and painful, but at least, I am able to get off my bed, looked out of the window and "explore" the little hall. My wife can take me for a short wheelchair stroll around the rehabilitation ward.

Avoiding Gust from the Fan

However, that one thing I still find difficult is the gust from the fan over my hypersensitive skin, especially at night. It is painful. As the ceiling fan is commonly shared by the four of us, every night my routine with my wife is to design my makeshift "tent"! I finally asked the nurses to move me into a single room. I have stayed in the single room in my first and second surgery. They looked at the availability and I was permitted to use that room.

My intent was to get out of the gust from the fan. Hopefully, I would feel better there without a fan. The room is at 7G. Basically, 7G staff will again come for the daily BP test, medication and other services. I really looked forward to it.

I was moved to the single room on the same day I made the request. I thought I will be fine without a fan, but once in the room, I have to deal with the cool gust from the cool air duct at the ceiling! Yes, I could feel the gust from the blower fan somewhere. In normal cases, the air from the air duct is rarely felt, never affect my skin, but it is different now! Furthermore, my bed is directly below the cool air duct!

So, my "Bear Grylls" mind quickly starts the possible "way out" of this survival situation. "Why not I get this duct blocked by a piece of paper, taped at the edges?" I thought to myself. I told my brother-in-law who happened to be there to help me with my "plan". "I can't stand the gust from the air duct too. I need the duct above blocked by a piece of paper. Please help me" as I lie down under it, helplessly, in pain. "Yes, you looked unhappy I know. Let me go buy some tapes. You hang on there" he said as he left the room.

"If you see any nurse, please get them to tell maintenance to switch off the blower to this particular air duct. I think they can do that" I notify my wife. My mind was focused on that gust from the air duct, nothing else. I do have visitors at that time, but my attention digressed. I am in pain. I think everyone can sense it from the frown on my face. I know, to block it, I must get off the bed and get someone to do it from atop my bed. I don't care which one comes first – the tapes or maintenance. I just want it done fast!

My visitors were helpful. They managed to seal it after a few attempts. "I am so sorry to trouble you, but I can't bear it. Who else will do it if not all of you?" I said, thanking them. I felt relieved for a while as I got my attention back to my visitors. "You looked handsome as before and a bit better now minus your wires and tubes on your face" one of them who had come before teased me. "What happens to your hair?" another person asked, commenting on my half shaven head. They shaved half of my hair. I don't know why. I could only say "I am now with a punk band". They all laughed.

"Yes, he begins to talk and jokes now. He is strong. In fact, he recovered quite fast from the anaesthetic!" my wife said. It was also the few instances where I could eat some of the fruits they brought as gifts.

I was quite content for a while. At least, no gust for now, but the paper and tapes looks as though it was not sticking that well. I expect it to tear off and fall apart in a matter of minutes or hours. It was a temporary, hastily done job anyway. I still have the maintenance and the makeshift "tent" as my other options. So, I am not worried. It was already evening and the probability of maintenance coming appears slim. I may have to live through the night by that paper and tapes up there!

As I was thinking about it, a nurse came. "You have requested to switch off the blower fan for this vent, right? We have informed them. It may not be possible as this is centrally controlled. I don't know, but see what they can do"

I know my request may be out of the norm, but I am trying. I am not going to suffer in pain, doing nothing. At the same time, I don't want to be seen as choosy and demanding. Hospitals have their rules, I know. After all, these people here knew me from my previous stay. They were all nice, compromising and kind to me. I don't want to rock the boat.

I survived the night even though part of the tape is not sticking the paper properly the next morning. The paper is half dangling off the ceiling. By noon, it is as good as not functioning, not blocking the cool gust from the vent. I have no way to mend the tape. I just have to wait because it was a Saturday. It is also, a six-hundred-bed hospital and huge. My request may not be in their priority list and that is expected. I was contemplating another night under the "tent".

However, it was better than that four-bed section. It is quiet here. I can rest in peace, but still, I am in diapers as it was quite difficult to walk to the toilet. My limbs are still weak, but for defecation, I chose to go to the toilet. "You can let me know if you want to urinate. The nurse has given me this urine collection bottle" my wife offered. "You just need to turn to your side on bed, and urinate into it. The nurse asked us to use it especially at night" she adds.

So, that night, we have to set up our "tent".

On the third day in the single room, the gust from the vent stops. Suddenly, the buzzing sound stops and the dangling paper at the vent stops moving. I didn't know when maintenance came and fixed it, but they finally did it. It was heaven! I can still feel air-conditioning from the walkway and hall outside. I can recuperate and recover better now, I thought to myself. My last few days in the hospital were in that single room.

However, I am not free from the dreaded bladder test though. They came a few times to insert that catheter and withdraw it. As usual, the pain is terrible. After a few tests, they asked me to measure my urine against a measured liquid they asked me to consume. It goes on for a few days until they are satisfied with the range and accuracy of the volume measured.

It was also here that the rehabilitation therapist began their more advanced exercises and training for me. They also did the numbness test on my limbs. Basically, they poke a tiny piece of sharp wood at parts of my body and limbs to gauge my reaction. They do it twice a day. I continue to be taught how to wake up, sit up, stand up and walk. This time, they do it a bit longer with more counts, sets and repetitions. I also got to sit on a normal chair, unaided.

The Pain Management Team

I am also regularly visited by the pain management team to deal with my body strains and pain. I like the name, pain team. Sounds like a bunch of sadistic guys out to derive pleasure by inflicting pain on me! No, it's not that at all. It is just my weird fantasy.

This team is headed by a nice lady doctor. She usually comes with three nurses from her department. "We are giving you medication for your body pains. We need to know how you feel. Neuropathic pain is agonizing because you feel it continuously" she explains. "We specialize in pain management. We have anaesthetics, drugs and many techniques to help you ease your pain" she clarified further. I spent the next few days "testing" the best drug possible for my pain control, I guess. I think they finally concluded the most suitable painkiller for me. "We have advised the ward doctor for your medicine. Just take it, OK?" she said a few days before I was discharged.

In this single room, they do not bathe me on the "ship" anymore. I have a private bathroom. "Please use the wet wheelchair to bathe, OK?" the nurse instructs us as she put the wet wheelchair in my room. "Madam, you must use this wet wheelchair. Don't let him stand while you bathe him" she reminds us. So, slowly and surely, I began a few bathing sessions sitting down. It was all the way my wife from bathing me, wiping me up until dressing me.

I am still weak and my balance is poor. I am also gaining strength to sit upright, but still unable to wear clothes. So, I am able to sit in a wheelchair and began to be pushed around the ward for a stroll. In my room, I began to learn to walk aided by a walking frame.

After a few days, I can slowly walk around the room. I am progressing well. I am able to take my meals off my bed, sitting on a chair. I am also happy for my wife because a sleeping sofa-bed is provided in this room. She can have a sound sleep after all day taking care of me. Once in a while nurses will monitor my condition. "Keep on exercising. Once you can run, we will send you home. Don't you want to be home, sir?" the nurse jokes. I know I am in the final stages of my rehabilitation at the hospital, but a long way to go until I can be close to normal! I have to face the hard truth.

Despite the walking exercise, I still have another problem. My bowel control is defective. At times I couldn't defecate and there are times where the urge is sudden. Basically, I can't control the urge to defecate. So, I still need my diapers! At night, my wife would occasionally change my diapers when I wet it. She has to do it. She is my nurse, the best nurse in the world. May God accepts her sacrifices and rewards her in Heaven!

> **"You want to see true love, caring, sharing and humanity expressed? Go visit the sick in the Wards and stay with them for a few days!"**

Doctors Who Work Hard For Me

Doctors are without a doubt, the most important person in any hospital. From the initial observation, analysis and plan for the patient at the clinic or emergency receiving area to the correct admission to relevant wards, to the procedures and care in the operation theatre, the ICU, the wards, the medication prescribed up until discharge and ultimately, production of medical reports, they are the ones who hold the keys. It is a long list of responsibility!

It is indeed a heavy, but noble responsibility because it deals with life and death. When we say life and death, we are talking about the life and death of a human being! Again, when we deal with a human being, we have to deal with their physical, social, mental, emotional and spiritual aspects of their life. It is not only dealing, but fulfilling all those needs. I do not know the pledge they make as a surgeon, doctors or physicians, but I think one of it must be putting the welfare of their patients and society above self-interest.

In any profession, we work in an organization. In any organization, there are stakeholders and each has sets of demands to be fulfilled. With medical profession, I guess the greatest demand comes from the patients. Doctors are also stressed with time pressure due to after-hours and on-call work. It may affect the family life! Apart from these, they have colleagues to work with and each has demands to be satisfied. Of course, finally the important aspects of the job are control, appreciation and remuneration.

As an outsider, I can only think of these general demands and stress. I can empathize with doctors because I am a patient and I know what I expect from them. I know my demands and I expect them to fulfil it. On top of that, I know doctors have to deal with many patients and each has differing expectations.

In my case, my surgery alone takes almost seven hours with the last surgery lasted for a staggering fourteen hours! Just thinking about it drained all my energy! It is fourteen hours of delicate plan and procedures. It is fourteen hours of full focus and concentration. I don't think I am any close to what they did and sacrificed. I must admit it is a tough job. They really have a high level of patience and persistence! Despite all the demands, they can still smile, be attentive, polite and courteous to me! This is amazing. I am impressed.

All the while, I didn't give much thought to the full scope of a physician's work, but after being hospitalized, my whole perception of them changed. I don't think thanking them is enough as a show of appreciation. For me, I go beyond appreciating them. I prayed for their well-being and wish all of them bliss forever. I was weak and helpless and they tried to save me. It is my life I am grateful for. I can never repay them. Of course God controls my life, but they are part of God's plan!

I can't remember all their names, but the two key surgeons who worked on me are definitely remembered. I remember their names, their faces and almost every single word they said. Also, I only come to know that in the medical fraternity, surgeons are not called using the abbreviation Dr., but Mr., mister! This is new to me.

I met doctors at the clinic, at the emergency receiving area, at the ICU and the wards. They are everywhere, always serving me along the way. I remember all the daily rounds they made. They are always alert and vigilant while I was confined to bed, unaware of anything and helpless. They keep my records and keep track of me while I can't keep anything, just being there, not even knowing the days and dates! They think of me in their daily meetings while I can't even think if I can survive the ordeal I am in.

For a moment, I am more than their children. They took care of me. They served me.

Nurses Who Work Hard For Me

Nurses are as important as the doctors. In fact, they spend more time with patients than any doctor. They are also closer to the patient, day and night! As a patient, the first person I see in the morning and the last person I see at night are the nurses. If I need anything, when I press the call button, a nurse will come. The ones who fed me through the dispenser is a nurse. They are also the ones who administer my medicine. The ones who cleanse me when I urinate or defecate are the nurses. They are also the one who would bathe, cleanse, dry and put on new, clean clothes on me every morning.

If there is any new procedure or test to be done, the nurse would be the one who informed me. If I am needed to be sent to any lab for a test, they would be the one to push me on a stretcher, carry my files and brief the officers at the lab. They would oversee the whole procedure, wrap it up and bring me back to the ward. If there is an upcoming surgery, they would be the one placing a request for blood from the blood bank. They would be the one to ensure patients are prepared for it including the requirement, like fasting.

As a patient, one of the most common things I observe on patients was the intravenous lines. Now, who manage these intravenous lines? It's the nurses, from looking for the main or prominent veins to inserting the needle and finally connecting the tube to the V liquid bag. They are also the ones replenishing it when it is due. I have been through this procedure many times. What I could feel is the initial cold sensation from the alcohol swap and of course that little pain when the needle was inserted. I don't really understand the whole precautions involved but to some of the more trained nurses, setting up the IV lines look easy.

Now, what else nurses do? I think, generally they are the ones observing and monitoring patient's conditions. In the wards I can see them moving around the wards looking at each patient regularly, looking at the drips, the supporting equipment, the monitors, the oxygen tubes and the dispenser. Apart from that, they are the ones recording and maintaining the patient records.

One of the most important tasks the nurses perform is communicating with doctors. In my stay in the ward, I hear a lot of verbal briefing by nurses to the doctors. Aside from the briefing during the morning rounds, at time doctors do come in and ask about patient condition at random. I think this is a key role as the doctors need to know the latest condition and status of all patients in order for them to plan their next action. Who else is more qualified to brief the doctors than the nurses?

Another important role is the correct feeding of patients according to the specified diet. I know nurses were the ones advising the dietary department for the right meals. At times for weak patients, they are the ones who would feed them manually. It is always pleasing to see nurses feeding patients with all the care and patience. It may look menial to us, but some patients have difficulty swallowing and may need extra caution when feeding.

Some of the other rarely mentioned duty is to calm down and control "difficult" patients. I know the anxiety level of patients is high. Apart from their physical impairment, they have mental and emotional stress to deal with. As a patient myself, I know it is not a simple issue to manage. In the wards I did hear patients screaming, crying, shouting, scolding and even spitting at nurses!

The Visitors that Enlightened Me

"The heart loves nice sweet things. Speak politely and bring gifts to others!"

Azhar is a friend of mine. We worked for an overseas project together in a far, distant country. We were together for around six months. He came with his wife. I didn't expect him to come, but he came, not once, but twice. He looks concerned and surprised when he saw me. He didn't give me much advice, but he left with some present for me. He asked if I need anything. I didn't say it, but the next time he came, he brought some water, from Prof. Dr. Haron. Prof. Dr. Haron is a well-known and respected Islamic medication practitioner.

I remembered when I just arrived in that far away city that doesn't speak English. He was in the company car that fetched me at the airport. I was dizzy after more than twenty-four hours flight. It was winter, but the temperature was in the teens. So, it's manageable. "Welcome buddy, you will be staying with me" he said, as we shake hands and got into the car.

Apparently, my accommodation has been arranged because I was given less than four days to be there after a five minutes international phone interview done by the project manager. The local office had faxed my resume earlier. "Please be here as soon as possible" reminds the project manager at the end of the phone interview. "Drawings for your discipline are piling up. You need to review and approve it" he adds.

So, in no time flight tickets were dispatched to my house and two days later I was somewhere over the Indian Ocean!

Actually, he offered himself to take me as a housemate there. I was told that there are others that came earlier than me, but he didn't take them. Anyway, I am glad staying with him because he is a good cook! Good cook? Yes, like me, he is good at reheating the ready-to-eat curry meals sachets in the microwave. He has a big stock of these ready-to-eat meal sachets. He also has various food-flavouring pastes for us to feel at home. So, food-wise, I am happy. I don't think I can survive on bread, butter, cheese, croissants day in day out!

Another thing that I have to adapt there is language. I asked him about language. He told me not to worry. "I just know the address of our office and our house" he said, happily. "For cigarettes, just show it", he jokes! We only commute by taxis to work, but for weekends, we ventured into their Subte which is the underground train and window-shopping! They have many well-maintained and good public clay courts too! So, you know what? Yes, both of us bought a tennis racket there! We got to polish our strokes and volleys!

Overall, it was a pleasant stay. I had a nice apartment and a good buddy. He is a simple, humble man and a good engineer. So, just imagine, we were happily together there in jeans and leather jackets, enjoying our short stint there and suddenly he saw me in a hospital, lying down, semi-paralyzed! He was taken aback initially. I am pleased he came to visit his "amigo"!

Mira is a friend of my wife and I knew her through connections and friends in my previous job. So, she is a common friend. My wife informed her of my hospitalization, I think. She is probably the first to visit me in my 3rd hospitalization. She came with her professional acquaintance. It was off visiting hours, quite late at night and she managed to get a special permission to visit me.

I think she was shocked and sad to see me the first few minutes. A few times I could see like tears in her eyes. She was like walking around my bed, a bit shaken and controlling her emotions. Who wouldn't? I knew she was sad to see me lying with a tube in my nostrils as I was under intubation with liquid food. I also had an oxygen breathing apparatus attached to the nostrils. She has a soft heart.

I was lying there in pain and it was delightful to know that someone is willing to sacrifice their time to visit me. "I had a meeting up north with him and decided to come here on our way back" she said, as she looks at her friend. "This is my friend. He is in your industry too" she said, introducing her friend. My wife wasn't around as she had left for home earlier.

Her friend then holds my hand and said "You know this verse I think" He then recites the verse to me. "Recite this verse. It has a strong healing power" he said. In times like this, just remember the Creator. Nobody can cure you except God! If anyone comes and say they can cure you, they are lying!" he said, convincingly! I had since then been reading the verse quite regularly and every time I read it, I remember these two special visitors! I remember the tears and the verse. May God bless them! We later became Facebook friends.

"Be the first to visit a sick friend. They will love you for the rest of their life!"

Lan Politik is an old college mate, he came a few times. Lan Politik is a nickname. He behaved like a "politician" long time ago so we gave him that nickname! We were housemate some thirty years ago, but still maintain contacts. He always came with a gift, his wife home-made cookies. I can't take any food manually at that time. So, I can only look at the cookies. He is always jovial and I really love his presence. We joked and talked about our naughty days when we were younger. He is one of the few visitors who made me laugh. I really laughed a lot when he came. Even the nurses realized it. He even visited me at home after I was discharged, again with his home-made cookies, his wife and family. I was touched by his care and concern.

It is normal for patient to get flowers, fruits and cards as a gift, but home-made cookies, is an exception. "My wife prepared this especially for you" he said, as he gave me the cookies. My hands were weak to even hold it and I couldn't take food normally, but the gift enlightens me. I appreciate the trouble both of them took, for me. These are those special little things that touched our hearts. Thank you buddy!

Pit is a nickname, a college mate from a different course of study. After almost twenty-five years, we managed to be in touch. This is one guy I didn't expect to come. He probably heard about my hospitalization from other close buddies of ours. He came when I was at the rehabilitation ward. He was lucky as at that time I am able to eat and talk. At least we can have a conversation. He spends quite some time with me as my brother was there too. He mixed well with my brothers. We then linked back through WhatsApp and has been in contact ever since.

Shukri is a neighbourhood friend and also a friend from our mosque. We became close from our religious discussions and exchange of information. I am not so much of a person with a strong religious background, but in the mosque, I did gather some small group of people and read out some religious advice from one book. He used to join us and he seems to like what he heard. In the mosque, after reading out the book, I will usually end the session like this "What we heard, we take as a reminder, practice it and relay it to others. At home, try to do this with your family. Find a suitable time, gather them and read out a few advice to them, like what I did" At home, I did the same thing. I will gather my wife and kids and spend a few minutes reading the advice from the same book.

One day, looking at his keen interest to learn, I quietly bought the book, went to his house and gave it to him as a gift. I didn't say much and left. A few weeks later he said "I have started reading out the book to my family. Sometimes I read it and sometime my son read it for us" I was excited at his ability to do that at home. I know it wasn't an easy thing to do, to discipline the children and sit in a small religious gathering with the distractions of television and internet. I think he did a marvellous job!

Basically, our relation revolves around my reading out sessions at the mosque. He did talk a little about his last job, as an airline officer. He had since retired and did his own business.

When he came for the visit, I couldn't recognize him because I have not frequented the mosque since I fell sick, probably for three years. "There is your friend to visit you, I think" my wife said, as she showed me to a gentleman standing a few feet away. He looks different too in a different attire not his regular clothes he used to wear at the mosque. He came close to my bed, smiled and I still couldn't recall him.

"You gave me that book, remember? You asked me to read it to my family, can you recall?" he asked, as he came nearer to my bedside. Listening to that, I immediately recall him, my mosque mate! "It's you! I am sorry I couldn't recognize you" I said, as we shook hands. He looks excited because I remembered him. I was touched that he made the effort to come and visit me. It was indeed enlightening to know that people who are merely a distant friend remember us and visit us. I was moved.

"Shaking hands touches the heart. Gifts enlighten it! People will never forget something that enlightens them"

The Direct Selling Salesman

When I was waiting for my surgery, I was fed through a tube as I could not be fed orally. At the side of my bed is the dispenser that released the liquid food from the bag to my nostrils. I was like that for a few days.

It was during this time that I was visited by one of my nieces. She came with her husband. "How are you uncle?" the husband greeted me. I could only nod and smile. Prior to that, the husband had messaged me that he is bringing some information on some medication which may help solve my ailment. I just replied positively as I think he wants to help and it is not nice to disappoint him. So, when he came he brought along a few brochures about some medicinal mushroom or herb. I couldn't recall. I tried to read the brochure that he gave. It has some information and some testimonials of "satisfied" users.

I was just trying to entertain him. I know it is not the right time to make a sales pitch. After all, it's a hospital. Even if I could swallow it,

I would not do it. I would not want to jeopardize my health by taking outside supplement no matter how good it may be! That's how firm I was, but I try not to upset him. I think he is sincere.

He then begins to explain the benefits of that herb to me. I just lend my ears and listen rather reluctantly. "One of my friends is coming here to explain to you further about this herb. He will be here soon" he said. A few minutes later the friend came. After a brief introduction of himself, he continues with the sales pitch. He explained about the product. He showed more brochures. I tried to maintain my composure so as not to upset them. He seems persistent in his pitching from the way he talks and the body language.

It is now slowly getting on my nerves. Then, he drops the bomb! "I think you should try this now!" he said, showing me a small sachet. "No" I said. "Why? No worries. This is just a supplement! It won't affect your medicine" he insists. Again, I declined to his requests. He looks surprised at my reluctance to take his supplement. He keeps on pestering me. By that time, I am getting a bit irritated. "Can't you see what that is?" I asked him as I showed him the dispenser at my bedside. He looks at it and tried to ignore my plea. "Oh that" he said.

Then, he makes another blunder! "I can tell the nurse to put it inside the dispenser" he said, ignorantly. This time I said it in an affirmative way! "No! No! No! Please don't do that. No, please" I said, shaking my head. I was irritated at his insistence.

He then stops his sales pitch and requests. I stop looking at his face. He finally said "I leave this brochure, CD and sachet for you here. Once you can take food normally, you must try this!" I didn't nod and neither did I smile. I just look at the ceiling, in anger. I think he reads my body language!

I could sense that my niece and her husband felt a bit awkward at my reaction and probably they understood. I tried hard not to upset anyone. I know the way the guy acted was improper, but I can accept his flaws. I understand the chemistry of selling as I was a sales engineer once. He may see me as a potential order, but he fails to learn a simple ethic in sales that is "know your audience", their requirement and if you can fulfil their needs! I think he is an amateur. After all, he is young. I can forgive him, but I just hope he won't get blasted by someone who may not be as accommodating as I am!

He may, by now, achieved his sales target and be rewarded handsomely. Who knows, right? I know many successful direct selling entrepreneurs. I have attended some of their seminars and met the Leaders. I personally believe in direct selling and mouth-to-mouth advertising. I respect these entrepreneurs for their independence, tenacity, sacrifice and positivity! I have seen Mercedes-Benz, BMWs even Ferraris at their seminars! It is by no means a small feat.

I know Robert Kiyosaki endorses direct selling! It is not a secret, but not everyone can succeed! It takes a special person to be successful in direct selling. I wish him luck, despite his torment of me then! If he is still struggling, I hope he can learn more about salesmanship skill.

"You will be more successful persuading than forcing!"

Sanusi is a neighbourhood and mosque friend. He is a quiet guy. He is the sort of guy, who is easy on everyone. He never talks politics or discuss issues that may bring about arguments. He stayed away from all that. In the mosque, he comes for prayers and quietly leaves after it.

He studied finance and now owns a company. He visited me when I was in the single room. He spends around ten minutes and didn't speak much. I think he understood the right etiquette of visiting the sick. After all, he is educated and religious. It is a breather at times when we get a gentle, considerate visitor. I know people are different, but everyone needs a good etiquette. I realized at times I talked a lot when visiting others. I may have annoyed others, I think. I learned about manners that day. In fact, it is a religious call too, but sometimes we forget. We are just human.

He is probably my first friend when I moved to my latest home. I remembered we had tea together in that new residential area. I was new and feel like a stranger in the new surroundings. So, I was quick to remember him. After all, we always remember our firsts!

Aida is a cousin of mine who happen to stay in the same residential area. She is that one single person I must thank and commend! She is my behind-the-scene caretaker. For a few months, she is the one replacing my wife taking care of my two kids at home. My wife is constantly in touch with her regarding the welfare of my kids when their mom is with me. At times she will pick up the children from home to school and sometimes from school back home. She even provides lunch and at times, buys lunch for my two children. She has a school going child of her own.

So, for a few months her schedule and route has to change to suit our child's timing and requirement. It is a big sacrifice for her. I can't imagine how difficult it would be without her help.

I felt guilty for not being a good cousin to her before. I should have visited her and her husband more than I did. They are a good couple, very humble and simple. I am glad I have people with sincere hearts around me in times of need. I don't know how to repay them. I can only pray for their well-being and a prosperous life. They deserved it! I think God gave me this sickness to make me a humble person.

Sohpian works for me in one of the companies I worked before. He was a fresh engineer then and has since progressed into quite a successful businessman. It is refreshing to know that someone who works for me some ten years ago came for a visit.

I was on a short wheelchair stroll around the ward when he suddenly appears from the Lift. "How are you, boss?" he greeted me with a smile. We shook hands and move back to my room together. "I heard you were like paralyzed, but now you looked fine, you can sit in a wheelchair! That's great" he said, as he gave me a small fruit gift hamper.

As we are in the same industry, we talked about business and some projects he is working on. "He suddenly becomes healthy when he talked about engineering" my wife told him, teasing me. "I like it when his engineering buddies come. He talks a lot when his engineering buddies come" she adds, as she looks at me. I think the time was different. He came when I am in the rehabilitation stage, off from all the tubes and wires on my body! Also, birds of the same feather flocks together, right? We are on the same frequency. It is in a way, therapy for me.

For a moment, I am like his boss again. The only different is the office is in a hospital!

Unnoticed Visitors

I must acknowledge the few thoughtful visitors who came to visit me when I was either in anaesthetic or somewhere in a test lab and clinics. I know a few close friends came during my surgery, especially the third surgery.

My wife told me of a close hometown buddy who came during my surgery. "He came with a few friends and they were all in motorcycle boots, glove and jackets" she said, describing that motorcycle "gang". I quickly realized that he must be one of my closest buddies in my high school days. I was right. He has since ventured into running a few gas stations. I forgot what bike he rode, but I remembered he said something like 1000RR. So, it must be a BMW. I guess he now rides a BMW S1000RR. He has an X5 too. He must be a BMW freak! Good for him.

By the way, he is well built and tall. He blends well with that S1000RR! He can surely handle that super bike. I was told that he waited to see me, but my surgery was too long, fourteen hours! He left after a few hours. He sent his regards.

At the same time, my old college buddy and housemate also came. He came with his wife. He also brought my old high school classmate with him. Again, both of them waited to see me, but the surgery was too long. They too left after a few hours. My sister and brother also came and they stayed for a few hours and left. I was told that the surgery started at nine o'clock in the morning and lasted until one o'clock in the morning, the next day!

It was a long fourteen hours wait and only my wife stayed for that whole duration! I can't imagine the anxiety, stress and test she went through! It must be unbearable and miserable for her! Only love could keep someone waiting like her!

Haji Ramlan is one of the most helpful of all my friends. He stays in a nearby residential area and once in a while, joined our congregation in our mosque. An accountant by profession, he is also a successful businessman, but live a very simple lifestyle. I know he has a few companies, is well connected and has vast banking, finance and contracts experience. He rarely speaks about his work, but talks a lot about religion. He is well learned in many aspects of religion. He spends a lot of time with scholars and even own and run a small religious school.

He is the first person to help me when I was looking for a cure. He brought me to a nearby practitioner and spends two hours, from picking me up at home, through the long wait and finally the session with the practitioner. He then sent me back, holding my hands up to the door of my house!

In another instance, he drove me one hundred and fifty kilometres south to see a traditional masseuse. He drives his car, paid all the fuel and tolls! It was easily a half day spent on me while sacrificing his free time. He is also the guy who brought me to the homeopathy clinic, not once, but for a few sessions! He will wait for me for the duration of the treatment and then, sent me back. He also accompanied me for the long trip up north to meet another masseuse.

After all that he has done, I was touched. He is not a relative, just a friend but he cared for me and loved me like his son. This is piety. This is devotion. This is religion. It is all about sincerity and love.

He has since left us. May God grant him Heaven as he rightly deserves. I know God is pleased with him!

Ramlan is my next door neighbour. He is one of the first who came in my 1st hospitalization. It is good to know that your neighbour come for a visit. I didn't know much about him as we are not that close, close. Do you know what I mean? It is not that I have any grudge against him whatsoever. I go to his house for all his feasts and invitation. He comes to my house for our religious festivities. We do talk to each other. We greet each other. I think I am a reserved type or I may look serious to him. I think I should be more approachable. I need to smile more I guess. I know he is a nice, gentle person.

It is probably because we didn't share a certain hobby. I know he plays golf, but I play tennis. I quit golf years ago. I don't know why. Probably, I didn't like the "social" side of it and it takes a lot of my time! At times, our flight took four hours just to complete nine holes! I can't blame anyone. We are not Tiger Woods and most of my buddies are not single handicapper.

I can't deny that golf is very interesting, exclusive and challenging. I like the golf course and its scenery especially in the morning when we have mist and birds chipping! The clubhouse at any golf club is always inviting, spacious and comfortable. The facilities are second to none! I love the restaurants, spa and pools. I love all that! Whatever, for now I am not golfing! I have two golf sets rotting in my store!

So, what else do we have in common? He rides a bike I just ride a bicycle. We have a few things in common though. He has four kids, two boys and two girls and so do I. He is an engineer and so am I. I think I should mix around more with him and probably pick up golf again, if my physical condition permits. Why not, right?

His visit was short and cordial. He didn't say much. I am the one talking more than him, just to warm up the atmosphere. Furthermore, for my 1ˢᵗ hospitalization, I can still talk normally and overall pain was not severe.

Baya and **Norsiah** were both my clerical staff in a previous company. At work, both liaise with me a lot as they are our sales clerk, sales coordinator and logistics officer. They are both seniors in our company. Again, these are staff from a company I worked at ten years ago! It is pleasing to know that I am being remembered. I think their visit is an expression of remembrance.

Initially, they were surprised to see my condition. I think they know how active I was in the office then. "What actually happened boss? Do you have an accident or what?" one of them asked. My wife chipped in and said "No, he has a nervous problem. He has some blockage at his spinal cord" My wife continued talking about my ailment to them. At that time, I was recuperating after surgery. I was able to talk, but my movement was still limited. I just let my wife entertain them.

Rafi was my sales engineer from the same company I worked at ten years ago. This guy is unique in a way because he had the same nervous problem like mine, but the difference is his growth is cancerous and its location is at the lumbar bones. In fact, he has to resign from that company due to his disorder. So, he had it much earlier than me. He is a good reference for me. I had communicated with him a lot regarding my disorder. He is my "self-help" group in a way.

He came with his wife, who is also a doctor. His wife was kind enough to encourage me and explain the ways to face the disorder. After all, she is a doctor and has a similar patient; her husband. "You will be able to walk again. Initially, you may need a stick, but eventually, you can walk" the wife said. "He was wheelchair bound for a while" she said, as she looks at her husband. "You will be fine! Just pray" she adds.

"You should maintain contacts with him" my wife suggests. "His disorder is like yours and he can help you recover" she said. I can see both of my visitors have full confidence that I can recover. My worry is that I may be paralyzed for life! It was quite assuring to know that I can recover and regain my limbs, especially when his wife, a doctor says it.

It was an enlightening visit from both of them. Basically, I am not alone. The problem is quite similar, blockage in the spinal cord. He has removed the cancer and my cyst may be sucked out, hopefully. He has since moved back to his hometown and his wife got a transfer to the same place. "I am not working anymore. My movement is limited and overall, my body is weak" he said. "I am a full-time housewife now" he jokes.

I have not contacted him for quite some time. I think he went through rehabilitation like me too. Hopefully he has fully recovered or at least, better than the last time we met.

Khairil is an old office mate. This is a friend from a company that I have been working for twenty years ago. We were both young engineers then. He has since progressed and becomes a general manager in one engineering company. I didn't expect him to come as we have not met for years. I have changed a lot and so does he. I have since grown a long beard and stop all my "naughty" off-work activities. He knows my "clubbing" history with the clients and I know his. We are in the same industry, but I think he is more successful.

We do, however, once in a while been talking to each other. Basically he knows where I am and what I am doing. He is humble. He always talks modestly about his achievement. I like his style, but actually, he is a good employee and has got a lot of rewards and promotions. On the other hand, he always speaks highly about me. I remembered he likes to say this "I have so many friends, but I think you are the most pious!" Yes, he always says that. Actually I am a bit ashamed of myself with that compliment. I don't know what he sees in me, but never mind. He is a nice guy.

So, as I was lying down in bed one afternoon in the single room I heard a greeting from behind the curtain. "I think you have a visitor" my wife said, as she stood up looking towards the door. From behind the curtain, this dear friend of mine appears. He stood at the edge of my bed, smiling. For a while, I couldn't recall, but a few seconds later, I remembered! "My old friend is here" I thought to myself. "How are you" he asked, as he stands there. "Thank God, I am fine" I replied. At that time I am already recuperating and in rehabilitation stage. So, I could see, hear and talk.

"I was at a friend funeral where I met a few of your friends and they told me about you" he said, starting a conversation. The friend who died is a friend of mine too. We met a few times in the course of my work a long time ago. "So, I come here today to visit you" he said.

I then updated him a bit about my disorder. I told him about the surgery and my current situation I was in. We talked a bit about work. "How are you? How is it like to be a big guy?" I teased him. "Oh that's nothing. I am still an employee, not like you. I heard you started a company" he said, trying to affirm what he heard. As usual, he remains humble. "Yes I did. The company is still there minus me" I joked. "No, you are a boss now. I still have a boss" he said, negating my praise of him.

In a way, it was a good meet after not seeing him for quite some time. I am in a way inspired by his success. Also, when someone from my industry comes for a visit, I get excited. At least, I am on the same mental frequency. I have something to talk about!

Roslan Air Leleh is a distant relative, my sister-in-law's brother. We were friends when we were kids. His village is next to ours. He came when I was at 7E, the rehabilitation ward. His entourage was quite big, about six of them. His style is different. He greets me and immediately announces to everyone there "Let us pray for him, God permits" He then starts his supplication. It was quite brief, but firm and assuring. He read a few supplications and verses from the Quran as the others answered his prayers. In a few minutes it was over. Only then did he lean forward, shake my hands and start talking.

"You will be fine. Just keep praying" he advised. "Once I am home I will get a religious scholar to supplicate for you, probably have a small feast for your remembrance" he said, as he looks at my brothers. "Your brother knows the man" he adds. "God permits, we will do it soon for you" he said, promising to do it for me. It was a short visit, but a heart-warming one. It is just different. I felt that there is hope and strength in what he did. Suddenly there was a sense of calm and peace. I am moved.

"Thank you for coming. I need all that spiritual help" I told myself when everyone left and I am back lying down, lonely, looking at the ceiling.

Jamel is a neighbourhood and mosque friend. He is one of my friends who visited me the most. When I was at home, before and after my hospitalization, he visited me many times. Also, each time he visits, he never missed bringing me gifts. It can be anything, from fruits, cookies to hot banana fritters! He is a thoughtful guy! Indeed, bringing gifts on a visit is our culture and a virtuous practice, but in our age and time, most of us have forgotten about it. I personally failed to do that at times. I admit! The very fact that he can do it delights me. Indeed, I have many good-hearted friends. I am humbled. I am nothing compared to them!

"You just can't fake good manners!'

He is a professional oil and gas engineer. He is a specialist contract worker who works on rigs all over the world. One day he can be in Libya, next few months in Uzbekistan, then in Saudi and suddenly in Vietnam. He works on exploration drilling rigs on monthly shift basis and will be in town for a month or so. He has been doing that the last fifteen years! He travels a lot. He makes a lot of money because I know the daily off-shore rates for specialist like him. He is a high-flyer, career wise, but he remains simple and humble. I have two things in common with him – the mosque activities and oil and gas industry. So, we blend along well. He is also a businessman and we do talk business too. We share our experience.

I couldn't recall how many times he came to the hospital. The last time was when I was recuperating. I remembered he brought me some fruits. He even helped cut it and gave it to me. He shows character and kindness. I think his religious background makes him such a pleasant, simple man. With all the travels he made and all the money he makes, he can brag if he wants. I think others in his capacity are easily carried away and showy! He is not. He remains modest and laid back. I like him.

We are Facebook friends now. Basically, we are in contact and he never stop suggesting me all kinds of treatments. He just wants to see me back on my feet and come to the mosque again, I guess!

Abang Man is my eldest brother and is a doctor himself. I was told that, at one time he was working in this very same hospital. He visited me a few times as his house is quite near. He looks serious and calm, but actually jovial when you can bring up a joke or topic that stimulates his mind! He is not that close to me when I was younger, but lately we do have some meaningful discussion about family, life and religion. I think I have grown up and the age difference is no more an issue. He has mellowed and I have changed, I guess. So, we have some brotherly chemistry now. I don't think he knows much about what I do though. I rarely talk to him about my "world".

I rarely talk to him about medical science either! I think he was a gynaecologist before, just guessing. That was what I heard. He later became a director at a few hospitals, probably this hospital too. I never asked him. He is semi-retired now, working on a yearly contract with the ministry. He trains young doctors too. By the way, I heard this from my nieces. That's how "close" I am with him! I think I am the "bad" brother. After all, he rarely talks about what he does! Anyway, he is my brother. I love and respect him no matter what. I think should have been more "friendly" with him.

In one of his visits, he gave me a scientific explanation to my problem. He stood close to my head and starts explaining. "See, your spinal cord is just this size" he said, showing his ring finger. "That is where all the nerves carrying all signals from your brain to your whole body. It is one delicate part of your body" he explains. "The surgeon has done their best to expand the passage at your skull and insert a shunt to suck out the cyst" he said, as he looks at me. "You will be fine. You will recover, no worries, OK?"

His short explanation jives with what the surgeon said, but since he is my brother, I felt more assured.

After he left, one of the nurses came over and asked "Who is he to you?" I said he is my brother, my eldest brother. "Oh he is your brother? He was our director here before, years ago" the nurse said. "I know he was a director but didn't know which hospital" I said. "He was here for a few years" the nurse adds. I finally came to know about my brother, from a third person! I am a bit embarrassed, but I think it is not all my fault.

My brother likes to keep a lot of things private. I think he is a busy man and his job is demanding. He wouldn't want petty things to bother him. I think it is his right and he acted wisely. Whatever the reason, I am not bothered at all. We still have a good brotherly relationship. That is all that matters to me.

Kak Izan is my sister-in-law. I couldn't recall when she came, but I remember how she reacted. I was still heavily tubed and wired, probably in the ward's ICU then. I was in pain at that time and I remembered uttering this words to her "What is happening to me sister? What can I do?" At that time I was heavily depressed and scared. I was down, almost giving up thinking about an uncertain future. I don't mean one or two years ahead, I am thinking just a few days ahead! I was close to being paralyzed, I thought.

I could still remember her reaction. She was standing at the bedside, near my head. Hearing my question, she looked down and I could see tears in her eyes! I mean I can see a few drops of tears falling off from her eyes! "I don't know what to say!" she said, with a sad expression. "I will offer the best prayer for you" she adds, in an affirmative tone. I don't remember what else she said, but one thing for sure she was visibly moved and saddened by my plain question.

I think there is no faking about sincerity. She was gravely concerned. I know this sister-in-law of mine and my brother does think a lot about me. I can sense it. They do call and visit me quite often since I fell sick. It is not that the others do not care, but each one is different in expressing their care and concern. I am also quite close with both of them. We do talk and at times share my problems with them.

I will always remember and cherish that moment. It is something I didn't expect, but from that moment my impression of her changed. I have more respect or her.

"We just can't fake emotions"

Azman is my niece's husband. He is an engineer and mostly reserved and quiet. His visit was short and brief, nothing extra ordinary. He didn't say much. I was still tubed and couldn't talk much either. In around half an hour he left. After he left, I just lie back and took some rest. There were many visitors that day and I was a bit tired.

I woke up and my wife came and said "Someone gave you this just now". She showed me an envelope. "Keep it in the locker" I said. Later, she opened it and said "Look at this, it's a lot!" I do get some monetary gift once in a while, but that figure is quite big. I don't know who, but it could be him. I do give monetary gift, but rarely that amount. I need to be more generous. What I learn is people have big hearts. People are generous.

Hanim is one of my many nieces and nephews. We are a big family! However, this girl is a bit unique. She lost both her mom and dad in the same year a few years ago. She is the eldest and had since then be the "Father" and "Mother" to her siblings. It was a tragic event in her family. She was even married in the absence of both her parents. It was a sad event, but life has to go on. The wedding was planned, organized and held. She now has three kids of her own.

In fact, after her, with the help from all of us she had organized four more weddings for her brothers and sisters! She really took the responsibility in her stride. She is a strong girl! When I think of my family, this girl always comes into my mind. They are close to my heart.

She came when I was still recuperating in 7G. I was happy to see her. At least, I am able to see her and know that she is fine. It was a brief visit, but at least she took the effort to rush through the rush hour traffic and come over. She stays quite a distance from the hospital. I was able to exchange updates about her brothers and sisters. Her husband came too, but having too many nieces and nephews I couldn't remember his name initially. What a blunder it was! So, I just talk to him as though I know his name! I felt a bit awkward, but I can't blame myself either! I couldn't even remember all the names of my nieces and nephews! Do you expect me to know the names of their spouses? What a "bad' uncle I am!

I hope all my nieces and nephews will forgive me. Uncle is getting old, but even though I didn't remember all your names, you are all like my children! I love all of you. Trust me!

"I can see that those tested with tragic event in life tend to be more humble"

Rahmat Nyah is my cousin. We rarely meet but, his presence enlightened me in a special way. We share our childhood days together even though he is a city boy and I am a village boy. We meet during school holidays and sometime we drove up to be with him in the city. Once we meet everything clicks! We were young and naughty. We were adventurous. Who's not, right? As a teen, we do and try all things! So, he never treated me "nicely". We call each other names, joked and teased each other a lot! When he was around, we painted the town red!

So, when he came the first thing he said was "Ah you are not sick! Wake up!" he jokes, in front of his wife and sisters. "You are OK! You will walk again!" he said, always teasing me. He suddenly turns the rather sombre ward into laughter. He shakes my hand and said "Just relax and everything will be fine. I know you!" He sounds positive and always smiling. He is a happy go-lucky guy! I didn't recall talking to him about any serious matter all my life, seriously! We never talk about family, children, religion and politics. We talk about all things boys and what boys do – sports and girls! One topic we share is play, whatever. We chose to be happy when we were together I guess! Even at this age, we never talk about anything serious!

In fact, I know his history a little bit. He used to own a few super bikes and is a "racer" himself, illegally, I mean! I knew he was hospitalized a few times with many bones broken! I don't know which bones, but he will ride again, crash again and breaks another set of bones! That's how "naughty" and "stubborn" he was, but I like him. He is unpredictable, always mysterious!

I know he is a big headache to his mom! His mom always smiles and shakes her head whenever I visit her and asked about him. I think through the years he may have mellowed a bit, just a little bit. From the way he jokes and teases me, I don't think he has changed. The boy in him is still there! He lives a thrilling life unlike me. I am a village boy. My games are a bit different!

I am glad he came. I didn't expect him to come. For a moment I felt I was twenty years younger. He changed the "weather" inside the ward. He is such an amazing guy full of intrigue. I don't believe he has mellowed. He may not ride Katanas, CBRs and GPZs anymore, but I think he must have a sports car now! Only a sports car can "carry" his image, his heart and soul!

So, what can I learn from him? Nothing! I don't see anything that I can learn from him. I can only see fun in him. It is just not him to be emotional and advise me! I do admire his simple philosophy towards life though. What is it? Play!

Aziz is my immediate elder brother. He has another sad experience just a few years ago. His wife passed away! I attended the funeral services, despite being unable to walk properly and the bodily pain. It was a trying moment for him because the time of his wife demise was when all the kids were still in school and dependent on a mother. In fact, the youngest of his children is just five years old! I didn't know how he coped with it probably because I was busy coping with my worsening disorder at that time.

He came to visit me with two of his sons. The moment I see him, I know he will give me a sound advice. I just knew it. He is much more disciplined, neat and well-organized than me. He has been tested by his wife death and I think he has been coping with it quite well. In fact, he quickly picked up the pieces and re-married. He chose to quickly get up and moved on, I guess.

He came over to me, hold my hands and only said this "Just connect and talk to God! Don't think of anything else" I can still remember his seriousness in giving that one sound advice. His advice is rather unique, different from the rest probably because he has gone through a tougher ordeal. From then on, I always "connect" myself with God when I am alone and free, especially at night. It is a bit different from prayers where we are engaged in remembrance, submission and a set of mandatory supplications and verses. Connect is more like "talking" directly without any specific words and time limit. It is more like focusing and deep concentration with the intent of seeking help by releasing our worries to God!

I have been applying his advice and it helps. I think we all need an escape channel, something divine to "listen" to our woes and misgivings. We all need this! I can't imagine anyone not having this one divine entity to talk to and seek help from.

"You will be taught a few lessons to make you a better person. The tougher lesson is to make you a tougher person!"

I wish I could emulate his emotional strength and steadfastness. I think his ordeal has made him a better person and the way he carries himself is inspiring. It is all about fate and our ability to accept it. We are not the same and our acceptance level varies. It is also about character. He is disciplined and when we were young, he is our mom's blue-eyed boy. He was good in school, got good grades and played in the school band. I think he was a school prefect too. These are all traits of a good student.

I am not like him. I do play hockey for the school, but other than that, I am just a normal student. I mix with a different set of friends and not as likeable to my mom as him. I am a bit like a black sheep of the family in a simple sense. I didn't do any horrible things and sent to jail or anything like that though. I am just naughty and "adventurous". I now know that it's good to have big family! It's fun too. We got to see a diverse type of character and we learned early in life to adapt to it all. We may face some disagreement, but the learning curve is faster! We got that early training to face the greater society outside and life as a whole.

I love it when all of us come back home and gather at one place during our yearly festivity. The whole house will turn into a big "market", noisy and crowded from the parking lot to the garden, the hall and the rooms all filled with people! We can see children playing and running around all day. Every year, we got to see new additions to the growing family. What a happy, blessed and grand atmosphere. How I wish my dad and mom could see that!

I am considered a grandfather in a way too. I have nieces and nephews who have kids of their own. It is a big family! In fact, I did try to count the shoes and slippers! It's a lot. Aside from that, I did try to identify each and every one of them to get their names! I failed in this department, but I keep it to myself so as not to be embarrassed! Can you remember thirty names? See if you can! All in all, it's beautiful!

Bibah is my elder sister. She sacrificed a lot helping mom raised all of us when we were young. So, my respect and love for her is strong. She also has that similar look with my mom. So, seeing her is like seeing mom. She loves all of us. She has shown it all these years from her calls, visits and help she gave all of us in many different form.

Her visits to see me are always uplifting. She may not say anything, but the bond, the love can be felt. In difficult and trying times, the presence of someone whom you know cared is heartening! One thing I learned is when anyone sincerely sacrifices for us we will automatically feel the gesture and be thankful towards them. So, it is important to give and give towards anyone all the time! In this world, everyone wants to claim their rights, but very few would forgo their rights to please other! You can count it with your fingers, right? Very few, right?

"What's inside shows on the outside"

She visited me a few times. I know she is busy with her family, her studies and her grandchildren, but she made the time for me. She is not that young and healthy either. It is not that others are not that caring, but most of them are staying in my hometown that is quite a distance. I have an open communication with her on many issues. It is just that with her I feel comfortable talking about some personal matters. I can seek her advice because I know she cared even if she can't help. I think a lot when I am in the hospital. I think God wants me to reflect and refresh! I need to be more thoughtful and thankful.

Haji Sabda is a friend that was with me in one of my religious retreats, overseas. I was the leader assigned to lead the congregation. It was an international retreat. So, he has a lot of respect of me, as a leader. He still calls me using the honorific title, leader. Since the retreat we become good buddies. He is a retired journalist with a reputable newspaper. He has a reasonably good life and speaks fluent Arabic. So, he has my respect too. When I was in the ward, I did send out messages to friends. One of the activities of a sick man lying in bed is toying with the phone. You would do that too, I think! So, I am no exception. It is boring and with that one toy, we can let the time flies by! It is therapy.

So, I did find his number and just send a "hi" message. In a few minutes he replied "I am now in a hospital. How are you?" "What? Which hospital are you in?' I asked. He mentioned to me the name of the hospital and his ward number. "He is in the same hospital as me! What a coincidence" I thought to myself, a bit surprised. So, I told him that I am in the same hospital with him and he sounds excited! I gave him my ward and room number.

In a few minutes, I heard someone giving me a greeting from behind my curtain. It is him, in a wheelchair with his wife! We spent a good amount of time talking about our retreat together and a lot of other issues. He is a jovial and knowledgeable person. So, talking to him is always fun and inspiring. I had a good session with him and felt relieved after he left. It is always interesting to meet old buddies who shared a common interest!

Shamri Mahligai is a neighbour in our previous home. He is a quiet guy, an engineer in an American company. I used to visit him at home when we were neighbours. We were on the same floor! So, we met regularly and I even got to know his wife and his mother-in-law, a friendly and approachable old woman. I think he was just married or probably not gifted with kids yet at that time.

I have not met him since I moved out from that condominium home. We never called each other, let alone meeting him. So, his visit to my room at the hospital was least expected. One day he suddenly appeared at my room! I was a bit surprised, but excited to see him.

Apparently, he was at the hospital visiting his "friendly and approachable" mother-in-law which we fondly called Opah. "I was looking at the patients list at the ward entrance when I see your name" he said, as we shake hands. "I didn't know your full name and was doubtful if it is you!" he explained. "So, I thought why not I just come here and find out! I am surprised it's you" he said, smiling at me and my wife. What a coincidence. It's a small world!

His mother-in-law, Opah always visits his house and she would greet us, talk to us and treat us like her children whenever we met at the lift or lobby. We felt good seeing her. In fact, all my kids are fond of her. She will share with us some of her home-made cakes and anything she may bring from her village. She is a good example of a village woman who is open, simple, humble and friendly unlike city women who are a bit reserved and suspicious of others. It is just my observation being a village boy who worked and lived in a city.

I can't blame anyone living in any city for being reserved and extra defensive. It is part and parcel of living in the city where the society is more diverse, individualistic and materialistic with a myriad of characters we have to live with. In a village, the society is much more connected and closed.

So, Opah is a picture of a village woman in a city. It is refreshing to see Opah with her simplistic view of people. I forgot why she was hospitalized, but knowing that she was there is already heartening. It brought some fond memories of her motherly affection towards us.

Domeng is a very close and good friend of mine. We went to the same technical college and later stayed together as bachelors in our first job! I will tell you about our first job later. You will love it! I am even smiling now thinking about it. We were so young then! By the way, Domeng is a nickname. You know boys, right? We are fond of giving our friends, nicknames!

So when he came for a visit, I am not surprised. I expect it. It was just that he came a bit late in my hospitalization because he works in a resort island some six-hundred kilometres away. He is a maintenance manager of a well-known international resort. After we left that company, I heard he worked at a few other locations and then went to the UK to further his mechanical engineering studies. I am happy for him as he has progressed to a manager holding an important and commendable position.

So, we spent almost two hours together, catching up on family, work and business. He also talks a lot about cars or anything with engines and wheels and business, his favourite subject. I forgot that I am sick. His visit was filled with jokes and laughter over all the "stupid" things we did together some thirty years ago.

Our first job was as technical instructors in a technical institute. This is a technical institute of a power utility company. As technicians, we are supposed to teach fitters and junior technicians of the utility company in our respective field. It is more of a technical intensive course designed for maintenance and operation workers. We work in labs and workshop with an occasional classroom lecture.

Firstly, we have to work there not because we want to be a "teacher" but we took the company's scholarship. So, we have to serve the contract. Of course we can be sent to any of their many installations, but it is destined that we are sent there! Knowing him and me, I think both of us are not designed to be teachers at all! We are not that studious and organized type of person in the first place! We are technical people. We only know wires, cables, equipment and workshop. In our technical training, we work in noisy, oily, dirty power generation plants. We see huge boilers and turbines every day.

We listen to Black Sabbath and Rainbow as our pastime, then and still doing the same thing. We keep long hair and are a laid back lot. So, logically teaching is not something we wanted to do! We can't imagine doing it either! It is something we were forced to do. We grumbled a lot, almost daily! It is not our cup of tea! It wasn't easy to adapt to a teaching environment. We were given some teaching methodology courses as a start. Even with that, we were not happy there. We were reluctant!

Secondly, the place is right in the middle of nowhere! The nearest town is eight kilometres away and a small village some three kilometres to the technical institute. I remembered the first day I reported for duty. I was sent by my brother and he left immediately, leaving me in that entirely strange place. I had no transport at that time. So, if I were to go out, I have to rely on a bus service that serves our place once every three hours! Can you imagine that? I am depressed just thinking of the place.

I was lucky to meet this friend of mine on the first day reporting there because at least he has a small, 100cc old bike. We were then proposed to stay at a rented house at the nearby village. One of the staff there helped us arrange our rental. Soon, we were at that modest, small, two-room house. We have a room and nothing at all, just the floor and the ceiling! The other room was occupied by one guy. We spend the first night with our arms as the pillow and a small mat we took off from the hall. It was fun. It's like the worst camping we had. We were bitten by big mosquitoes from a nearby stream and bush.

We stayed there for a month before being given rooms at the institute meant for trainees. What a breather! We even have decent meals at the cafeteria. Our life changed, but still, we remain reluctant as teachers! We grumbled a lot.

Thirdly, our students are mostly old trainees. Most of them are older than us. After a short registration, I met my new boss. I love how his first impression of me was. He looks surprised. He might be thinking "Can this guy teach?" I sat with him for a while in his room as he talks a bit about the institute, the department, the course modules and my job description. All the while, he looks "doubtful" but he remains friendly. He even made some jokes. A few days later, in private he gave me a few good advices. I couldn't remember all, but one thing I remember up until this day is to cut my hair! I think he was right. My appearance should be neat and tidy. I must look "studious" and carries the teacher's image.

We were then put through a few educational methodology courses conducted by the methodology department. Slowly we began to absorb in the "teacher" chemistry and grow up.

So, that reluctant guy, in a strange place and supposed to teach old trainees began his working life! He is lucky to meet a friend who is as reluctant as him! At least to share a common grouse! Not only that, we stayed in the same room. We were roommates! I must admit that the facility is world-class. Our room is quite spacious and serviced daily by the janitors. Our three meals are served in a huge cafeteria. So, now I have a room and food plus a 100 cc bike! It is a good start.

The whole complex is equipped with a big football field, gymnasium with two badminton courts, tennis-courts, a huge lecture theatre for almost a hundred with pitched floor and state-of-the-art labs and workshops in nearly twenty blocks of building. It has a library, an audio-visual lab and even a million-dollar simulator to teach power plant operations! I should be happy, right? Well, not so.

So, when my roommate came and visited me after many years, we have a lot to talk about. We spent a good two hours reminiscing around our early working life. We remember how we all waited for Fridays then. How we wished every day is a Friday! We rarely stay there on weekends. Almost everyone, instructors and trainees will leave for home or make short travels away from the complex.

We talked about the "beautiful" girls or probably someone's wife serving us meals and cleaning our rooms. It is basically a utility company and is male-dominated company. So, most of the instructors and trainees are males! We do have a few ladies in the office and as instructors.

We were young and jovial, despite the sudden change of character we have to carry! Inside, we remain the same! In our room, we still have Black Sabbath and Rainbow! We even have a music studio in the complex! Yes, we have drums, guitars and all! So, at least we have a channel to express ourselves and escape from the loneliness of that huge, state-of-the art, well-equipped complex in the jungle. Unfortunately, we are not good musicians, but some of our buddies there are professionals. One of the instructors is an artiste. He even has a band and makes record albums!

So, once in a while we got to have a jam session! It helps kill our nights in that isolated and haunted place! Haunted? At night, it is definitely eerie. We did hear of ghostly sightings! I wouldn't want to elaborate because I had not seen anything personally!

In those days, we do not have Internet. We were still using floppy-disks and the only application then was word-processing. We wouldn't be that bored if we had Internet then! For presentation, we still use overhead projector and carousel-type slide projector. I guess some of you would remember this old presentation equipment. It was state-of-the-art then!

Visitors to my House

Kak Rohani is my cousin. I feel obliged to mention her in my book. She is without doubt, the most frequent visitor visiting me, at home. She didn't visit me at the hospital because she stays some six hundred kilometres on the East Coast. I didn't expect her to come either. However, at home, before and after the 1st surgery and in between all the surgeries up until my rehabilitation stage, she visited me many times.

People can say she has two children staying near me so she can visit me. Well, that is beside the point. The point is she visited me. I know there are other cousins and relatives passing through my area, but didn't drop by and see me. In fact, our age difference is quite large and I rarely mix with her when we were growing up in our hometown. How can she be so courteous and kind enough to visit me? I think she has a good heart. That is all I can say.

In her visits, she never forgets to bring me gifts. This is the culture she held on to strongly that is commendable – visiting the sick and offering gifts. This is a noble, sacred practice in our religion. As a sick person, visit and gift brings joy and enlightens the heart. It may not cure us, but it will help ease the pain and burden at least for an hour! She has come with her husband, with her son, with her daughters and grandson. All the time, she will try to bring something, even dried fish! It is not so much about what is being brought, but the effort to bring a gift, as remembrance.

I hope to emulate her when I feel better. I hope to visit my cousins and relatives more. I know I missed a lot of visiting the sick, some of whom are my cousins and relatives. It is not that I am busy, but I don't have a heart as soft as her! If I am not sick, I wouldn't know how bad I fair with my cousins in the area of courtesy and remembrance. I have a lot of time to reflect. I admit I failed. I will improve.

Thank you to this dear cousin of mine for "teaching" me a valuable lesson! I will try to fly to her place one day. I have never visited her there and yet, she came and visited me many times!

Deq Man is a cousin of mine. He didn't visit me at the hospital, but visits me at home many times since he knew that I was sick. As cousins, he would just call me last minute and just drop by. We defy any "protocols". He is family. We were quite close living nearby in our village. He is a well-learned and philosophical person. So, in his visits we ventured into mature subjects like politics, human relations and religion. These are also my favourite subjects. He is also my friend on Facebook. So, he knows my inclinations and interests.

He still lives in our hometown. He lived in the capital city for years, but finally returned home. Once in a while, I do get updates on the "political weather" back home. Politics is rive and lively in our country. The "tension" is always high even among families! His father used to hold a key political position in one small local principality. When his father resigned, the position was contested among our cousins! I didn't know who won and he didn't tell me. I think one of his favourite cousins lost to another cousin. I didn't ask, but from the way he grumbles and complaint, I think his candidate lost.

Anyway, whoever he prefers is irrelevant. As long as we remain mature and close, I am fine. In his visits we did talk about religion. As a younger person than me, he almost never gives me any advice. It is our culture and as a courtesy, I think. However, I did remember one profound statement he made. He said "All your religious experience and your many retreats you made was to prepare you for this, your sickness". It is indeed a profound statement something that could only come from a thoughtful, philosophical guy like him. I cherish this advice. I must share it with everyone! How often do you get one remarkable observation and advice like this? He was definitely right!

I couldn't imagine how I could cope with all these hardships, depression, pain and despair if I wasn't strong enough spiritually. I did fall, but I have some cushion to absorb the impact – God and prayers. I was down, but not out because I have a place to "go" and "tell' about my predicament. At least, I am not like the many others who took a long time to accept their fate. I am blessed to have so many kind and sincere souls that churns out excellent advice for me.

"All your religious experience and your many retreats you made was to prepare you for this, your sickness"

Busu Said and **Mak Dek** are my uncle and auntie, the last few still surviving. They used to come to the city to visit their two children staying in the same residential area as mine. Both of them are around eighty years old and frail. So, for them to travel hundred and fifty kilometres from down south to the city must be exhausting, but they did it. In fact, I know they did it a few times for the duration I was sick. How do I know? Well, they never forget to drop by to visit me! Yes, they will come.

Visit is our culture and greatly encouraged by our religion. Another great culture is to bring gifts during visits. However, this beautiful culture is slowly being forgotten and ignored by our society. This is something I personally admit. I rarely visit my cousins and uncle. I do visit them once a year during our festivities, but even that, we do miss them sometimes. I am ashamed of myself.

I used to visit almost everyone in the village when I was young. In our society, the young visiting the old is a respected act. Also, almost every relative are like family and we visit each other regularly. In the villages, it is normal even for relatives to have meals at each other houses. For visits, we almost need not have any appointments. It is always an "open house".

So, for an old couple from the village to visit the younger one, in the city now is a big display of affection and gesture. It is a show of love and remembrance at its best! Of course they are not driving, but their intent to divert and connect with the bigger family is highly respected. I was moved when they came. They may just come for a few minutes, but the warmth remains for month even years. This is what I loved about the old people in our society. They are still holding on graciously to the age-old, beautiful culture of visits and bringing gift! It is heartening to know that some among us are still continuing with this forgotten culture.

I promise to make more visits to all my siblings, uncles, aunties and cousins when I regain my health. I want to see this culture flourish and I want my children to carry on with it. I know this world will be better if everyone starts visiting each other. Let us all start with our families and later extend it to neighbours and friends, near and afar!

"What will happen to this world if everyone visits each other?"

Zaul and **Rahim** are my overseas buddies when I was a student. I did expect both of them would come as I was close to them then and both are simple, humble people. In just a few days upon knowing about my situation both came for a visit. It is always inviting to know that your close buddies remember you after some twenty thirty years!

We met and talked, but at times we seemed lost as all three haven't met for so long and each had gone separate ways in one owns career. So, it was more like updating each other. Suddenly, one has become a manager in a big communication company another is an officer in a huge government agency and me, a "crippled" old engineer!

I still remember the different kinds of "rugged laid-back" lifestyle of one of these guys. After graduation, I simply left for home, but this guy made a grand tour of China. I remembered in college, he was fond of his camera. He loves camera. I think his camera set, plus the lenses cost him thousands. That was his favourite pastime. So, hearing that he makes that tour doesn't surprise me. In fact, a few years after he came back, we did meet and he gave me a book he wrote documenting his travels.

He travels alone as a backpacker covering the whole length of China from the eastern side to the western-most regions of China! Yes, I think he flew in into China, and from then on took buses and trains. I rarely read travel books, but since it is a friend's book, I guess that was the first time

I read a travel book! At least, I have a traveller-author friend. I am quite proud of him. His book may not be a best-seller, but knowing he writes in it is an achievement. Knowing him, I never thought he could write. The other guy was working in our embassy then. Basically, he is a working man and we were students. He lives in a beautiful condominium unit in the plush area of town while we are just renting homes in we-do-not-care-where area of town as long as it is close to school. He has a car, but we just ride the subway and buses. The best part is he was still a bachelor then and he can spend time with us as much as he want, no commitment whatsoever!

Also, we speak the language of that country whereas he only speaks English, which is not the first language and neither is it a second language. So, for him, getting around would be a hassle and he needs us! I can't imagine his life without us and I know he was happy to befriend us then.

The few years we spent together there was memorable. We shop together sometimes we go bowling, clubbing and travels. Talking about clubbing, with him once in a while we got to go to a few affluent, posh and costly international clubs at luxury hotels. I remember that one Irish pub in one posh hotel up on the hills of the city!

Otherwise, as students, we could only afford some less-expensive clubs. To me, a club is a club and it is how we mingle and enjoy the people especially the girls inside not so much the name of the club. At that young and energetic age everywhere is fun and a club is definitely a plus! It is usually fun during long summer and winter vacation. We paint the town red!

We talked and laughed over all the things we did together. It was a good visit. We all need to rekindle old memories and laugh at it. It is therapy, a good one!

Ah Chong and **Zamri** are my two old college buddies. We were in the same course and one of them is a housemate. It has been thirty years since we last met. Not only that, I didn't know where they are and what they do. So, it was a big occasion for me. I was delighted. I remembered both of them dearly. Why not? They are basically the first new friends I know aside from my hometown high school buddies. It was a time when we first left home for studies. So, it was "freedom" to me away from the daily routine and discipline under the watchful eyes of my religious, serious and strict father. God bless his soul!

I think having a big family with almost all were growing up boys and teenager, one do need a strict parent. My father fits well in that role and had facilitated our growing needs in a strict, but wise regiment. He did it with patience and love. He rarely scolds or punishes us. His silence and looks is enough to us as a deterrent! I know he has succeeded in his role. Prove is we all grew up to be good people if not the best and have descent work and life.

As friends, there would be some special traits in them that we hold on for years and remember. I remembered Ah Chong is very religious. He never missed his daily prayers. This is his trademark. After all, he is my roommate! How could I not see him praying? He is also an organized and neat person. He loves jeans and t-shirt, most of them black with pictures of Kiss, Queen and the likes emblazoned on it.

So, guess what? He is an avid "rocker" and also well-versed in music. He listens to Led Zep, the Stones, Sabbath, Rainbow and all names of hard rock and metal bands. He can tell you everything about rock bands, from what Freddy Mercury likes to what guitar Ritchie Blackmore plays! He can sing along almost all the rock songs even though one could barely understand what this noisy band and vocalists sings about! He is definitely cool!

The good part is, despite his "heavy metal" head, he is still a good young man, a nice student who shines and remains strictly religious! I think he influenced and "spoiled" me to switch from someone who likes old Malay pop songs to the world of Ronnie James Dio and Ritchie Blackmore!

I was nowhere close to him. I am playful and not as religious as he is. I wasn't neat, a bit clumsy and disorganized! On music, I have almost zero knowledge except for the few Santana and Deep Purple songs I heard my brother played on vinyl records at home. So, religion and music-wise, I am inferior to him. He is my mentor! Ask anyone, they would acknowledge that Ah Chong is a good young man and that one knowledgeable "rocker". Slowly, I began to follow him and be like him!

I bought few pairs of Lee jeans and black, rock-emblazoned t-shirts and start acting like a rocker. I think I am a fake one!

So, when that "rocker" came to visit this "crippled" old friend, it was heart-warming. He has since progressed into a telecommunication engineer in our telecommunication utility company. He holds a good regional position. Good for him. He deserves it.

I don't remember much about Zamri. He didn't stay with us and he does things I don't. He plays soccer, but I did not. He is a sportsman, I am not. I didn't see him in black, metal t-shirt either! He is clean and lived a healthy lifestyle. I know he did not even smoke.

One thing I remembered dearly about him is that he is a funny guy. He jokes a lot. He is likeable. He has a thick northern accent and I don't think he can change that! He can mimic almost anyone, anything! One of his best imitations is the Hawaii Five-0 theme song! He mimics that fast drums in the theme song! It is so real! Remember Jack Lord? I think those living in the seventies would recall him!

So, the first thing I teased him when we met was about Hawaii Five-0! After shaking hands and a mild hug, I said "Hawaii Five-0!" He laughs and said "Do you still remember that?" Immediately, I request him to mimic that Hawaii Five-0 theme song. He did! He did, but at a much lower volume. The speed of the drum is still there though! He smiled, looked at me and said "I am an old man now. So, the volume is lower!" He then softly told me that he had a by-pass surgery a few years back. "I have to remain calm and relax now" he adds. He now heads a state fire department and do golf once in a while.

I was touched by their visit because I really lost touch with both of them for thirty years! We tried to recall our heydays in that short one-hour visit. We couldn't do it all, but it was a jovial get together. I cherished that visit and their remembrance of me. I was in pain, but for a while, I seem to feel healthy!

Burn is a college mate and hometown friend. He is a close friend and one of the most contacted and met among my friends. We regularly met, before and after my ailment. He is one of the friends who visited me at the hospital while I was undergoing surgery. I was struggling for life in the fourteen-hour marathon surgery and he waited outside. I was told he came with his wife. His wife is in fact lived in the same village as me. So, I am considered close to both of them.

I remembered the many times he visited me at home. He will call and say "Can I kidnap you this morning? Let's go have breakfast together". If I say yes, he will come and fetch me. I know he just wanted to entertain me. It is difficult for me to go out especially with my hypersensitive skin and having to bear the inconvenience and pain of wearing a shirt, but for him, I will relent. I do not want to disappoint him and in fact, I like it too. I know I am in good hands. Every time he comes to fetch me, my wife would remind him "Take good care of him. He needs help sometimes" Indeed, he took care of me.

Once I was in pain, depressed and bored. I called him and said "Let us go to the Lake Gardens". He immediately came and off we went. I loved the Lake Gardens and have not been there for quite some time. It is quite a vast area in the city, some twenty minute drive away. On the other hand, he has forgotten the place, but he drove me there anyway. It was quite inconvenient for him looking at the signs and checking the route. However, we managed to reach there.

So, anyone taking me out should know that I have to be close to a seat or a bench. First, they need to be patient with the way I get off the seat. It is very slow and quite strenuous for me. They need to help me a bit, wait for me to stand and gain balance before walking. I will need my walking stick! So, I was happy to be at the Lake Gardens. The first stop is the flower shop. There are a lot of orchids, roses and many kinds of flowers. It is a different feeling after being confined to bed at the hospital and home. What a breather.

We then move our car to the vast grass, landscaped area of the Lake Gardens. I walked slowly with my walking stick and he holds my hand, looking at every single step I made. It was a beautiful scene with trees, shrubs, flowers all over, a lake and many inspiring spot to just let go and relax. It is therapy! All the time, I will be looking for a place to sit because of my weakening muscle motors. We took photos and shared it on our

WhatsApp group. On the way back, we stopped for dinner at a "floating restaurant". It is just a restaurant built on a small lake, and it's all wooden. It was a good outing!

It is good to know that you have friends who are willing to accommodate your disability. It takes a special person to tolerate the needs of a disabled person. It takes a soft heart that can sacrifice their time and feelings. I remembered when we stop for our prayers. First, he has to help me take off my shoes as I hold on to a wall, standing. He has to help hold my glasses and watch. Then, he has to help with my ablution. I can do it standing, but bending over to wash my feet is a bit dangerous as it is slippery. So, he has to pour water over my feet and help wipe it with his hands!

Next, he has to find a stool for me to pray. He went to the restaurant, borrowed a chair and brings it to the prayer hall. Once my needs are met, he starts with his ablution. At times I feel like I am bothering him, but he looks calm and pleased to do it for his "crippled" buddy.

I think he can come every time I call him. I know he is always ready to please me. He knows I need the short "excursions" here and there. He has brought me to a few restaurants and of course, to my friend's bamboo resort! At restaurants that offer buffet-style service, he will get me seated and go fill my plate before he serves himself. My needs will be his first priority. He will also find the nearest parking for my convenience.

His offer is always open. "Just call me and tell me where you want to go" he would say. He is now my Tour Guide and a private "chauffeur". It is just that my reluctance is about the pain when I have to put on the shirt! Over time, the pain subsides, but sometimes, it didn't! So, every time I want to go out, my mind would think of the pain! However, if I want to go out, I know my dear friend is ready for me. Always ready and willing! Thank God there are so many nice people around me at times like this.

John is a college mate more than thirty years ago. He lives in a nearby village setting, near a small town. In fact, we are both staying in the same municipality, on the outskirt of the city. We are close then and now, like brothers. I have great respect for him when it comes to friendship. He is nice, kind and respectful towards anyone. I don't remember having any grudge towards him or quarrelling with him, on anything, ever the last thirty years or so! Also, I rarely hear anyone talking bad about him, on anything, ever. He is one kind of a guy!

He is one of my frequent visitors! He visits me and at times, become guides and bring along some friends to visit me. His house is near, less than ten minutes and he can just take a motorcycle to come here. Talking about motorcycle, he is an avid rider. He once owns a grand touring bike, the Honda Gold Wing. I think he owns an easy rider too. He has travelled the whole length of our country many times and in fact, went across the northern border into our neighbouring country!

He has all the gear to match his riding appetite. He has a full face helmet for riding his Gold Wing and the German, half helmet to go with his easy rider. Of course, he has the Hell Angels black leather jacket and the bandana! He has since switched to a pick-up truck and an MPV. He still rides a modified scooter. "I am an old man now. This scooter is enough" he quips.

He was working in a bank before and now owns a resort of around ten bamboo chalets. Yes, his chalet is made from bamboo! It is a unique resort. It is a scenic resort in the middle of a small forest area, up on the hills. It is cool and refreshing. It has a small wading pool using natural streams from the hills. Do you know what? He constructs the chalets himself. He designed the layout and landscaping! He knows every single plant there because he planted it!

In fact, he spends a good two years shuttling between his home and his bamboo masters in a nearby country learning and studying about bamboo! He is a skilled constructor now and has appeared many times on national TV talking everything about bamboo. He is now the bamboo master himself! He used to joke "A rich man stays in a brick house, but a wealthy man lives in a bamboo house"!

His resort is frequented by nationals from all over the world. He used the concept of volunteering. In the course of building his chalets, he got help from all these volunteers who are mostly backpackers from Europe, US, Japan, Korea and Australia. He lets the volunteers "have a hand" in building up the chalets. So, the backpackers have a "sense of ownership" to the chalets. Of course he leads in the construction, but all the backpackers volunteered "in the making" of those chalets. Most of them are repeat customers and they themselves brought more backpackers to stay there. It is a laid-back, simple concept. I don't think he charged much because I can see the backpackers are so happy staying there as volunteers! In fact, he has an open kitchen and barbecue stove for his clients. Anyone can buy anything and cook themselves. He even reared some chicken and has a small fish pond. I once asked him how about his client meals. He jokes" I have a fish pond and reared chicken here. They can cook the fish and the chicken" I did talk to some of his clients and I can see the happiness in their faces. Indeed, they have a great person as a host!

So, his visits are always interesting and enlightening. He talks about politics, religion, the arts, motorcycles, and girls and as always bamboo. He talks about his seminars and seminars held at his resort. He is a well-rounded, seasoned, rugged and jaded person. He has a long, wavy hair and at times, tied it into a ponytail. He was a lead singer in a local band too and played in clubs in the city years ago!

So, with him, I can discuss anything from bamboo, to chicken and fish, to politics, landscaping, to Van Halen and Led Zeppelin! In fact, among friends, we all call him Robert Plant! His favourite band is Judas Priest! The best part is his offer. "You can stay at my resort. Please come any time! I will give you a good chalet to stay" Yes, how I wish. I am still in need of a suitable bed with built-in bathroom. Furthermore, his resort is quite hilly with many steps. I will have a hard time moving around. Anyway, I will try to stay there. "My BP was around 145, but after a few years living in the jungle building up this place, I am off the BP pills!"

Do you know what? Just writing about him and his resort makes me happy. Yes, goodness and kindness is contagious! I should learn to be like him. He is so experienced, creative and most of all relaxed! What a great combination.

Appointment with the Psychiatrist

I think what the hospital did to me was incredible! From the pre-surgery test, the surgery, the pain management and rehabilitation, I was also offered a psychiatrist! "You will be sent to a psychiatrist to help you manage your depression due to your disorder, OK?' said one of the pain management team doctors. "For a start, we will call him to your room. We have arranged a slot for you" she adds.

"Why did they direct me to a psychiatrist?" I asked myself. "What do they think? Am I getting insane or what?" I said, as my first impression. Later, I told myself to just let it go. I will go with the flow. I have got nothing to lose anyway. I lie back and think about my situation. I managed to get rid of my negativity, let it go and look at it positively. I know I can definitely learn something new! So, I waited for the appointment, not eagerly though. I was reluctant.

Two days later, the chief psychiatrist, a doctor himself came with two beautiful lady assistants. He looks immaculate in a neck-tie with a white robe. He is in the fifties I guess. "Good morning! How are you sir?" the doctor greeted me. I just smile and nod in affirmation. "I am here to help you with anything to ease your emotional stress, if any" he explains. "Tell us anything. I have with me two trained psychiatrist" he said, glancing at the two beautiful ladies. I didn't have much to say. I just lay back and listen.

"You look relaxed and calm" said one of the ladies. "You will recover well and be back to your family. You like to see them, right?" she jokes. "Actually, you will recover faster at home than here" she adds. I think she was right. Now, I discovered that there are a lot of elements that help in recovery.

After that initial visit by the psychiatrist, I had a few other appointments with the psychiatric department after being discharged. In one session, I had a casual "interview" with the chief psychiatrist in his room. "How are you today?" he asked politely. "I am fine" I said. He looks as usual calm and composed, friendly. "I think you won't have any problems coping with your disorder" he said, looking at me with a smile. "You don't look depressed, like the others I met. You are so relaxed" he said, commending me.

We then start talking about life, family and children. We ventured into social media, sports and what's on the news. "I need motivation from you" I said. "It is your field and you know better" I sounded him, with an intent to hear his advice. He smiled and said "You are a motivated person. The way you talk shows that you are not that depressed" I just laugh at his comments. "I have a few slides I used in my seminar at the hospital. Give me your email. I will mail it to you" he said, accepting my requests. The slide is purely motivational. You will like it!" he said.

I think as a chief psychiatrist he has been looking at my body language, reactions and my overall disposition. We continue talking about filling our time. We talk about friends. We talk about having people who understand us. "You should spend time meeting people like yourself and share your experience" he suggests. I nod in agreement. He asked me to look for groups that have similar experience to talk it out.

We talked about social media and the internet. "Do you have a Facebook account?" he asked. I said yes and my wife chipped in "Yes, he spends quite some time with Facebook, always with his smart phone now". I think he wants me to have an escape channel to share my difficulties and divert my mind from my pain.

"We need to stimulate our senses. We need to go out, feel the air, the breeze, see the trees, the birds, hear the sounds of things out there" he starts being philosophical and at the same time, motivating. "Here, we encourage patients to leave the hospital as soon as conceivable because patients recover better at home, outside when all their senses are stimulated" he adds, with a sense of seriousness. He then asked my wife to, once in a while to push me outside the house. He suggested a few minutes stroll under the sun.

"I have difficult patients here" he said, talking about his work a little bit. 'There is one patient with HIV, she got from her boyfriend, a foreigner" he starts talking about a patient, as an example. "We have a hard time consoling her because her boyfriend left her and her family sort of disowns her!" he said, looking down as he spoke. "We meet her regularly. She is beginning to talk now" he explains.

We even have sessions with patient caretaker here. "Caretakers are depressed too. We need to counsel them on the art of care taking" he said, as she looks at my wife. "Your wife is your care taker" he said. "So far, how are you coping?" he asked my wife. My wife just smiled.

We talked for nearly an hour. It was an enlightening session. He gave me a few advices and I couldn't recall all but this one, I noted. This is probably the best, the most assuring and the most profound statement I have ever heard all my life!

"You are still alive because you have some unfinished business with your Creator"

Indeed, he deserves to be the chief in the psychiatric department! He has the poise, calmness and mind of a motivator. I still keep his motivational slides and once a while, I flip through it. I also had a few other sessions with his department, but with his assistants. I can sense from my visits there that most of the patients are highly depressed. I can see it on their faces.

I am grateful that I am given that little strength from God to face this ailment. I still have my mind and can comprehend fate and life. I am glad to have such a beautiful nurse, friend and caretaker, my wife.

Rehabilitation Stage

My life as a Syringomyelia patient doesn't end at the ward. The surgeon and doctors have tried their best to treat me and restore me to the best possible condition. In the medical fraternity, they have a term called MMI, maximum medical improvement. I forgot where I came about this term, probably in the medical report or from one of the many doctors I met.

As I said, the doctor's focus was the two areas – enlarging the passage for the spinal cord at my skull and reducing the cyst in my spinal cord. The fact that I have regained my swallowing capability and able to be wheelchair-free are testament of the success of the surgery.

The overall sensory, motor muscles and digestive pain and discomfort is still with me, but manageable. I simply use the term "manageable" in describing my condition when people asked me. It is difficult to explain my "pain" inside as people tend to think I am healthy from the outside. I do try to use the pain score to describe my pain. In my many consultations in the hospital, slowly I began to gauge my pain score. This is specific to bodily pain. It is between mild and moderate. When I put on my clothes, it goes to severe. This is what bothered me the most!

For my muscle motors and digestive, I can say that it is around 60% to 70% from where it was before. I still have muscle strain, cramps and imbalance that led to loss or limited movement. I do not expect to be restored fully to my condition before Syringomyelia, but will go through rehabilitation to maintain and improve the remaining nerve function. I can only conclude that my nerve function is still there, but its efficiency has been reduced. If not, I would have been paralyzed. However, I am prone to any eventualities as the cyst may grow! I just hope it doesn't get worse.

So, my next journey is rehabilitation. After discharged, we were asked to come for rehabilitation at the hospital rehabilitation clinic. Is it at the "haunted, old WW2 military barracks' again? No, not this time! This clinic is in the new hospital complex. It was a weekly routine from our home, through part of the busy city traffic to the hospital. It is an hour and a half journey! I was still weak and wheelchair ridden.

So, my "chauffeur" has to stop at the main lobby, carry out the wheelchair, help me out of the seat, take my hands, bring me to the wheelchair and push me into the lobby. She then has to "look" for a parking slot, most probably outside the hospital and walk that long three hundred meters to the main lobby!

The clinic is close to the main lobby. It has a moderate sized gym for physical training and another hall for occupational training. I was first introduced to the chief therapist. "Welcome sir!" he greeted me. He is a young doctor. He looks fit, but doesn't seem friendly. Maybe it is his "square" face that I find intimidating. I don't know. He opened my files, looked through it and said "Yes, you are a spinal patient. Here, we do three main things. First, is the range of motion. We try to help patient regain their basic limbs, body and head movement. Next, is strengthening and endurance" he gave a short briefing. "You will be assisted by our many therapists here, OK?" he adds. He then introduced me to two therapists.

My first equipment for that day was the stationary exercise bike for warm-up. "Come try and have a seat here. We will do a little warm up" said the therapist. "Try this exercise say a hundred rounds. Look at this counter" he instructs as he showed me the counter. "I'll be here for you. If you feel tired just stop for a while" he adds. My wife was given a chair and sat nearby. I was closely assisted and monitored through my exercise.

It is here that I began to look at the different types of conditions of the patients. I couldn't recall everyone there, but I know my condition wasn't that bad. Just beside my exercise bike is a lady, in her mid-thirties, cycling with her weak leg. She could hardly cycle! One complete round seems like a big burden to her! She is quite persistent though. I can see her grimacing face each time she presses the pedal! Her mother sat patiently near her looking at her doing that exercise.

After the warm up, I was brought to an exercise table. The first thing they did was to let me lie down on my back and they start lifting, bending, extending and testing both my legs for the different kinds of posture. I think they want to gauge if my legs still have that flexibility for the different range of motion. They also gave me a few stretching exercise and muscle power tests. I was told about the proper stretching and exercise for the different sets of muscle. It was quite thorough. Again, they train me to wake up, sit up and stand up, like what the therapists at the ward did. However, here they are more comprehensive.

I am drilled through different position like waking up from lying on the right side and left side. The exercise "bed" was also raised to different height and I am put through the same exercise for the differing heights. It was more detailed here. They also kept taking counts and notes. It was a good first day.

Looking back, I realized all my life, I never really thought about all these little "pleasures" of standing, walking, squatting, waking up or sitting up. I never thought much about it. Now, in this room full of disabled, I am distressed to be one of them. As much as I would like to deny it, I am forced to accept it. It wasn't easy emotionally! I am disabled. I will have to live with it!

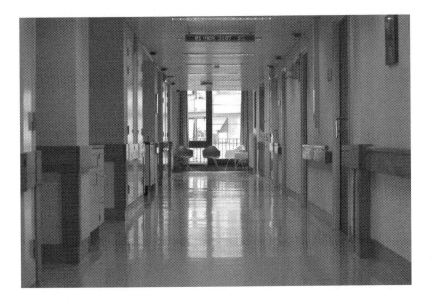

The Rehabilitation Hospital

M_y rehabilitation journey leads me to a new rehabilitation hospital. After a few weeks of travelling fifty kilometres, to and from the rehabilitation clinic at the hospital, we were advised to continue my rehabilitation at a new rehabilitation hospital. It is a hospital only for rehabilitation.

This facility is new. It is also close to our house, just nine kilometres away! So, I do not have to wake up at six in the morning and endure the one and a half hours morning traffic crawl. My wife can look forward to a less demanding drive. It would be less taxing for her. Do you know that I have passed by that place a few times before, but I never knew there is a rehabilitation hospital there?

I think I have become more knowledgeable about places around me now. All this while I only knew my regular route to my office! I have a few routes I can take going to the office and one of it did pass by this hospital! I didn't see it then. I guess I couldn't care less about hospitals. Why should I? I was healthy then.

The parking space is ample and for patients, there are many lot provided just a few steps from the lobby entrance. It is efficient. So, my wife doesn't have to go through the daily three hundred meter walk any more. Apart from the location and the facility, it is the "positive, smiling and friendly" people who work there that I really cherished! It's not only the physiotherapists, even the doctors are different! I think they are trained to "give us back our life"! They may not say it, but I can feel that they exude hope. I think because of this, all the patients there are happy! Yes, it is an enlightening atmosphere! I can feel the warmth, concern, respect and sincerity of the people there. I am happy too!

30 Year Old Man without Both Limbs!

Just like 7G, this place is never short of trauma and human courage. In one of my sessions, I saw this one guy. He lost both his limbs from an accident. "He had an accident with a lorry. Both his limbs are crushed" his mother told us as we managed to start a conversation with her. "It is his fate" she reflects as she looks at his son. His son came with two artificial limbs and two walking sticks. He sat on a stool close to me and starts removing his artificial limbs. We were side by side with me facing a wall-bar and doing simple sit-ups drill holding on to the bar. He is on a floor mat, facing the mirrored wall.

"How are you?" asked the therapist. "I am OK. I am OK" he answered with a big, happy smile. A few minutes later he was on the floor mat doing some sitting drills with the help of a therapist. It looks like he has to sit up from a lying position. With his strong arms, it looks quite easy for him. He seems positive and talkative. It is obvious that he is not new there. He must have been here months before I came.

"Pity him. Like this who wants him?" her mother said as she let out a long sigh of sadness. "He is very courageous though. He exercises hard and consistent. Now, he is back to work" her sad face glows with delight as she talks about her son. "Is he working, auntie?" I chipped in with a question. "He works in a telecommunication company, as an engineer. His employee takes him back. He now drives to work!" she seems content at her son's recovery. I am impressed too! I can't imagine how devastated I would be if I am in his situation. I am much luckier than him, but I am so negative. How I wish I could have his courage! I learned another lesson.

"He was married with one kid" his mother said. "After the accident, he left his wife" she adds. I didn't say anything. My wife just looked down. "In the beginning I was miserable, but now I think I am over it. He seems fine" she lets out a sigh of relief. I was saddened at his tragic fate. I am still sad, now! Every time I think about him my heart is moved. He is a million times stronger than me! "I think he did the right thing by divorcing his wife. He is young. His wife is young and he knows his wife deserve a better man" my wife told me, later. I also found out that at the time of the accident, he was twenty-eight!

"Look at him. He never gives up. See, he even sweats!" my wife nags. "Try to be like him, OK?" she commands. I know I fret a lot. I sometimes vent out my frustration to her. She has been with me all the while. Surely, she could see my negativity and weakness. Deep inside, I accept all her comments. After all, it was for my own good and she just wants me to recover. She wants me back!

I could still see the young man walking with his walking sticks. Every single step looks strenuous, but he did all that calmly, with a smile! He is such an awesome gentleman. He is way pass the denial mode. He overcame his grief. He is "back to life again"! That was what rehabilitation is all about, giving someone's life back! I am still struggling to accept my fate. I still asked why me. It is not easy to overcome any predicament. It is easy to talk about it. We can advise others, but when we are the subject, only God knows how depressing it is!

I came across him just a few more times. Every time during the rehabilitation sessions, he always displays a positive attitude. It shows from his smiles, his jokes and his overall flair with the therapists there. I think his main training, using his artificial limbs and his walking stick has been done. From the way he managed to walk, he can be independent.

Still, I can't help thinking how difficult his life would be. At that ripe young age, he has to cope with a tough life and future. At twenty-eight, I was at the top of my life. I have a young family, a job, travels and tennis! I never met him again. I don't know how he is. I think he can cope with it. He is awesome and inspiring! That much I can say about him.

Can I be like him? How I wish, but the fact is, we are all different. I do not want to set unrealistic goals and starts feeling frustrated when I can't achieve it. I remembered a sound advice I heard before "Try not to do things that are beyond your control. Just do what you can control" In my case, I can't control when I can fully get my life back, but I can do everything towards it like exercising, trying to increase my range of motion, increase my strength, add some endurance and positive thinking. I know I can control all this! In short, do not change the things you can't! We can't change fate, but we can hope.

As a patient myself, I know that a piece of advice is good, but it is the implementation that matters. Now, who will have to implement it? Me. I have to do it. Now, I can attest to you that it wasn't easy. So, when anyone gives me some advice, I just listen to it. I got many kinds of advice while I am sick. I forgot most of it. Why? It's simple! I am in pain and I am focused on getting rid of the pain. The truth is, I couldn't be bothered with those advices, but at the same time I couldn't refuse it. Advice serves as a temporary relief though. You just say "Oh thank you for your advice" Nothing happens from that advice!

A Very Thin Boy Trying To Walk

We just talked about a man without two limbs. He has his set of challenges to face. In the gym, in my weekly physiotherapy sessions, there are many others with differing conditions and fate. Apart from the many stroke patients learning to walk, some accident victims with artificial limbs and some diabetic patients with limbs amputated, there is one boy that is a bit unique. I don't know the exact name of the disease, but this boy is so thin, his muscles seem wasted or wear away.

He is around twenty years old and is tall. He comes in wearing the ward clothes. He is an inpatient. Just looking at his physical condition is saddening. I couldn't lay off my eyes from him. After all, he is at the open area, at the centre of the gym where most "walking" training is conducted.

It was strenuous just watching him. It is apparent that he has to live by his two walking sticks. There is no way he can support his figure. In the future he may be able to walk, but not now.

The physiotherapist patiently helps him synchronize the placement of his walking sticks with his steps. At the same time, he must be held firmly at the waist. The walking distance is just around ten meters, but clearly that looks like a hundred meters to him. He has to struggle every single step. I think he is new in the walking training's regiment. I just hope that one day he could walk, like me.

I was initially wheelchair-ridden and slowly, but surely, the physiotherapist put me through the parallel bars drill. It wasn't easy. My limbs were weak, strained and numb. I couldn't "feel" my feet touching the floor and my balancing is poor. It takes me more than five long sessions just on the parallel bars! My hands were also cramped and numb. So, even with the parallel bars, my grip on the bar wasn't strong enough to support my weight. Now, two years later, I could walk!

I sincerely hope the boy is walking now, somewhere. I would be happy if I could see him. I think a lot about him. After six months, I could leave my wheelchair and walk. It was a huge milestone in my life! At that time, I used to cry inside thinking about my fate. How could I live in a wheelchair? I used to sit and ponder if I could ever walk again. Looking back, I regret the days when I sometimes cursed my skinny limbs. I never thought of nearly losing my limbs. I was at the verge of it, but miraculously, the last surgery and with God's consent, I was saved.

The Student That Fell Off a Building

One of the many patients in our session at rehabilitation is a teenage boy. He fell from his hostel. I don't know how many floors he fell from, but whatever, there must be a reason. Apparently, he injured his head, had an operation and now, undergoing rehabilitation. He is wheelchair-bound, his speech stuttered and movement is limited and slow.

As usual, the person accompanying a child is always the mother. It is the mother that will lift the wheelchair out from the car booth, sit him onto it and push him for the registration and into the hall. She will feed him with drinks and goodies, to make her son happy. I came to know that he came from a reputable college and it is unfortunate that he had to quit his studies. His mother must be disappointed and her dream of seeing her son shines in life shattered. The boy looks sharp in his occupational tests. He seems to complete the tasks given satisfactorily. He is an easy patient to the therapists there.

Having a son his age myself, I can't imagine how devastated I am if he is my son. What future will he have? However, looking at his mother, I didn't see much sign of disappointment. She smiles and maintains her composure all the while. She would always encourage him, stroked his head gently and pat his back. She is tireless. I met them many times and she is always smiling and calm. It is an affection of any mom to a child even in difficult circumstances.

"He looks intelligent" my wife said about the boy. "He is of the same age as our son. So sad to see him like that" my wife said, reflecting about our son. "The mom must be sad, I know, but she looks calm." my wife commended.

I think the mother has passed the denial stage and accepts it as fate. She may not have any expectation from his son anymore. She wouldn't be that calm if she is still in the denial stage. Sometimes in life, we tend to put high hopes on ourselves be it financially and career-wise. I think, the higher the hope the bigger is the disappointment if we fail to achieve it. I looked at the boy and reflect on me.

I think I know why the mother is calm.

"Do not change things you can't!"

The Physiotherapy Exercises

If you asked me how many types of exercises they taught me, I would say a lot! If I were to do all the exercises they taught with the same three sets and each set with ten repetitions, I would easily spend around three hours for physiotherapy and three hours for occupational therapy daily! In the rehabilitation hospital, the physiotherapy and occupational therapy are separate departments and a separate training area too. It is well equipped and well-staffed. It has a lot of exercises, but actually broken down into three types – the range of motion, the strengthening and endurance. It is systematically organized and sequenced!

So, now at home I just do an hour on physiotherapy and one hour of occupational therapy on alternate days. When I look at it, generally physiotherapy relates to rehabilitating the lower abdomen and limbs and occupational therapy deals with the neck, arms and the hands. Is one hour enough? It is enough because after two years in rehabilitation, my range of motion is basically restored although not entirely, but acceptable and I just need a set each day. The rest is on strengthening and endurance. I didn't do all either. I just choose the key ones for each set of muscles.

So what would be the key exercises? What do you think?

The key exercise I saw taught mostly to everyone is the wake-up exercise. Yes, wake-up exercise is important. You need to wake up well-stretched before doing the other exercises, right? It consists of a few exercises while lying down and after we got into a sitting position in bed. While lying down, first is the back-stretch. Simply lie down with the knees bent and feet on the bed. Pull the right knee to the chest, hold on for a few seconds and release it back down. Do the same for the left knee. After that pull both knees to the chest, hold it for a few seconds and release it back down.

Next is the simple ankle stretch. Lying down with the leg straight, just pull our feet backwards three or five times, for both the right and left. Next is the straight leg raise exercise. With both legs straight, lift the right leg for twelve inch, hold it for a few seconds and put it back down. Do the same for the left. Still with the leg, lift it for twelve inches, swing it out, hold it for a few seconds and back to the original position and put it down. Do the same for the left leg.

Then, do the hip exercise. Lie down with knees bent at 90 degrees and simply sway it down to the right and do the same for the left. Next is the hip and pelvis exercise. Just lie back with knees bent at 90 degrees and simply lift the pelvis off the floor. Do it three or five times. The last leg exercise is the side-lying leg lift. Just lie on the right side and lift the left leg and do it for three to five times. Then, do for the right leg by lying on the left side. We are done for the lying down position exercises. There may be more, but this is enough for me.

In the sitting position, we do the knee exercise by simply lifting the leg straight and pulling the feet inwards. A few more exercise for loosening up of the fingers, ankles and it is done. Next is a short stretch of the waist and hips. I still do this exercise daily up until now. It really helps in the overall flexibility of the joints and muscles. So, after we wake up, what do we do next?

The parallel bar is probably the next most important piece of equipment. It is to rehabilitate the lower limbs and walking. I can see almost everyone is put through this parallel bar regime. It may look simple, but when our own limbs are weak and muscle motors are not functioning as expected, it is a tedious exercise. It is just around ten feet long.

Usually, the wheelchair is parked and locked at one end. Then, the patient is helped and made to stand and asked to hold on to both bars. The patient is then aided to make the first few steps while holding on to the bars. In a session, if a patient can do five or six times walking through the whole length of the parallel bars is considered acceptable. I think it took me around five, twenty-minute sessions before I could walk comfortably through the parallel bar.

"It was not easy to learn to walk all over again"

Being able to stand is basically the basis of all other leg exercises. Once a patient is able to stand, they may proceed to walking. Parallel bars would be a start and next progression is walking using a walker and slowly upgraded to using a walking stick. I bought a walker during my early rehabilitation stages in the ward. I still have it and maybe I will have a small museum to display it. My wheelchair is also another item for the museum! Anyway, the eventual target is walking without any walking aid.

Once I was able to walk, I am put through a series of balancing and strengthening routines. I forgot the sequence, but I think the few exercises were for balancing. I still remember the one leg stand routine on a foam pad. I think it was for balancing by strengthening the muscles at the heel, the ankle, the feet and probably the calf. It wasn't easy because besides the general weakness due to muscle motors failure, my legs were also partially numb. I couldn't feel the full touch of my sole to the floor. I spent a few sessions on the one leg stand exercise on the foam pad, switching between the right and left leg.

Once I was quite efficient on the foam pad, a rocker board is used for me to stand on. I think it is for both balancing and strengthening. A rocker board is to train how my whole body react when both my feet tilts to the right and left and also, forward and backwards. The foam pad and the rocker board is an excellent exercise for balancing and strengthening the legs. It is kind of fun too. It's like a toy, old man's toy!

Next, is another tricky exercise, still using the foam pad and the rocker board! A ball is thrown towards me and while standing on the foam pad, which is unstable, I have to catch the ball. The ball is thrown to different points in front of me, sometimes to the sides and sometimes at different heights. I think this exercise is for eye-body coordination too.

Thinking back, I had never thought of playing ball games like basketball although I like to watch the NBA. Now, I have to play this simple catching of the ball game. After a while, it becomes fun. I even asked the therapist if I could throw a few balls into a basketball hoop. In fact, they have a basketball hoop set in an adjacent hall and I did get the chance a bit later to be "Michael Jordan" throwing three-pointers!

I was also put through walking on a series of foam pad arranged in line. It is a step by step walk after merely standing and balancing on the foam pad. Basically, it is about walking on an uneven base to train balance and muscle strengthening. After a few sessions, I gained a certain amount of balance and strength of my legs.

Next is the big application of the balance and leg strength capability so far trained. It is called the heel toe balance exercise, the tandem stance or sometimes called the "catwalk". We were put to a walk exercise where the forward movement is gained by putting the feet forward, where in each step the heel of the forward moving feet touches the toe of the other feet behind. The steps must all be on a straight line drawn on the floor and placed in front of the other feet in a straight manner. All the while, both knees must be kept straight.

The whole stretch is around ten meters in the middle of the hall. Usually, we were put through three or five rounds of the stretch. This is a tough routine. Suddenly, we become like someone drunk unable to walk straight and look like as though we are being blown by some strong wind! We have to use the strength of our feet, the balance attained through previous exercises and our overall body adaptation to the feet movement.

I think this is one of the toughest drills. It took me a few weeks to walk without tilting and getting off the line. I must admit even now, at home, I still struggle to perfect this "catwalk" routine. I think once we mastered this routine, we can perform as a tightrope walker in a circus!

If you think the "catwalk" on the floor is tough, wait until you see what obstacles they introduced on that line drawn on the floor! A portion of the stretch then includes a few two-inch high foam pads! We are supposed to do "catwalk" on that foam pads too! Just normal walk on the foam pads is tough enough for patients like us. Can you imagine doing "catwalk" on these foam pads? Probably, this is a progression from beginners to intermediate level of "catwalk".

So, it was a lot more fun, more tilting, more swaying and getting off the line! We looked like we had more beers than before! On top of that, they also placed small wooden blocks on the straight line as obstacles where we have to cross over it.

The following drills are more for range of motion and muscle strengthening covering the calves, hamstring and quadriceps. It is more of ensuring flexibility of joints and leg muscles. Initially, we were asked to stand on our toes and fingers as a start. Then, we went through some sit up exercises, initially from a chair, a stool and eventually from a squatting position. One of the basic exercises to rehabilitate sit up is a Stall Bar. It is just a ladder-like structure build at a wall and a small stool for us to sit. We will then try to sit up with the help of some pulling of our hands holding the bars.

Eventually, we sit up without holding the bar for the pulling force. The bar then become as a precaution so as not to let patients fall.

Talking about sit-ups, it is the most painful of the many exercises. Let's not talk about sitting up from a squatting position. Just trying to squat is such a painful, strenuous ordeal! So, I took a few sessions to be able to sit up from the stool and from squatting position, I still can't do it now. I think I lack practice or along the way, I deliberately skip this drills. It is just so painful!

Actually, at home I did try to squat down and I managed to do two or three times. I forced myself, but seeing how difficult it was for me, from the grimaces of my face, my wife advised me to skip it to a later time when my joints and limbs are more flexible. "Take it easy. Don't hurt your legs" my wife said. "You can walk and do stationary march. That's good for now" she would say when I exert myself doing the squats.

It is a far contrast from the therapist at the rehabilitation hospital. The therapist would say "Go down lower! Yes, lower and keep it there for ten seconds! Don't cheat!" What, ten seconds? I can't even squat for one second! Luckily I am married to this "therapist" at home!

Looking back at all the equipment and drills given, I know that the amount of effort put in by the medical fraternity to make us all recover is enormous! I can't even remember the names of muscles on my legs, but these physicians and scientist have designed specific equipment and drills for specific set of muscles! They even merge certain exercises to rehabilitate the muscular system and the nervous system, like the balance exercises. It is quite confusing to me, but they made it look well-organized, coordinated and sequenced!

I am thankful to all the souls behind all these efforts. Definitely, there was an enormous amount of time spent on studies to perfect all these routines! It is also an expensive facility. I saw big robot-like equipment used to rehabilitate patients to walk. It must be expensive, probably a million. I look at myself and reflect.

"What have I done to benefit others?"

After all the basic range of motion drills and strengthening exercises, resistance training was introduced. We were then moved to various weight training stations like the leg extension and leg curl stations. I also did the leg press weight training. On top of that, we also did weight training for our arms and shoulders. There are a few pull and lift weight pulleys in the gym that we used for this purpose. For strengthening, the static bicycle and treadmill were also used.

One of a key training I went through is regarding the steps. In rehabilitation, one of the targets is for patients to return to their normal life of which climbing up of stairs is one of it. This test combines strength and balance. We have to step up and down the stairs first by holding the railings and later, without holding it. In a later routine, our movement was timed to see our speed and how we progressed in our stepping exercises.

After going through the range of motion, strengthening and endurance test in the gym, I was tested for the overall progress. It was then concluded that I need further training for my strengthening and balance. They told me that my balancing is still deficient. I need more balancing training. Now, where did they send me next? Hydrotherapy! Yes, to the pool!

Hydrotherapy is part of physiotherapy. So, it falls under one department and the hydrotherapy hall is just next door. I used to pass by the entrance never knowing what it looks like and never expected that I would need that either. As it is a wet activity, the preparation is a bit different. We need to bring along our swimming trunks and t-shirt.

So, we need to go to the changing room. As I am still weak and imbalanced, my wife will have to accompany me into the changing room. I still need help wearing my trunks and shirt. As we enter the hall, prior to entering the pools our BP is checked and later, we need to cleanse ourselves at the shower. Then, a floating device is put over our shoulder and some weight is attached to our ankles.

The hydrotherapy hall has two pools. One has a fixed platform for general leg exercise and the other is a pool with an underwater treadmill. However, both the base of the pool can be raised and lowered. It is raised for patients to enter and lowered for the exercise. I was told that in a pool setting, buoyancy helps support our limbs in our attempt to adapt to proper balance. It was hoped that all the underwater routine could be done when patient is off the water.

So, what are the routine a patient needs to do off-water? In short, what are the movements a patient needs to learn and do after rehabilitation?

The first is walking with the right posture and balance. So, the patient needs to learn to walk with the right posture and balance underwater first because buoyancy will help support the patient in the exercise.

As a start, patient will be asked to walk forward while holding the side railings in the pool. In the beginning, it is quite confusing as the water resistance and the weight affects the steps. It is in this water resistance and the counter-resistance of the weights that "balance-off" the steps made. Also, in the right posture of walking, the chest must be out and hips kept straight. In an underwater setting, the hips can be "pushed" to a straight position during the walking by buoyancy.

For some patients, they tend to bend while walking out of fear of tripping. However, it is not the correct way of walking. So, this is what hydrotherapy tried to assist! The patient is "trained" to walk with the hips straight.

In the ensuing exercise, patients were asked to walk sideways and backwards all the while holding the side railings. In all this movement, the therapist standing inside the pool kept a close watch at the posture and immediately correct and advise the patients. Slowly, after a few sessions, patients will have to walk with the correct posture without holding the railings.

Next is walking in the middle, across the length of the pool. Once the therapist is satisfied with the posture, a water jet is introduced to the patient. It is a tedious step-by-step progression each patient went through.

What else is taught? I can remember single leg stand, "football kick" swing, step-back lunge, forward lunge, squatting, static marching and even underwater steps! It is all balance-related routine. Yes, you need balance to make a one-leg stand, right? You need balance to do a "football kick" swing too. Static marching is a good exercise as it involves a series of one-leg stands and needs a lot of balancing powers!

I realized that only after learning, practicing and doing all these routines underwater, I can do it off-water! Indeed, hydrotherapy helps us balance by initially supporting us through buoyancy! In the underwater settings, our mind "remembered" the instructions it sent to the right muscles and once off-water, it just duplicates that same instructions! This is purely my understanding based on some of the instructions given by my therapist.

So, in the pool, I was able to be with many kinds of patient. Once, I was with a semi-paralyzed patient. He can't even walk as he is wheelchair-ridden. So, the purpose of his hydrotherapy session was just to let the water support him and push both his arms and legs to open and close. He wears a full flotation at his shoulder and legs and in a lying, floating position, he was asked to just open and close his limbs. The therapist was extra cautious with him as he needs full support and help from the therapist. I was also once with an amputee. So different patient has different types of exercise designed for them.

In the underwater treadmill pool, our walking is monitored by an underwater camera and shown on a screen in front of us. The speed can be adjusted by an operator at the panel in front of the pool. I spent around ten sessions in hydrotherapy and finally managed to do a few of the routine off-water. I am still not confident of the "football kick" sway though! I think I need more training.

The Occupational Therapy Exercises

This is one area where the exercises are "small". Basically, it involves the arms and the hands and everything the hands need to do. It also dealt with other senses and a bit about the brain. For the arms and hands, just like physiotherapy, it starts with the same thing –range of motion.

I remembered the first few sessions were about my arms and shoulder range of motion. The aim is to restore back the distance and direction of my shoulder and arm. It involves the "activation" of the joint, tendons, ligaments and muscles. "In most spinal patients the tendons and ligaments of the shoulder and arm may be frozen" the therapist explained in one of the beginning sessions. Yes, I remember this word "frozen". It means the tendons and ligaments are not elastic or flexible as expected due to some physiological disorder. "Here we try to first check the range of motion of your arms and shoulder" the therapist adds.

So, the first thing the therapist did was to check my arms overall extension and flexibility. At that time my arms were so weak. Basically, both arms just droop down, hanging without much power. The therapist would slowly lift, twist and turn my arm and as she did that, at almost all positions she will ask if I feel any pain or not. After the initial check, they can identify which set of ligaments and joints are "frozen".

At the same time, they feel the mass and texture of my muscles. "We will give you certain exercise to activate back your joints and muscles" the therapist said. "Overall, it is not that bad. It can be improved. You can do it" she said, as she keeps "loosening" my arms by lifting and twisting it. She then asked which the weaker arm is. I said the left one. "We will let you use your right arm to help your left arm" the therapist explained further.

One of the few exercises given in the beginning was to gently and slowly get my shoulder moving again. I was given a stick. I am supposed to use my stronger arm, the right arm to help push my left arm up, in front of my body. First, I hold the stick at both edges with my right and left hand with both arms straight and lowered down at my thigh. Then, with a bottom swoop of my right arm, I slowly try to push my left hand and arm up. It wasn't easy at first. It is so painful probably because the ligaments and muscles are stiff. It doesn't get straight up, but maybe half the height. I think I did that more than ten times and it doesn't break that barrier. I was asked to rest and try again. It is one of the ways to get the weak shoulder move again.

Once I could push my left hand up in front of my body, I am then asked to push my left hand up at the side of my body, still using the right hand to push. Again, they want to see it done ten times!

Next, still with the weak left arm, I am put through a shoulder arc exercise. Simply, there is a half loop wheel on the table in front of me with a few rings in it. The task is to move the rings through the whole length, height and curvature of the loop using my weaker arm, the left. It is to "force" my shoulder to lift the arm through the whole length of the loop.

For a start, I am allowed to use my right hand and arm to help lift my left arm and move it through the arc movement. Again, this is a slow, tedious process. It is so painful just to lift one ring and pass it through the arc! Do you know how many rings the put there? I think around a dozen! Once I moved all twelve from left to right, I will have to move it back to the left and that is counted as one set! So, how many sets must I do in a session? Guess what! I have to do three to five sets.

As painful as it may be, my therapists are all friendly and courteous. They will always let me rest. They are never hard on any of us. They are always smiling and positive.

I went through both the "stick push" and the arc movement a few times. Eventually, I could feel some looseness of my left shoulder and arms. Next, is getting the left arm, up the back. They need to see how far the left arm can move up my back. In the first try, my left arm could barely move up. So, they devise a way to get my left arm to move up my back. How? Again, using my right hand to pull it up! What I did was to hold a short plastic band in my right hand and throw it backwards over my right shoulder to my left hand that is behind my back. With my left hand, I catch hold of the other edge of the plastic band. So, with my right arm, I pull the band upwards thus pulling my left arm slowly as far as I could. As usual the resistance is hard. The shoulder blade and the shoulder are so painful. It was hard. I could barely do five pulls!

Luckily, we have nice, sweet your lady therapists around. They never scold me. They just smile. For this arm moving up the back exercise, I have to do for my right arm too, unaided. It was a bit stiff, but I managed to do it.

Once in a while, I am asked to do some light shoulder circles, forward and backwards. Again, they said it is for the shoulder and the arms to be activated again. After a few sessions, they check my overall looseness by lifting, twisting and turning my arms and asked if I feel any pain. Still with the range of motion drills, my next exercise is simply to pass a piece of short stick from my right hand, over my shoulder to my left hand at my back. It is actually a dual purpose exercise to see how far my right arm can reach down from behind my right shoulder and how high my left arm can move up my back. It is very strenuous, but after a few repetitions, for both the right and left arm, my shoulder felt a bit loose and flexible. I realized now that this exercise at least serves one important purpose - to use my towel to wipe my back after shower!

For lifting of my arm, I went through one small routine at an arm robotic station. It is just to aid my frozen shoulder and arm to move again. I simply sit on that station seat and my arm is placed and wrapped onto a robotic arm at my side. The robotic arm is slowly raised to a certain angle up. Initially, it is minimal, but later the angle is gradually increased. I liked it very much there because I don't have to strain myself. Unfortunately, I just got to do that "lazy exercise" twice!

Another "trick" these therapists used to loosen up our shoulder and extend our arm upwards is using a pinch tree. What? Pinch a tree? No! It is simply a thin flat pole with height grading, standing on a small base and placed on a table. From a seating position, I am asked to place clothespins onto the pole starting from the bottom to the highest possible height I could clip the clothespins. It sounds simple but to a patient with muscle motor disorder, I felt sore all over my arm!

Do you know what? I am given some fifty clothespins! That's a lot! Again, after I clip it on, I must clip it off again and that is counted as one set! How many sets must we do? You know the answer, right? By the way, at home I never touch any clothespins. Don't tell my wife, OK? I am lazy. I rarely help her hanging clothes. Once in a while, probably once a year I did help her with the clothes!

The last few range of motion exercises are more like doing it unaided and some stretching exercises. I am asked to raise both my arms to a horizontal position in front of my body. After a few sets, they switch it to the sides. I now have to raise both my arms from my sides up to horizontal position. It was heavy. Both my arms felt heavy as though I am holding a heavy object. After a few repetitions and sets, the arms felt really strained. I remember the pain lasts until I reach home! This is what happened when the signals from your brain is not fully reaching your muscles!

"In rehabilitation, we try to activate new sets of muscles to compensate for the muscles that may not function due to your nerve failure" I remembered one of the therapists said before. He even adds that our body has a special way of accommodating weaknesses in other parts of the body.

In the following sessions the bar is raised. Now, I have to raise my arm in front of my body, straight up, vertically. I then have to raise my arm from the side of my body, straight up, vertically. Again, initially it was just five repetitions per set, but gradually increased to ten repetitions. These two exercises is one of the toughest. My arms felt so heavy. The whole shoulder and arm was strained.

I think those are the range of motion exercises I could recall. Even now, I still find it "heavy" to raise my arms! I can barely lift one kilogram now. I think I need to focus more on strengthening, but it wasn't easy though. My body is constantly in pain and exercises increased the pain and I needed to take a long rest after it!

At times, I felt depressed. I am facing all that alone and I don't think any of my friends know what I went through. In fact, I wouldn't want them to see what I went through. I am trying to use my arms and hand again. I can't write because my hands are numb and stiff! It is so sad! Negativity did creep in once in a while. However, the atmosphere in the rehabilitation clinic is always warm and happy. The therapists are friendly and great. It really helps boost our mood! I believe, whatever the situation, nobody can motivate me, but myself!

"Self-motivation is telling yourself "I can" a million times!"

After the range of motion drills, they proceed with strengthening of the shoulder, chest, arms, hand and even fingers! In occupational therapy they use elastic bands to exert resistance. They do not have exercise stations and heavy weights as in the physiotherapy gymnasium. I was given some elastic bands to work on my chest, shoulders and arms. It is not just an elastic band though. These bands are graded according to the resistance level. I am given the red and green bands of which the green has a higher or heavier resistance. I still have the red and green band here with me, at home, but it has been lying there, unused! I procrastinate!

So, the few exercises I can recall are first for the shoulders and chest. It is called pull-apart exercise. We simply hold the two edges of the band in front of our body and from that position, pull it outwards, pulling it apart by stretching both our arms straight, outwards to the sides. I forgot the names of the muscles, but this is for the shoulder and chest. I started with the red band for a few repetitions per set and a few sets in the beginning. Gradually the number of repetitions per set was increased. Later, the number of sets were increased too.

Another pull-apart exercise involves the muscles at the back of the shoulder. To do this, the band is pulled in the same manner, outwards with both arms stretched straight to the sides, but this time, the band is behind my neck. Again, I started with the red band and repetitions are a few in the beginning. I think it helps strengthen my shoulders. "Your shoulders must be strong to support your neck and head" the therapist said, in one of our pre-exercise briefing. As my surgery was at the cervical, it is important to increase the muscle mass and strength of my shoulders. In fact, I did feel the difference before and after these drills.

Another exercise is called the external rotation for the shoulder. With the upper arm fixed to the body and elbow bent ninety degrees, one edge of the band is tied to a fixed point before the band is pulled outwards to the sides. I can feel the shoulder muscles especially the ones at back are being worked out. It is a good drill. For the internal rotation, one edge of the band is tied to a fixed point and in the same elbow bent position, the band is pulled inwards. The same is done for the other arm. Again, we started with the red band with a few repetitions and sets. This exercise is done when seated. I remember sitting by the window and the band edge is tied to the window grilles. Another type of pulling inwards exercise or internal rotation is done with the elbow straight. This is a bit more strenuous as more muscles are involved.

There are also simple pull exercise for the triceps and biceps. In a sitting position, with the upper arm fixed to the body, we step on one edge of the band and the other edge is held in front of the body and pulled upwards by the forearm. Another drill is, from the same sitting position, the band is pulled upwards with the elbow straight. The next drill is in a standing position, with one edge of the band stepped on, the band is pulled upwards by the arms at the front of the body, with the elbow straight. One more drill is still in a standing position, with one edge of the band stepped on, the band is pulled upwards by the arms at the side of the body, with the elbow straight.

Actually, there are a lot of shoulder and arms exercises devised by the scientists and shown to us by the therapists. I am an old man. I couldn't remember all! As I said, I could not remember all the names of the muscles, but I think it was thoroughly thought and each set of muscles has its own exercise devised. I wish to express my gratitude to all these scientists for their great effort!

Apart from the elastic resistance band, occupational therapy does have a simpler arm shoulder workstations. One of it is the pedal arm exerciser. It is just a static cycle fixed onto a table with some dials to increase the resistance of the cycle and record the number of rotations, speed and a small timer. This is a mix of range of motion and strengthening workstation because it tests the upper extremity and reach of the patient arms plus some resistance for muscle strengthening. A five minutes drill on the pedal exerciser is very good to the arms. I can feel the muscles there being worked out. It is strenuous but the effect after exercise is good. I can "feel" an increase in muscle mass and it makes the muscles stronger too! I was given this drill quite a few times. As I progress, the time is set to ten and later fifteen minutes.

Another small workstation to tests the upper extremity and reach of the patient arms and muscle strengthening is an inclined board. It is designed with various adjustable angles of the ramp inclination and is placed on a table. The inclined board has a railing on both sides and a box with a handle at the sides, in between the railings. A few weights are put inside the box for resistance. We are required to, from a sitting position with the inclined board in front of us, push the box up along the railing, hold it for a few seconds in the uppermost extension of our arms and bring it down again. This is tougher than the pedal arm exerciser because of the effort required by the shoulder and biceps muscle to push the load up the ramp. I was also given this drill a few times.

I have been talking about the exercises in the occupational therapy hall, but where is my wife? She was always with me, seated nearby watching all my drills and at time toying with her Android. In fact, every time we come for our rehabilitation session, she is the one driving me, registering my turn, pushing me in the wheelchair into the hall. Later, when I can walk, she still holds my hands as I gingerly walk to the hall. In short, she is "working" all the time. A session lasts around an hour and every session she has to "wait" for an hour. I don't think waiting for an hour, every single session is a leisurely activity.

At times, I can feel her stress and boredom waiting for me doing all that "little" things. One hour, doing nothing, can be a long time. Just try waiting for ten minutes! She sacrificed a lot. She never stops sacrificing for me. She is one mentally, emotionally and physically strong woman! Taking care of a disabled man is demanding. So far, she shines! She has given what she could, without fail! May God grant her Heaven in the hereafter! I am pleased with her!

Let's get back to the occupational therapy drills.

The next series of exercises are for the hands, fingers or as they call it, exercises for the fine motors. It starts with some squeezing. I was given a small rubber ball to squeeze! For this, there is no repetition. You just squeeze it! Easy! Then, I was given a hand grip to strengthen my hands and fingers. Again, there is no repetition. You just do it until you are sore! I was also tested for my gripping power. The Therapist uses a hand dynamo meter, small hand grip equipment with some spring resistance added and a small pressure gauge to measure my gripping pressure.

We then progress to the fingers. They devised a strange exercise to activate my numb and "dead" fingers. They have one small container containing modelling clay, commonly called Plasticine. In the Plasticine they hid around ten marbles and we are supposed to use our fingers to squeeze and spreads open that thick Plasticine to bring out the marbles. This is strenuous for the fingers and repeating the process really strained, but improves the finger's flexibility and strength. What am I playing with? Plasticine? I can't imagine my burly, rugged engineer friends see me playing with Plasticine, like kids!

For my fingers, they also asked me to screw and unscrew a nut to a fixed bolt. What now, nuts and bolts? Well, at least this sounds "engineering". This "Screw Board" has fixed bolts with threads and nuts of differing sizes. This exercise is for the fingers fine motors. It is very tiring.

Next is the finger pulleys exercise. From the sound of it you can imagine what it is, right? No? It is a small pulley and weight setting on a table. It is basically a table fitted with five pulleys hanging from a steel frame. Five nylon strings pass through the five pulleys, with one end fixed with a small finger-size loop and the other end tied to a rod that passes through a hole in the table with hanging weight at the bottom end of it. So, we are supposed to hook our five fingers into each of the loops and pull it towards us in a horizontal pull. It exercises the finger muscles and also the hands and forearm. We have to alternate between both our hands and weights are gradually added as we progress.

As usual, the therapist will be by my side, checking if I cheat! No, I am joking! I can't run away from that repetition and set thing. It is part of my life there! My life as an occupational trainee! I am no more an engineer giving instructions. I am a student!

After the finger exercises, there is also a finger grip test! They use a key pinch gauge. It measures my pinching strength between my thumb and my index finger. It also measures my pinching strength between my thumb and both the index and middle fingers combined. All the readings were recorded in my file. Every time I come in they will flip back the previous session records to see my progress!

The last few exercises I remember is about picking up tiny objects like coins and transferring of grains from plates. This is to see how our fingers coordinate to perform a certain task. It is quite tedious. There are also peg boards drills. The peg boards has tiny grooved holes of different shapes and we are supposed to pick up the tiny iron sticks of differing shapes and slot it into the pegboards hole.

One of the other interesting drills is the PC game. It is like the normal games we play on a PC. The difference is, I don't have a controller or mouse to move around my pointer. Instead, my whole movement of the pointer is through a robotic arm and a ball-type squeezer to click my "mouse". My weak arm, which is the left is placed and strapped onto a mechanical arm. The mechanical arm has a soft ball at the end where my palm is placed. First, they calibrate the extreme reaches of my mechanical arm in all the directions to synchronize with the extreme reaches of the pointer on the screen. This takes a few minutes as different patients has different reach lengths.

So, let's recap. The movement of the pointer is by the movement of my mechanical arm, which is controlled by my arm. The clicking of the mouse is by the squeezing of the soft ball by my hands. Got it? OK, game set! This game is a combination of arm extremity test and finger control plus mind coordination. So what are the games? I forgot all ten games, but remember shooting down some birds and picking up groceries and putting it into a shopping trolley. I shouldn't be playing these games. Anyway, for someone who rarely plays video games, I scored a combined average of 90% of all ten games! Cool, isn't it?

In occupational therapy, they also help me control my neuropathic pain. In one session, I was put in a sound-proof studio for relaxation music therapy. The room is dimly lighted with one crystal-ball disco light above us. The room has an audio instruction guiding me to relax and slowly "melt" my body to the reclining sofa and forget about my pain. They then play some relaxation music for some ten minutes. It was supposed to ease me of my neuropathic pain. Do you know what? It didn't work, but I didn't tell my therapist. I am just being courteous.

They also taught me how to desensitize my pain by applying soft touches using cotton or soft clothes to simulate normal clothes that has been causing my neuropathic pain. They even tailored me a tight shirt that is supposed to help me desensitized. They went to great length to help me. I am impressed and really grateful.

I can still see and feel the entire atmosphere of the occupational therapy hall. I can see the friendly, courteous faces of the therapists. I can also hear the tears and laughter of my fellow patients. I am now at home trying to do all the many drills and exercises. I may not be able to do all, but I try to do my best. I know each of the therapist wants to see me "back to my life" doing what I did before. In fact that is what their profession is all about – helping us return back to our normal life. What a noble profession.

I must share this beautiful quote by the therapy unit where I spent time rehabilitating. I got it from their video. Just read this.

"We are no magician. We are no healers. We are no shaman. We can't create miracle, we can't save life but what we may do is to give them back their life"

I have got back my life although not to where I was before. I wish to thank all of them!

Indian Stroke Patient Working Again

Among the many patients undergoing rehabilitation, there is one Indian man who managed to survive his stroke and got back to work. I met him many times at the gym and occupational therapy hall. He smiles a lot. He walks like a typical stroke patient, but the way he carries himself is different. I can feel his pride looking at his stride. He is calm and confident.

I was with him once in a hydro-pool for our underwater strength and balance exercise. It was quite a long session on the underwater treadmill. I managed to start a conversation as he looks approachable and friendly. "I have seen you a few times. Nice to meet you" he said, as he offered a handshake. "Your face is a bit gloomy. Are you in pain?" he asked. I said my body is hypersensitive and wearing the swim shirt is very painful. "No...no sir, never say the word pain. Try not to, OK?" he suddenly makes that remark. I was a bit shocked. "I was in pain, but I train my mind not to think about it. Just don't think about it. Try" he advised as we slowly walk on the treadmill. I just nod as I listened to his "motivational" talk.

"My pain is on my muscles. When I make any movement, the cramp and pain is unbearable" he said, showing his arms and the left side of his body. I asked him how he managed to "forget" about his pain. He smiled and said "I learned some meditation. I just focus my mind away from the pain. I do it a few times in a day" he explained enthusiastically. He seems excited sharing his experience. He told me that it took him a few months to be able to train his mind. He suggested that I try meditation too.

He stared at me for a moment, smiled and said "I know you must be a religious man". I gathered he made that remark because of my beard.

"In your prayers, try to ask your God to help you" he said. "Your prayer is in itself a meditation" he adds. "Important thing is never thinks about your pain. Try that first. I know you can" he said, motivating me again. He sounds positive. "Now I am back to work. I was a clerk doing a lot of paperwork and moves a lot. Now, the department took me back and gave me an easier task, as a librarian.

"What's inside shows on the outside!"

In the beginning he went through that same "acceptance" phase. He said for the first six months, he didn't do anything. He was negative, depressed and sad. I can understand his predicament. Later, he started to go for treatment at the hospital for six months and end up at the rehabilitation. "Rehabilitation can teach us the exercises, but we must do more. At home, continue working. Do anything to cure us" he said, with conviction. I think what he said was true.

I did get positive comments about him from a few therapists. He is proud of his recovery and he sincerely wants to see me recover. Indeed, it shows from the way he talks to me. We had a good pool session and a great deal of sharing too. I left the session feeling positive. I told my wife about that Indian guy. "You must be like him. He is positive, but you complain a lot!" she said rather sarcastically, but I know she didn't mean to scold me. Yes, it was a good session. I learn something from a stranger in a pool. We don't actually need a classroom to learn. We can get lessons of life, anywhere!

The Weeping "Rich" Woman

In my weekly rehabilitation session, I was able see many different patients displaying many levels of strain. It can be physical or emotional. I remember one woman. She is one character I find it difficult to forget because of her constant crying and tantrums. Even my wife will wink at me when we see her in the hall or gym. "There she is. There she is" my wife would hint me if she is around. "She always looks like that, see? She is always sad" the same comment from my wife about her moody looks. She will come in a wheelchair pushed by her daughter. Her daughter is always smiling, a big contrast from her mom's gloomy face. She has a pleasant disposition and greets us sometimes.

I think the woman must be someone influential from a big company or the wife of a wealthy man from the way she dressed. She looks neat and proper. Her sudden disability may be too upsetting for her to accept. It must be too depressing for her to be deprived from enjoying her influential lifestyle because of her ailment. Her daughter speaks fluent English. The girl looks neat and proper probably from her wealthy upbringing and lifestyle.

I realized that the woman will start crying the moment she fails to complete a simple task or exercise. A few times I sat close to her. It must be hard for her to accept the sudden limitations and change. I was told that she has lost her ability to speak and one of her arms is crippled thus affecting her ability to do those tasks. In occupational therapy, we were given simple cognitive test tasks like arranging puzzles, inserting certain objects into a container according to their shapes and sometimes, buttoning shirts. It was tough for me to do some of the tasks, but I may have overcome the "acceptance" mode. She may still be struggling with her emotions to accept her disability.

"Don't cry sister. Never mind. It's OK. Just try to do what you can, OK?" the therapist would console her. She will weep uncontrollably and moans. Her daughter will gently and patiently pat her back and sometimes wipes her tears. It can be heart-breaking seeing her crying. She sounds so sad! "It's OK mom. Nothing is wrong. Take a rest, OK?" her daughter comforts her.

I pity her and I think everyone sympathize with her. "If you want to leave, they will allow you mom. No worries" her daughter tries to console her. A few times she would just throw way all the things in front of her. She will cry continuously at times. The therapists there were all aware of her condition and everyone chips in once in a while to encourage her. If she is in the hall, she would be the centre of attention.

"If you are always attached to each other or the things you loved, you will suffer when those things are detached from you! Learn to detach yourself from those things regularly!"

It is frustrating. I know because I am a patient too. Simple things we take for granted suddenly becomes a big hurdle for us. It is not that I didn't have the urge to shout and complain. I do have at times, but I kept it to myself. I suppressed it! I am not strong too. It is expected. Probably I didn't lose as much as her. All the while she may be adored and respected. Her life may revolve around influential and dignified people. So, being crippled is taking a big toll on her self-esteem. It may be difficult to accept. I understand the psychology of being crippled now. I try hard to tell myself "You must face it. You are not normal anymore. Do not try to change the fate. You can't."

Yes, I do shy away from friends and I still keep my ailment a secret to my colleagues, friends and even relatives. It is partly pride. I know I shouldn't feel bad over something which was never my fault, but it is just about emotion. For me, I rather not tell more than I need to because I am ashamed and I do not want others to see my deficiency. At the same time, I rather not make my friends feel shocked looking at my disability. I have a different personal and emotional sensitivity to preserve than her.

I didn't see her situation improves for the many times I was together with her for our rehabilitation. She is still in denial mode or maybe she is the type that demands perfection. At times, she just stares at the objects and training material without doing anything. She refused to do the exercises. Her daughter would quietly whisper to her ears and tries to persuade her. The girl is adorable. She always smiles and gentle to her mom. She would pat her back, talk to her and wipe her tears. She always sits beside her for the whole one hour. She is friendly and cheerful.

I think God made her a patient and gentle person to face her mother's misery. I don't think many people could be patient enough to tolerate her mother's demand and at times, irritating behaviour. Just like me, I am depressed and demanding too. I just can't help it. It is part of the psychology of being disabled, crippled and in pain. I am lucky to have a loyal and patient wife. She has all the qualities of a good wife and more. I can't imagine going through "hell" the last few years without her. I know it wasn't easy. She coped well.

Most of us are not trained to treat the ills among us. It needs a lot of psychological training to understand the many emotional states of a patient and how to react. I think the number one mandatory skill one needs in the medical environment is anger management. Actually, it is not so much about anger, but the ability to "ignore" and "pretend" not to be perturbed! It is the ability to exude a calm disposition in those conditions. Also, this skill is needed all the time, day and night regardless of the types of wards. I can see most of the nurses and doctors have these "special" skill. In layman terms I called it "cool heads". As patients, we have lost our cool heads because of the pain, discomfort and emotional stress. We are negative. So, we need a positive charge to blend the situation to an acceptable level.

It has been two years since I met the weeping woman. I can only hope she recovered at least to the acceptance state that she is crippled. I know she has an excellent "nurse" in her adorable, calm and cheerful daughter. I remember a piece of advice "Do not be so intense over something. It is not good for you". I got this advice from a friend because of my tensed character in an argument. I have the tendency to prolong an argument just for the sake of winning. At times I regret for being such a nuisance, but there are times when friends admire my ability to comprehend an issue and present my stance.

What I am trying to say is not so much about the argument, but the emotional intensity. I think from my ailment, I have mellowed a lot. I still show some level of intensity, but it is very much reduced. It is not good for me. I know it now. My ailment and hospitalization taught me a lot.

I may have all the perception about that woman, but from her I learned something valuable. What is it? "It is definitely alright to release our despair, depression and pain. It is only natural to be disappointed because we have lost something from our life!" Even now I do cry quietly at night just to console myself that I have lost something! We all need that channel to escape. She chose to cry and I do it too! I find it relieving because I do try other techniques to relieve my emotional stress and in my case, continuous pain, but crying helps. Yes, just cry. Do not feel embarrassed. We are all humans. It is life's natural way of telling God that we are sad.

She may lose a lot emotionally. I may not lose as much as her, but we have one thing in common. We are disabled and crippled. The intensity may differ, but we are both disabled. It is something we have to live with. Others may sympathize, but we have to face it every day!

The Rehab Clinic Appointments

All the rehabilitation, physiotherapy and occupational therapy, was planned, designed and instructed by the doctors at the hospital and the rehabilitation hospital. After discharged from the wards, we have monthly appointments with the neurosurgery doctors. It was a continued effort to monitor and care for my recovery.

After a few months, the frequency of appointments was reduced to one appointment in two months and later, one appointment in three months. My appointments with the hospital was eventually stopped and taken over by the rehabilitation hospital. The rehabilitation hospital has its own neurology department. As usual, the doctors in this rehabilitation hospital are as positive, friendly and motivating as the therapist. I had a good and satisfactory review, follow-up and advice. I remember coming to these clinics in a wheelchair, later with a walking stick and finally, walking on my own. The doctors are excited at my progress.

I was also referred to the sports unit to help rehabilitate my shoulder. They have a few extra stretches they taught and also the use of strength bands as resistance. The physician is very helpful and showed me all the necessary drills in detail. The other help the hospital gave was by assigning me to ten sessions at the acupuncture unit. This unit is manned by a few Chinese acupuncturists and some trained in China. The objective was to see if acupuncture can help ease my neuropathic pain.

The overall scope of rehabilitation given to me is thorough. The rehabilitation hospital has extended their full attention and care for me. I am grateful to all their efforts.

My Concerned Neighbours

As a patient, apart from the training at the rehabilitation hospital, I was asked to do exercises at home. At home, we may not have the necessary equipment, but some of the exercises can be improvised for training at home. One of the simplest exercises is walking. In my case, I am wheelchair-free but it is advisable to use a walking stick when walking. At the hospital, I was trained to walk the proper way as my walk is rather stunted due to poor mind-muscle coordination, imbalance and weak muscles.

"You walk like a robot!" my wife used to tease me. Not only that, I bend forward when I walk. Part of it is because of my weak shoulder muscles and the stiff neck. "Sometimes you are like a penguin too" she jokes. I walk by moving my feet a bit side by side rather than stepping forward. I walk with a slightly bent knee not straight like a normal person. I realized that my walking style is awkward, but I didn't do it intentionally. It is all about keeping me standing and walking with all the limitations I got from my disorder.

In fact, a few of the masseuses we met said the same thing. What actually happen is, if I were to stand up straight, chest out, I feel like falling backwards! Also, me feet are partially numb thus minimizing the sense of touch at the base of my feet. So, I need to gently and slowly train and adapt myself to the proper way of walking.

At home, for muscle strengthening, simple sit-ups and climbing up of stairs can also be performed. For the arms, we were given stretch bands of differing strengths to perform simple bicep, triceps and shoulder muscle strengthening. We can also use dumb bells for strengthening. At the hospital, we were given the basic counts, counts per set and number of sets for each exercise. So, based on the advice we can still do the same types of drills given at the hospital, at home. Every morning, I would do lower limbs and upper abdomen exercises. Initially it was tough, but I have gradually improved.

At home, I will take a brief walk with a walking stick around my residential area. At first, I have my wife to accompany me. We just try a few meters at first. Gradually we increase it, always under the watchful eyes of my wife. A slight knock can render me out of balance and tumble. So, the first few attempts, my wife held my hands. It wasn't easy. After a few months, I tried walking on my own, with a walking stick.

So, it is normal that I got some curious look from my neighbours who are used to seeing me walk normally and cycling before. In fact, not many of them knew what happened to me. I think some of them were surprised seeing me with a walking stick and walking like a penguin! "What happened to you?' some of them asked with a curious look. "Since when are you like this? I didn't know. I am sorry" another remark from another neighbour. "No wonder I rarely see you on your bicycle!" came another comment. In fact, everyone is concerned and sympathize with me.

Along the way, there is no short of offers for help that I got from them. My immediate neighbour offered me some Chinese incense to treat my itchiness. She said she got it from China. Another old lady showed me a kind of herb from her small garden. "You blend this with apple juice and drink it. It is good for your body" she said to my wife, as she plucked a few leaves for me.

On the other lane behind my house, another Chinese lady greeted me and said "You look like you have a nerve problem. Wait a minute" she said, as she stopped sweeping her porch and went inside. She came out a minute later and said "Here is a very good Chinese masseuse. Try to see him. He is good. My back pain is gone" she said excitedly as she gave me a business card. Her husband encouraged me too.

Another help comes from my neighbour in front. He came over and offered me herbal drip. "See, my factory does packaging for a lot of products, including medicinal herbs. I think this may help your nerves" he said, as he gave me a small bottle. "This drip has special qualities. A few people have tried and they said it's good, effective" he explained.

In my daily morning stroll, I was able to meet many of my neighbours. One of them is and old woman, but she looks healthy. She used to walk to a nearby shop to buy her newspaper. She used to see me and one day she stopped to have a conversation with me. "I heard you have a nerve problem. Maybe you want to try a Tai-chi exercise. My friend gave me a video, but it is in Chinese" she said. "Never mind, give me your hand phone number, I will WhatsApp it to you" she said as she pulled out her smart phone. I read to her my number. "You may not understand, but just follow how he did the simple exercise on the video. It can cure a lot of disease just by swaying the hands" she said as she swayed her hands forward and backward. "Yes, just like this, roughly" she explained.

One of my many neighbours is a retired Indian man. He used to walk his dog in the morning. So, in my morning stroll we used to meet each other. One day, he stopped over in front of my house and asked me about my problem. I briefly explained my disorder to him. He then suggests that I try alkaline water. I had a few years ago tried alkaline water. In fact, I bought a jar-type manual dispenser which converts the normal water to alkaline water. I used it for a while, but did not continue as I did not replenish the filter. So, that was it.

"Why not you try it?" he asked. "I have been attending the seminar and many people have bought the alkaline water dispenser. I have one at home" he said. "You can come over to my house and I can explain it to you. You can also take the water from us. Just bring an empty bottle with you" he proposed. So, I told him one of the days I will come over to his place.

One day my wife and I went over to his house, just a few units away from my house. We just walk over with our bottle. He welcomed us in an introduced us to his wife. "Please be seated" he ushered us. "Let me show you a short video about the product and its benefits" he said, as he flip open a laptop on the sofa table. "It's a very short video" he said, as he scrolls looking for the video. The house was quiet probably because their kids are grown-ups and may be on their own, I guessed. His wife just sat there, smiling. We then watched the video. It was quite informative. At the end of the video he said "You can Google this name and there will be many YouTube videos about it. Spend some time watching it to learn more"

He then invited us to his kitchen where the dispenser is. He briefly shows the dispenser, point to us the simple tubing connections and its dials and functions. It is quite simple. "You just set the pH value you want, put your bottle at the outlet and press this button" he explains, as his wife stood by watching. "Why not you fill your bottle now" his wife said. We filled the bottle and went back to the living room.

"You can come here every day and take the water. Your wife can come. There will always be someone home" he said before we left. "Just try it. It may help with your problem" he adds. So, I went back and start browsing the Internet for the product. From that day my wife starts frequenting his house for the alkaline water. I consumed it for a few weeks and finally stop as there was no major effect. Anyway, we are thankful that people around us cared and are concerned about us. I wouldn't have known this Indian man if I was not sick. Indeed, there is a blessing behind all things that happen.

There is also an old man, like me, walking with a stick. He told me of his problem. "I fell ten years ago and my back is injured. Since then I have been walking like this" he said, as we walked along together. "Hospital asked me to exercise every day. That's all". "Ten years like that?" I thought to myself. I think I am luckier than him!

I also met an engineer with the same predicament. He works in a shipyard that is familiar to me. "I have to quit my job at the shipyard because of this" he said, showing his twisted left arm and legs. I know the pay was good as I have friends working in that shipyard. He told me he is the lead mechanical engineer. So, he must earn a handsome five figure income.

"I am not alone. There are others like me, some worse than me"

Generally, what I learned is, people are good. At times I think others are individualistic and couldn't care less, but God was I wrong! I learned from my neighbours that, despite being of a different race and religion, they are all human at heart! They care and they tried to help with whatever they have. Yes, I was wrong. Let us all learn to stop having any kind of perception of others. I have learned a lesson. I hope we all learn.

"Everyone is fine until we come out with our perception of them!"

Where Do I Go from Here?

So, now my life revolves around my daily exercise and sleep. I couldn't do much. My upper body is constantly in pain, the gripping pain and the burning sensation. My limbs are partially numb, strained and weak. I can walk, but the balance is not as good. In fact, after my exercises, I usually feel tired and fatigue because of the muscle motors not accepting the right amount of signals, probably. I am basically "forcing" the muscles rather than letting my brain to direct it. Whatever, I must rest after the exercise. I will feel fresh when I wake up.

So, how long have I been living like this? Well, a good measure is by looking at one woman pushing her granddaughter on a baby stroller. I have been walking the last two and the half years. The little girl was still in her stroller then. Now, she can walk beside her grandmother! She is already a big girl! Every morning when we passed each other, I would say "hi" to her and being too young, she can only wave back and smile. Now, she greets me and wave at me first! She recognized me! She has grown up.

When I look at her, I felt hopeful. She gave me hope. With her fresh and lively face, her smile and her excitement seeing me every morning makes me feel life is worth living for. There are days when I feel down, but when I see her, my whole morning changed! I may be crippled but to that girl, I am her "excitement" every morning. I want to be there for her, every morning. I love her and when I didn't see her, I missed her! There is already a bond between us. I love you little Nathalie! I really do. She may not know what I wrote about her, but maybe one day she may come across my book and remembers me, as "that uncle with the walking stick"!

To Nathalie, I have this to say "One day, uncle will be fine!"

I found strength, love and hope from all those who have touched my life as a Syringomyelia patient. Indeed, I am in pain and almost in vain, but not!

I thank God for keeping my cognitive intact, despite the deteriorating physical ability.

Our mind is greater than our body! Our mind is the one that has the free will to think and direct our body to act and produce results that we want! So, mind what you think! You may be in pain, in agony, disabled, frustrated, but try to tell your mind that you will survive. There are many "Nathalie" out there who still want to see you happy! Do not disappoint them please!

For me, I still have my wife and four wonderful kids who want to see me fit and healthy again. They want to see me happy, travel and go for vacation with me. I wanted to see them grow and have a meaningful and blissful life. So, I will hang in there for them. I will fight for it! Yes, I am in pain, but I will not be in vain.

Life goes on!